THE WARS OF AMERICA

CHRISTIAN VIEWS

Edited by Ronald A. Wells

WILLIAM B. EERDMANS PUBLISHING COMPANY
Grand Rapids, Michigan

255 Jefferson Ave. S.E., Grand Rapids, Mich. 49503

Printed in the United States of America

Library of Congress Cataloging in Publication Data
Main entry under title:

The Wars of America.

Includes bibliographical references.
1. United States — History, Military — Addresses, essays, lectures. 2. War and religion — Addresses, essays, lectures. I. Wells, Ronald, 1941-
E181.W28 261.8'73'0973 81-15194
ISBN 0-8028-1899-4 AACR2

CONTENTS

PREFACE

THIS BOOK WAS WRITTEN BY EIGHT HISTORIANS under the direction of one of them. As editor, I assume responsibility for the book's contents, but if praise is due, it must be shared equally. Throughout the nearly two years it took to bring this project from idea to reality, my seven colleagues were helpful and patient, as was our publisher, Marlin VanElderen of Eerdmans.

Specific thanks are due many people, without whose help and encouragement this book would not have been completed. The idea of it first came out of a discussion with Lee Nash; a helpful and corrective reading of an early draft was done by Arthur Roberts; the initial encouragement from the publisher came from Reinder Van Til; time away from teaching duties at a critical stage was given the editor through the support of the Dean of Calvin College, Peter DeVos; important contributions to my thinking, which find expression in both introductory and afterword essays, came from two authors, George Marsden and Ralph Beebe; the diligent typing of most of the manuscript was done by Helen Meyers Ysselstine.

While the eight contributors to this volume are all members of the Conference on Faith and History, the book cannot claim to be a reflection of the common mind of that Conference. However, we would be remiss if we did not acknowledge that we all first became acquainted though the work of the Conference, and we probably would not have embarked on this project had we not thought it worthwhile to do what the Conference encourages — to bring our Christian commitments to bear upon the study of history.

In this case, we ask whether or not it is possible for historians to speak of "just wars." The essays that follow, in all their diversity of views, are honest attempts by historians who are Christians to answer that question. We hope and trust that a potential reader will think it time well spent to consider the wars of America from a Christian perspective.

Grand Rapids
July, 1980 RONALD A. WELLS

INTRODUCTION

WAR IS COMMON TO ALL HUMAN HISTORY. While the history of war is not the history of mankind, mankind's history cannot be studied fully without reference to war. Moreover, the way in which a nation wages war reveals a great deal about its basic values. Thus, the illuminating qualities of war should be of greater interest to the historian of society than the actual stuff of warfare, such as armaments, battles, and tactics. To examine a nation's experience of war, and its response to it, is to learn something fundamental about a nation's values and its social order.[1]

That war should be as common to American history as to the history of other nations was a condition that many of the "founding fathers" did not anticipate. It was their belief that the United States would be signally different from Europe in many ways, but especially in its elimination of war. In the new environment of the new world, the "new man" of America (in Crèvecoeur's phrase) would rise and live out the potential for mankind that had never been allowed by the decadent and decrepit institutions of Europe. Americans would turn their backs on the nations of Europe, which, as Jefferson wrote, "are nations of eternal war. . . . On our part, never had a people so favorable a chance of trying the opposite system, of peace and fraternity with mankind and the direction of all our means and faculties to the purpose of improvement instead of destruction."[2] Jefferson was able to express this belief because it was part of a larger philosophical perspective on the "American experiment" itself. The very word "experiment" was significant for him, because what happened in the United States "laboratory" of self-government would be of great importance to the watching world. To James Madison he wrote that in 1789 Europeans were already citing our experiences as though they were "the bible." To John Hollis he wrote, in 1811, that

> The eyes of the virtuous all over the earth are turned with anxiety on us, as the only depositories of the sacred fire of liberty, and . . . our falling into anarchy would decide forever the destinies of mankind, and seal the political heresy that man is incapable of self-government.[3]

In claiming social uniqueness for America, Jefferson was the most eloquent spokesman for a tradition in American thought—perhaps shared by a majority of the Revolutionary generation—that American political procedures were a novelty in the history of civilization. To some observers, "the rising glory of America" represented the final stage of human evolution. Writing in 1772, Philip Freneau and Hugh H. Brackenridge spoke in glowing terms of the peaceful and progressive future for America:

> This is thy praise America thy pow'r,
> Thou best of climes by science visited,
> By freedom blest and richly stor'd with all
> The luxuries of life. Hail happy land,
> The seat of empire the abode of kings,
> The final stage where time shall introduce
> Renowned characters, and glorious works
> Of high invention and of wond'rous art.[4]

The hyperole of patriotism—in America, Fourth of July rhetoric—is common to all nations. But in the United States the hyperole about the uniqueness, greatness, and future prospects of the realm seems to outstrip that of other nations, and the American appeal to destiny seems to set this nation apart from other modern nations.

The rhetoric of a grandiose American consciousness was always at some variance with the reality of the American experience on the North American continent. The United States was born with ideas about itself that demanded its special place in human history. Americans imposed upon themselves the requirement that they either be the greatest success in world history or the worst failure; nothing else would do. For Americans to have regarded themselves as having to bear the common burdens of humanity was to have adjudged themselves failures. To be a nation like any other nation would be to accept a theory about man and about the future of "the experiment" that most Americans found unacceptable.[5]

America's founding fathers fixed their eyes on the future; the historian fixes on the past. In trying to reconstruct historical reality the historian must cut through a web of mythology. "Mythology" has several meanings: there is a sense in which "myth" can mean historical untruth, and therefore deserves to be exposed to the light of "truth"; there is also a sense in which myth can mean historical truth *as perceived* by those who perpetuate the myth. It is in the latter sense that historians must be wary of simple "demythologizing," because "truth" does not come to us unambiguously. Mythology is necessary for nation building; it is vital for a sense of peoplehood. Therefore, myth is not important as history but rather as a method by which history can be used to build a consciousness of a nation and a people. Because of their special "calling" in history, Americans were a people before they were a nation, or, as Michael Kammen has observed, "they had a mythology before they even had a country."[6] Americans believed that their birthright was unique, and that they were "born heirs to freedom." Thus, their revolution was "conservative" in that Americans "revolted not to create but to maintain their freedom." This people of paradox was able to live in a dichotomized world because from the first instance there were two levels of consciousness—the rhetorical and the real—that rarely coincided.[7] While the sensitive historian must avoid a too facile debunking of myth in American history, he must strive to bring the "rhetoric" of the American past into at least a dialectical relationship to "reality," lest in repeating the mythology of the past he continues to affirm the pretentions of the rhetoric.[8]

The American claim to uniqueness as a society was, of course, pretentious, especially in its belief that the United States could be a nation free from war. Many Americans still hold to the belief first articulated by Franklin and Jefferson that the United States would be a peacable nation, and that it would only go to war under the most optimally just circumstances. This belief has been held despite the 1775–83 war that brought the United States into being; the 1812–15 war with Britain a second time; the 1846–48 war with Mexico; the 1861–65 war with itself; the 1898 war with Spain; the 1917–18 war with the Central Powers; the 1941–45 war with the Axis powers; the 1950–53 Korean War; and the 1964–74 Vietnam War. As Maldwyn Jones writes, with decided understatement, "This bloody catalogue, extending over the whole span of American history, demonstrates that the American claim to uniqueness is subject to at least one major qualification."[9]

How should the historian approach the history of a people whose agreed-to version of their past (myth) is at substantial variance with the reality of those events (history)? Some conceptual terminology may help, especially if one can distinguish between pathos, tragedy, and irony.[10]

A historical situation can be called pathetic if it is a situation that on the one hand elicits pity, but that on the other hand, neither deserves admiration nor warrants contrition. A possible example of a pathetic situation is a genuine natural disaster for which no reason can be given, nor guilt ascribed, such as the San Francisco earthquake. The people trapped in that natural disaster were doubtlessly "pathetic" victims who deserve the historian's pity but not necessarily his admiration, and, since there was no question of "fault," there is nothing of which anyone need repent.

A tragic historical situation consists of the conscious choice of evil for the sake of good. Men or nations make tragic choices when they do evil in good cause, or when they accept the guilt for actions necessary to the completion of what is in their view a high responsibility. John Brown would be a good example of a tragic figure in American history. He was willing to murder, and to incite others to murder, for the "higher good" of liberating slaves from the injustice of slavery. Since he was convinced of the "sin" of slavery, and since he believed that there could be no remission of sin without the shedding of blood, he was willing to accept "the call" of God to be the agent by which the land would be purged with blood. Brown's tragic end elicits our admiration as well as our pity, because it combines potential nobility with guilt for wrongdoing.[11]

The ironic element in a historic situation obtains when fortuitous incongruities are discovered not to be merely fortuitous. Incongruity can be merely comic, eliciting laughter. But irony is more than comedy if the incongruity reveals a heretofore hidden relationship. Incongruous situations become ironic if virtue becomes vice because of a hidden defect in virtue, or if strength becomes weakness because of the vanity to which strength may prompt the mighty man or nation. Historical irony is different from tragedy because the responsibility for the action in question is related to unconscious weakness rather than to conscious resolution. It is different from either tragedy or pathos because when the people involved in an ironic situation become conscious of it they can dissolve their participation in it. Such awareness involves some realization of the hidden vanity or pretension by which the incongruous comedy has been turned to irony. This realization either must lead to an abatement of the pretension, which means contrition, or to a desperate accentuation of the vanities to the point at which irony turns into pure evil.

The United States was founded upon a confidence in its own innocence and virtue that was to place it, by the mid-twentieth century, in an ironic situation. The belief that "Nature's God" was intent on beginning again with man in the new world was the fundamental pretense of American consciousness that energized the nation for its first 150 years. But American practice was always wiser than its theory. While the theory spoke of the potential for the new American man, the Constitution was "based upon the philosophy of Hobbes and the religion of Calvin."[12] This warning, sounded by founding fathers like Adams and Madison, went largely unheeded by the mythmakers of the American consciousness. It went unheeded because Calvinism's contention of the ambiguity of virtue was domesticated in America to reflect the confidence in the virtue of "the elect" American. Thus, the two great religious-moral traditions that informed our early life—New England Calvinism and Virginia Deism—came to similar conclusions about the nature of the new nation and of its destiny.

The spiritual pride of the United States consisted in acting innocently upon the pretense of its special calling despite the fact that it was almost constantly at war, either with Indians at home or with other nations or peoples on this continent or abroad. Reinhold Niebuhr observes well that "Nations, as individuals, who are completely innocent in their own esteem are insufferable in their human contacts."[13] Niebuhr continues:

> The American situation is such a vivid symbol of the spiritual perplexities of modern man, because the degree of American power tends to generate illusions to which a technocratic culture is already too prone. This technocratic approach to the problems of history, which erroneously equates the mastery of nature with the mastery of historical destiny, in turn accentuates a very old failing in human nature: the inclination of the wise, or the powerful, or the virtuous, to obscure and deny the human limitations in all human achievements and pretensions.[14]

The irony of American history, therefore, consists not so much in conscious choices of evil but in America's acting upon a pretentious view of itself, a view that suggested its moral superiority to other nations and peoples. The historian's sense for the ironic situation in American history depends largely, although not entirely, upon his prior acceptance of a Christian world view. Irony cannot be experienced directly. Since the participant in an incongruous event typically cannot be self-critical enough to know it, the recognition of irony is usually reserved for observers rather than participants. Christianity tends to make the ironic view of human evil normative because it is based on "the belief that the whole drama of human history is under the scrutiny of a divine judge who laughs at human pretensions without being hostile to human aspirations."[15] To the Christian historian, "the evil in human history is regarded as the consequences of man's wrong use of his unique capacities. The wrong use is always due to some failure to recognize the limits of his capacities of power, wisdom and virtue. Man is an ironic creature because he forgets that he is not simply a creator but also is a creature."[16]

The importance of an ironic perspective on the past is that it emphasizes the dire consequences of vain pretensions, since they are ironically refuted by actual experience. Consciousness of an ironic situation can help the observer to encourage the participant to dissolve the irony by moderating the pretension. The Christian historian who accepts the ironic view of evil can be of help to his society if his disclosure of the ironic can encourage that society to repent of its pretensions. As to the wars of American history, the ironic perspective can be of help in human understanding if we begin an analysis by suggesting that no American war was begun with a conscious choice of evil, even if for a higher good. American wars, largely, were begun on the basis of the society's prior acceptance of the pretentious view of itself and of its role in world history.

The Christian historian is uniquely placed to be an ironic interpreter of American society, and especially of its wars, because he will hold fast to universal religious truths rather than accept the absolutizing of the pretensions of a nation-state. A Christian historian, as Herbert Butterfield has noted, "is particularly called to carry on his thinking outside the framework which a nation or a political or social system or an accepted regime or a mundane ideology provides."[17] The very nature of compassion—so vital to Christianity—requires, in wartime, that that compassion be extended to the enemy, even a diabolically evil one, such as Germany during the Second World War. Moreover, and of great importance, compassion requires the Christian "to be diffident about believing that his own nation's cause is absolutely the righteous one, and all the wickedness on the side of the enemy."[18] The diffidence of the Christian historian is required by the fact that his ultimate allegiance is never given to a nation state but rather to the kingdom that has come and is to come.

For Christians, the obvious places to begin an inquiry about war are the Bible and church history. But, alas they are not unambigious sources, and several plausible theories about war and peace can be argued.[19] During the first three centuries of Christianity's existence, the church generally refrained from politics. When the political task was forced onto the church from Constantine's time onward, Christians borrowed models of behavior about war from Jewish and classical cultures, from which it borrowed other things as well. Thus, the "Christian" ethic of war that emerged after the fourth century was not distinctly Christian, but rather was based on Hebrew, Greek, and especially Roman ethics, accomodated to the needs of a "Christian culture."

In general, Christians have advanced three attitudes about war and peace: pacifism, the just war, and the crusade. The early church, largely because it eschewed the entire political task in the pagan Roman world, was pacifist, and it rejected the claim of the state to the believer's participation in the wars of the state. Although pacifism was abandoned by most Christians in subsequent church history, there has remained a sizable minority of Christians that has consistently maintained that their Christian witness required them to be nonviolent in all their social relationships.

The argument of pacifist Christians springs simply and spontaneously from the Bible. They try to act on Christ's commandment to love enemies. They agree with the Quaker leader George Fox that for them Christ has taken away "the occasion of all wars." For the Christian pacifist, life is sacred because it was created by a loving God, and thus there can be no justification for the taking of life. If the pacifists are correct in believing that nonviolence is the will of God, they will not be moved by suggestions that it is "impractical." Indeed, they are prepared to assert that nonviolence is practical, because the example of courageous Christians in history demonstrates to their satisfaction that the force of love is more powerful than any worldly powers.

After the fourth century, when the church became closely associated with the state, Christians took over theory extant in Roman culture, the just war. This theory, with some variations, has been the official policy of most churches since the time of Constantine, and a large majority of Christians would accept the theory as describing their position. The first and most notable exponent of the just war theory was St. Augustine. The just war is to be fought under the authority of the state, and is to limit its goals to the restoration of justice or the preservation of peace. Moreover, the just war—in order to be just—must be a last resort, entered into only after all methods of solving disputes nonviolently have been exhausted. Further, the just war must be fought "justly," that is, with special care taken to protect noncombatants, and with the level of violence strictly limited to the minimum necessary to accomplish the goal of "justice," that is, the restoration of peace or the preservation of justice. This position does not spring as simply and spontaneously from the Bible as does pacifism, but a majority of Christians would concede that the just war theory agrees with the spirit of the Bible—that while God requires love of his followers, he also requires justice in his creation.[20]

The third position that a minority of Christians have held—the crusade—emerged in the Middle Ages. A crusade was to be fought under the authority of the church or of a charismatic religious leader, but not by the state itself, although it might potentially be conducted by a theocratic state. The goal of the crusade was not to be limited to restoring peace or preserving justice; the goal instead was to uphold, preserve, or expand the dominion of the church itself against the threats, real or imagined, of its enemies.

As Roland Bainton has suggested, the Christian's attitude toward "the world" was crucial in determining which of the three options were to be accepted: "Pacifism is thus often associated with withdrawal, the just war with qualified participation, and the crusade with dominance of the church over the world."[21]

To the writers of this book, the concept of the crusade is philosophically unacceptable, because crusades have typically been acts of arrogant imperialism in which the church, if only a small minority within it, has sought to impose its will on an unyielding and recalcitrant world. Therefore, the just war and pacifism are the models for our analyses. One author, Ralph K. Beebe, while discussing the War of 1812 from the perspective of its potential justice, is nevertheless a person who believes that his Christian commitment entails a commitment to pacifism. The other seven authors accept the philosophical implications of the just war theory, and analyze a particular war from that perspective. But as the essays will suggest, the prior acceptance of the plausibility of the just war theory in no way commits a Christian historian to a conclusion that the war under review was in fact just. Insofar as our Christian viewpoints will emerge in these essays, they will consist of the attempt to judge whether or not particular American wars conformed to the twin requirements of the just war.

With the desire to demythologize but not neccessarily to debunk, impelled by a sense for the ironic, and restrained by diffidence, we have examined not war in general but American wars in particular.

1 GEORGE MARSDEN

THE AMERICAN REVOLUTION: Partisanship, "Just Wars," and Crusades

THE CHRISTIAN'S CHARACTERISTIC RESPONSE TO VIOLENCE, as I understand Jesus' teachings, should be nonviolence. This is just the opposite of the wisdom of the world and the apparent instincts of human nature, which suggest that force is best met with force. The follower of Jesus characteristically is to turn the other cheek. Any view that says that Christians should regard violence or warfare in the service of their nation as simply matters of course seems to me to be less than faithful to Jesus' own teachings. Christian citizens should be willing to kill at the command of their national leaders only in cases in which the killing is the only means available to protect the innocent and thereby promote justice and restore peace. This, I take it, is the essence of "just war" theory.

One of the strongest arguments against such a "just war" theory is that it is too theoretical—it does not take into account how people actually behave. While during almost any war citizens on both sides have been entirely convinced of the justice of their cause and the total unrighteousness of their opponents, we can see in retrospect that only in rare cases were such judgments anywhere near being correct. Often neither side fought primarily for the cause of justice. Often, in cases in which one side had a technical point of justice in its favor, warfare was a solution disproportionate to the seriousness of the injustice. Yet almost without exception, especially in the modern era of the popular nation state, the citizenry has regarded its nation's side of the argument not only as just but also as the most righteous of causes, endorsed by whatever deities there may be, and warranting the wrath of vengeance. Christians in such countries have not usually been exceptions to this rule, but rather have characteristically been in the forefront in turning their "just wars" into such crusades. These modern crusades, however, have not been ones in which the church dominates the world; rather the nation has set the agenda and the Christians have supplied the flags and crosses.

The American Revolution is a pivotal instance for understanding how modern nations have transformed supposed "just wars" into secular crusades. It is pivotal for considering other wars of America, since the patterns of nationalism and civil religion established at the time of the Revolution became important elements of the mythology that determined American's behavior in subsequent wars. It is also important in terms of the wider picture of the development of the modern nation state, since the United States was in many respects the model for modern nations built on popular support that was characterized, among other things, by the citizens' army.

As soon as we look at the rationale offered to justify the Revolutionary War, we should be struck by a most revealing feature of its justification. The American revolutionaries, despite the Christian profession of many of them and the Christian heritage of almost all, seem generally not to have felt any need to provide an elaborate rationale for resorting to violence and killing. Although the Revolution was resisted on such grounds by the peace churches, such as the Mennonites and the Quakers,[1] the revolutionaries with whom we are here concerned seem to have regarded the resort to warfare as almost a matter of course. The war, in fact, broke out in 1775, almost as a spontaneous culmination of ten years of bitter dispute. In the sense that through all those years most of the violence had been against property and many efforts at relatively nonviolent resistence had been made, warfare was a last resort. But for the participants, the idea of shifting the resistence from an essentially nonviolent to an essentially violent base required no special theoretical justification.[2] Significantly, what they were far more concerned to justify and far more reluctant to engage in was revolution, not warfare. Fighting against one's established government was for them a far more radical act than simply fighting. In practical terms, of course, the two issues were inextricably connected; revolution inevitably meant warfare, or more correctly, warfare had led to revolution. The Declaration of Independence was in fact an attempt to justify and to enlist international support for an already existing state of war. Yet, significantly for understanding the long-standing assumptions of Western culture, the framers of the Declaration directed their efforts not toward providing their rationale for a just war (where mere soldiers would be killed) but toward rationalizing a just revolt against a king.

Nevertheless, because of their scruples concerning rebellion against God's annointed, the revolutionaries defended the justice of the Revolution (and incidentally of the war) as carefully as any strict just war theorist might desire. Their care in defending the Revolution reflected the conventional wisdom of their day, which held (as just war theorists would say for any war) that such radical acts should be undertaken only in the most extreme of circumstances. The Puritan revolution in England, during the civil wars of the 1640s, had established the principle that God's law stood above any person and that therefore even kings might be judged as criminals. If a monarch characteristically, blatantly, and continuously violated God's laws, then he or she was no longer God's ordained but had become something else: a tyrant. In such cases it was the monarch who had rebelled against God. Persons who resisted such a criminal-tyrant were champions of God's law and good order. Nonetheless such instances of justified violence against a monarch were extremely rare and were to be pursued only when demonstrated beyond a shadow of a doubt.

John Locke, who supported the "Glorious Revolution" of 1688, provided in effect a more universally applicable version of these views, basing it on natural law rather than on explicitly Christian grounds. Reason, he said, tells us that governments would have arisen out of the original state of nature only for the purpose of preserving certain self-evident human rights, such as the rights to life, liberty, and property. If a pretended government ceased to perform this protective function and in fact did just the opposite—took away citizens' lives, liberty, or property without due process—then reason said this was not true government, but a tyranny. Resistance in such rare cases was in order.

With some modifications the American Declaration of Independence essentially followed Locke's arguments.[3] The revolutionaries especially agreed with him that such resistance to constituted authority must take place only on rare occasions. "Prudence will dictate," they said, "that governments long established should not be changed for light or transient causes." Yet in this case, they were convinced, "a long train of abuses and usurpations . . . evinces a design to reduce [the colonists] under absolute despotism." In such an extreme case, it seemed their right and duty to resist, even to pledge their lives, fortunes, and sacred honor. Though the fact that the war to which they pledged themselves was a revolution accounts for their scrupulousness, seldom has the justice of a violent cause been argued with more care.

One of the aspects of the revolutionaries' stance that is most puzzling—and this puzzle is the focus for the reflections of this essay—is how they came apparently to believe that theirs was one of those extreme and exceptional instances when revolution, and hence revolutionary war, was justified. Even if we grant (which many historians will not, although I am inclined to do so)[4] that they had legal precedent on their side in the issue of taxation without representation, their claim that they faced a case of extreme tyranny seems extravagant. In retrospect it is difficult to believe that British government of America was designed to create utter despotism. To include the American colonies before the Revolution in the same category as today's notoriously criminal governments, such as Hitler's Germany and Stalin's Russia, seems wildly inappropriate. And rightly so. In fact most people of the world, both then and now, have lived with much less freedom than the Americans enjoyed under the British. How could they possibly think that theirs was one of the extreme cases?

Twentieth-century interpretations of the Revolution have been divided, speaking in very broad terms, into two camps, one of which would find the central question of this essay intriguing and the other of which would find it far less so. The one that does not pursue our central question suggests in a variety of ways that the Revolution was not primarily fought over the principles stated in the Declaration, but rather that the war occurred to advance the economic or class interest of a limited group of revolutionaries. Such interpreters, then, explain the extreme claims of the Declaration as basically some sort of rhetorical flourish that shielded, intentionally or unintentionally, the true aims and interests of the revolutionaries.

Early in this century, during the Progressive era, Carl Becker announced the theme of those who propounded a social or economic rather than a primarily ideological interpretation of the Revolution. The Revolution, said Becker, was not simply a contest over home rule, but it was also a struggle over who should rule at home.[5] Charles Beard in 1913 advanced a similar thesis in his famous *An Economic Interpretation of the Constitution of the United States*. Arthur M. Schlesinger, Sr., supported such claims regarding the Revolution itself in his *The Colonial Merchants and the American Revolution* (1918).

The major influence of this Progressive school of social and economic interpretations continued until approximately World War II.[6] After that war, corresponding with a general return of some faith in the American nation and its principles, the older "Whig" interpretation of the Revolution, maintaining that indeed it involved high principle (so that the Declaration should be taken seriously), regained considerable prestige. Having learned from the Progressives that social settings and interests cannot be neglected, these historians nevertheless argued that in the case of the American revolutionaries, principles and self-interests genuinely coincided. Bernard Bailyn, for instance, expressed a version of this theme in his widely reprinted "Political Experience and Enlightenment Ideas in Eighteenth-Century America" (1962), which argued that the colonial experience, marked by practical self-rule and representative government, predisposed Americans firmly to accept advanced Enlightenment political opinion. Bailyn's *Ideological Origins of the American Revolution* (1967) supported this interpretation by demonstrating that Whig ideology, learned from a vigorous school of eighteenth-century religiously dissenting British political writers, often known as the "Commonwealth Men," was not appropriated by the Americans simply for the occasion of their revolution, but had solid and deep roots in American colonial political and religious thought. Gordon Wood, who placed an account similar to Bailyn's in the broader context of a full-fledged history of the Revolution in *The Creation of the American Republic 1776–1787* (1969), produced what is usually recognized as the magnum opus of this new "Whig" interpretation. Edmund S. Morgan, who has provided many of the outstanding presentations of this view, has also summarized its most telling criticism of the older social-economic interpretations. "Both before and after the struggle," he grants, "Americans of every state were divided socially, sectionally, and politically." "But," Morgan immediately adds, "these divisions did not with any consistency coincide with the division between patriot and loyalist, nor did they run so deep as to arouse the same intensity of feeling."[7] Morgan, who frankly speaks for the "consensus" school of interpreters, has emphasized that the most important developments of the Revolutionary era were the emergence of a binding sense of American nationality, sealed with ideological ties, rather than the acknowledged social and economic conflicts of that era.[8]

Nevertheless, the mood in the later 1960s and accordingly that of many of the new generation of historians who published in the 1970s, often did not agree with such consensus views as were still strongly represented by Bailyn, Wood, Morgan, and many others. If one trait most often characterized the host of books accompanying the advent of the bicentennial, it was a search for what the Revolution meant to "the people." A small galaxy of historians, often influenced by "New Left" or neo-Marxist categories, suggested new versions of the old class-conflict interpretations. Another group concentrated on the loyalists, that sizeable number of Americans who totally rejected any emerging consensus. Similar interest was high concerning other groups outside the circles of the revolutionary elite, as the poor, the artisans, or members of the militias or the Continental Army. John Shy's *A People Armed and Numerous* (1976), which relates the impact of military experience to the wider context of American cultural ideals, and Robert A. Gross's *The Minutemen and Their World* (1976), a fascinating study of the responses of the people of Concord to the war, are two outstanding examples of such recent trends that supplement and confirm, rather than challenge, the consensus views. As to the motives of the leaders of the Revolution themselves, opinions still are sharply divided basically between the "Whig" or consensus view and the newer expressions of class and social interpretations.[9]

My own view of the matter is that, despite the efforts of the "New Left" and other social interpreters of the 1970s, it remains easier to explain why twentieth-century historians are so disposed toward seeing practical considerations of economics, class, or upward status mobility as primary causes than it is to find any clear correlation between social and economic interests and commitment to revolution. In fact, if any correlation has emerged clearly in the scholarship of the past twenty years, it has been the link between religious affiliations and revolutionary activity.[10] While such affiliations indeed involve strong social components, they suggest also that ideological commitments may play a larger role in determining people's actions than many present-day idealogues are willing to admit.

More positively, there seems good reason to suppose that people in the eighteenth century, such as those who provided the justification for the American Revolution, more often took their ideological commitments seriously than do, let's say, most American's today. This seems likely because the eighteenth-century idea of "truth" differed so markedly from the prevailing views of the twentieth century. Ideas were not regarded as essentially or properly the creations of the persons who expressed them. Certainly they were not regarded as properly being simply "instruments," as in modern pragmatism, propaganda, or advertising. Rather, even when rhetorical flourish was used in the art of persuasion, the assumption was that the goal was simply to lead persons to see the truth, which was essentially an objective and fixed entity.[11] Truth was discovered like Newton's laws; it was not a theoretical construct as in the world of Einstein. Status loomed large in all areas of eighteenth century life, and the truth had status.

Let us assume then, for the sake of the present argument, that the Revolutionary leaders and the people who followed them believed and took seriously the justification for the Revolution, and incidentally the war, that was summarized in the Declaration. In this view, then, we have a fairly good instance of an attempt to demonstrate that a military cause was just.

If we assume, however, that the revolutionaries acted, at least in part, on high principle, we are left with the puzzle. Even after discounting the aspects of the Declaration that can be considered as rhetorical flourish, how could the revolutionaries honestly have believed that they were describing an actual state of affairs? How could they honestly have believed that they were acting in one of those rare instances of opposition to extreme tyranny such as they described?

The answer to this question raises an important set of issues concerning human perceptions, issues that should be taken into account in any attempt to apply a just war theory in a real life situation. People's perceptions are strongly influenced not only by the well-known factor of their partisanship but also to a considerable extent by the theories that they already hold. That is, even under the best of circumstances, we do not view facts—political facts for example—wholly objectively. Rather, we fit the facts into categories that we have previously adopted, and these categories actually shape our perceptions of some of the facts themselves. Nothing illustrates this phenomenon better than the American perceptions of what was happening during the Revolutionary era.

Political theory in the eighteenth century—which was considered a rather exact science—taught that it was a law of politics that republics eventually turn into tyrannies. The writings of the "Commonwealth Men" especially emphasized this point. History and experience seemed to confirm this law—particularly the history of the fates of the republics of Greece and Rome. This scientific law was quite simple. Republics were based on virtue. Virtuous republics soon got strong. When they did, they gained empires. Empires brought riches and luxury. But riches and luxury inevitably brought corruption. So, the law concluded, empires would lose their republican virtues and be turned into tyrannies. This seemed to be both a thoroughly rational principle and one scientifically confirmed by collective human experience.[12]

As the highly partisan contest over rights to self-taxation developed after 1765, many colonists could readily be persuaded to fit the facts into this reputable framework. Their partisanship, of course, was crucial to the emerging rationale for the justification of their cause. Only a few British observers, who had the same theoretical framework available, saw the facts as the potential revolutionaries perceived them. On the west side of the Atlantic, however, the heat of controversy helped color perceptions, so that many of the best minds and most responsible citizens perceived the relationship between the facts and the well-established theory of tyranny as virtually self-evident.

To them the events leading to the Revolution fit alarmingly well into the predicted pattern. When the British in 1764 announced frankly that the new Sugar Act was a tax to raise revenue, and not simply a means to regulate trade, several colonies registered strong but polite protests through their legislatures. When in return the next year they got the direct tax of the Stamp Act, the protests over taxation without representation turned into civil disobedience, minor riots, intimidation of tax appointees, and effective nonimportation agreements. While the economic boycott brought repeal of the Stamp Act in 1766, the Parliament would not concede in the least its full rights to tax. Rather, they and the colonial administration, seen from the colonist perspective, determined one way or another to prove their point, as though breaking the will of disobedient children. In the process, it seemed they were willing to despoil and corrupt their colonial progeny, who the colonists themselves considered to be far more virtuous than their rich and profligate parents. Not only did the Parliament impose one illegal tax or custom duty after another but they also sent (as the Declaration later put it) "swarms of new officers to harass our people and eat out our substance." The fact that the Boston Massacre of 1770 took place in front of the customs house was evidence of the colonial resentment of the export to America of the corruption of office that pervaded the politics of the British empire. The Coercive Acts of 1774 and especially the closing of the Port of Boston in reaction to the Tea Party, together with a series of acts that removed Massachusetts' traditional legislative and judicial checks on the executive power of the royal governor, seemed conclusive evidence that Parliament would sooner ruin the colonies economically and destroy any vestiges of self-rule than allow them their rights not to give up their property without due consent. By 1776 this hideously corrupt empire was making war on her dutiful children and had destroyed whatever natural bonds of affection may once have bound them.[13]

How could this aberration, this unnatural alienation of affections, be explained? Very well indeed if one knew the laws of the course from republics to empires to riches to corruption to tyranny. The colonists, so they thought, had found firm evidence of a scientifically established law. Given the pattern, the future could be plotted as certainly as one might predict the increasing acceleration of a falling object. By 1776, having already endured a year of war with the mother land, they were convinced that they must act now before it was too late and they be reduced "under utter despotism." This conclusion, they were assured, was not mere prejudice, but confirmed by science and reason.

As it turned out (as we now know), the colonists were very likely wrong. Even if it is conceded that they had a somewhat stronger legal case than did their British opponents and that the economic and political treatment of Massachusetts in 1774 was both outrageous and ominous, the rebelling colonists nonetheless appeared to have been dead wrong in concluding that without armed rebellion absolute tyranny was inevitable. While the British treatment of Massachusetts appears unjust and to have removed ancient liberties, it is not clear that these extreme measures were more than an inept attempt to teach a lesson and that a compromise might have been reached by measures short of warfare. Careful modern studies of the British administration of the colonies have revealed not only that the British had a quite plausible legal case but also that their failings were not extraordinary as governments go. True, there was a fair amount of corruption, intrigue, and of course some incompetence surrounding the crown and its appointees; but on the whole, it is now usually agreed, its policies were responsible, some say even quite benevolent.[14] Certainly nothing has been found to support the claim of the Declaration that the crown's policies "evince a design" to establish utter despotism throughout the colonies. To see how wrong the colonists were one need only look at the administration of Canada, which, despite continued British rule, developed along lines not clearly inferior to those of the United States. Even taking into account whatever lesson the British may have learned from the loss of the thirteen colonies, the actual administration of Canada during the next century seems far more consistent with the direction of British civilization than does the conspiratorial scenario of enslavement that the revolutionaries had come to believe.

Whatever lessons might be learned from this about the frailties of our perceptions in identifying a just cause in time of war become all the more disconcerting when we consider the responses of Christian colonists who presumably held to something like a just war theory.[15] This excludes, of course, Christian pacifists, such as Mennonites and Quakers: who asserted that no war could be just. Of those remaining, the only groups substantially opposed to the Revolutionary War were the Anglicans, who opposed the war not on religious grounds, but because they traditionally tended to side with the Crown. Of the others, we find among the vast majority of Congregationalists, Presbyterians, Baptists, and the fledgling Methodists not merely acquiescence with the arguments advanced by the Revolutionary leaders, but enthusiasm for the war that often surpassed that found among their compatriots. Not only did they perceive the cause through the eyes of partisanship, and not only did they accept the scientific confirmation of their partisan perceptions, but their religious orientation raised their perceptions of the American national cause to the level of a crusade.

To them, good Protestants that they were, the history of tyranny had a strong religious dimension. Their historical memories went back to the 1600s, to the conflict between the Puritans and Parliament on the one hand and the bishops and king on the other. To Calvinist heirs of that conflict, liberty and true religion were always on one side; tyranny and hierarchical episcopal power were on the other. More broadly, this lineup seemed to go back to the Reformation, with Protestantism and liberty alligned against Roman Catholicism and despotism.[16] This pattern had been reconfirmed in the English Protestant mind with the so-called Glorious Revolution of 1688 when King James II—suspected of Roman Catholic sentiments—was replaced by a Protestant prince; whereupon John Locke developed the new Whig theories of liberty.

Throughout the next century this association of Whig principles of liberty with dissenting Protestantism was perpetuated by the Commonwealth Men, who not only opposed political tyranny and executive power but also strongly opposed the Anglican establishment. The name "Commonwealth Men" for these Whigs suggested in itself their ties to the tradition of the Puritan Commonwealth. Their writings had a strong moral flavor and had a great deal to do with convincing many eighteenth-century political thinkers that hierarchical powers in church or state went hand-in-hand with moral degeneracy. Such interpretations were immensely popular in America, where of course there were strong Puritan roots to feed such prejudices.

One of the influences of this partisan Protestant and Whig political tradition was that it infused the American Revolution with much of its conspicuous moral dimension. The Revolution was not waged simply over administrative abuses and high taxes' it was also a contest of national morality versus moral corruption. In the colonists' view, morality was still found commonly in America, but corruption was spreading alarmingly in England, especially in high offices. Separation from England thus became an act of righteousness—almost a form of national sanctification.[17]

Moreover for these evangelical Americans the Revolution had a distinctly religious dimension. One of their fears, fueled by the commonwealth tradition, was that England was about to appoint a bishop for America—and episcopacy was tied in their minds to political and religious tyranny. This antibishop craze has been referred to by one historian as "the great fear." Another fear was the spread of Roman Catholicism—had not England just recently in the Quebec Act of 1774 recognized the legitimacy of Roman Catholicism for the conquered provinces of Canada? The forces of Antichrist were encamping roundabout—moral degeneracy, episcopacy, political tyranny, and Roman Catholicism—all threatening to destroy both virtue and true religion in Protestant America.[18]

The result was that by 1776 most American evangelical Protestants—especially the clergy—were regarding the Revolution as the most righteous of righteous causes. Among many examples that have been traced, a particularly striking instance of this extravagant clerical support for the war is found in the development of American interpretations of the millennium during the Revolutionary era. During the eighteenth century the prevailing view of the millennium was a form of what is now called postmillennialism, which maintained that the present era would culminate in a millennial golden age and that currently one could see fulfillment of biblical prophecies preparing for that great day. Political and religious aspects of these developments were not clearly separated, since some of the main evidences of currently fulfilled prophecies were the various setbacks of the Antichrist, who was assumed to be the pope. In the cold war atmosphere between Protestant and Catholic world powers, punctuated by outbreaks of open hostilities, Protestant Americans in a predominantly Catholic hemisphere saw strong religious implications in the political contests of the day. The various eighteenth-century wars with France, culminating in the Seven Years War from 1756 to 1763, especially had this mixture of political, religious, and millennial dimensions.

During the Revolutionary crisis after 1763 a remarkable transformation took place in clerical interpretations of the meaning of the Antichrist. As the British administration became increasingly harsh, the colonists, to their horror, began to conclude that their British protectors were taking on the very despotic traits indelibly associated with Roman Catholic powers. England herself was being corrupted by the beast of political tyranny. In the midst of this political struggle, the traditional interpretations of the contest in terms of actual religious affiliations faded, and the political dimensions prevailed. As the Rev. Samuel West told the Revolutionary Massachusetts legislature in an election day sermon in 1776, the Antichrist "better be understood as political than ecclesiastical tyrants." The British army, in West's view, had become the "horrible wild beast" of the Book of Revelation, which led West to announce, "We must beat our plowshares into swords, and our pruning hooks into spears."[19]

West's bald statement could be paralleled by many others. In the fervor of an emerging nationalism the gospel has been turned upside down. The biblical hopes for peace have been forsaken for images suggesting that Christians, with muskets in hand, are to do the avenging work of Christ. The approach of the millennium is identified with the advances of the Continental Army; the American Revolution is seen as part of God's redemptive plan. The chosen people, the new Israel, is no longer even simply the elect of the church, as it was for the Puritans; it is the entire American nation.[20]

We can see, in summary, three interrelated steps in arriving at this Christian justification for the Revolutionary War. First is simply the influence of partisan perceptions. Second, the colonists had inherited political-religious categories, especially from the Whig tradition, that served as a framework for organizing their perceptions and gave them a rational-scientific credibility. Third, the religious dimensions of these perceptions, especially for those who took biblical categories seriously, raised such perceptions to cosmic dimensions. Not only did most ardent evangelical Protestants view the revolutionary cause as just; they also saw warfare as a sacred duty.

The irony in this development and its value for throwing light on our own righteous pretentions are heightened if we grant that on the whole the revolutionaries' cause was a good one. The liberties that the British had removed from Massachusetts in 1774 and which the colonists defended were indeed part of their most valuable heritage. The principles embodied in the new governments of the states and of the United States likewise were admirable. Yet the American revolutionaries had taken a good cause, the virtues of which they overestimated because of their partisanship and their political preconceptions, and they had vastly inflated its importance by sanctifying it with biblical imagery. Thus the good cause, as good causes especially are prone to do, became an idol.

Perhaps the most important outcome of this process was that in it a new religion was born. This new religion is the now-famous American civil religion in which the state is an object of worship, but the imagery used to describe its sacredness is borrowed from Christianity.[21] Church and state in the Western world since the time of Constantine had been intimately connected. Indeed it has been this close association of religion and politics that has been one of the greatest obstacles to a genuine Christian critique of the political order, specifically of its military ventures. Now in the new American situation, even with the disestablishment of the church, the religious-political intimacy was maintained by applying sacred rhetoric to describe the status and mission of the secular government. This civil religion, growing out of the ironic amplification of the American good cause during the Revolutionary era, has continued to shape, and indeed to distort, American visions of her own justice in subsequent wars.

Such observations concerning the extravagence of some Christians' support for the Revolution need not make us despair of just war theory entirely. Indeed, as Mark Noll has shown, some who supported the Revolution did so in qualified and reflective ways that made clear that their quest for justice against the British did not blind them to the shortcomings of their own cause.[22] Their highest allegience was to the city of God, and that city was not to be equated with any earthly civilization. Given the frailty of human perceptions, such a well-developed sense of higher allegiences seems prerequisite to any realistic pursuit of justice in time of war.

2 RALPH BEEBE

THE WAR OF 1812

Blest with victory and peace, may the heav'n rescued land
Praise the Power that hath made and preserved us a nation.
Then conquer we must, when our cause it is just,
And this be our motto: "In God is our trust."

WRITING IN A DARK MOMENT DURING THE WAR OF 1812, Francis Scott Key believed God would bless the American war effort, a cause he considered to be fully deserving of divine intervention. In this persuasion Key echoed the patriotic sentiments of many of his countrymen, including President James Madison, whose request for war had called upon Americans to use force "in defense of their natural rights" and to commit "a just cause into the hands of the almighty Disposer of Events."[1] Key and Madison believed that the God who had "made and preserved" the American nation could surely be counted upon for its continued protection. Human beings, of course, would be God's instrument in this just cause.

The purpose of this chapter, notwithstanding the author's own pacifist convictions,[2] is to determine whether the War of 1812 can be justified in the minds of those who see some wars as necessary, others as unnecessary. This requires a study of the evidence to determine and evaluate the war's causes. Unfortunately, however, those causes are difficult to assess. Historians have long debated the many factors that led to the war.[3] Yet those 2,260 American men who died must have felt they fought for some purpose, and those who took British lives must have felt there was justification for the killing. Although different people undoubtedly fought for different reasons, it is possible to identify certain major causes. The desire for trade and the desire for unrestricted access to the west and expansion into Canada and Florida stand out. Underlying these causes were patriotism, national honor, and the defensiveness of a young nation flexing its muscle against the exaggerated indignities it believed it suffered at the hands of older European powers.

The War of 1812 must be seen against a dual backdrop. First, America was a new nation with an ironically ambivalent self-image that stressed its freedom from the old world's propensity for war, while at the same time the nation pursued a strongly materialistic "success" ethic that caused its people to engage in pursuits that were certain to lead to conflict. Second, Europe was still engaged in the war in Europe that had begun in 1792 when radical Frenchmen tried to export their revolution while autocratic powers tried to contain it, and that had continued until 1814 as a death struggle in which England and her allies resisted the despot Napoleon.

The military involvement of the United States was confined to the last thirty months of a more than twenty-year war. Her tardy entrance into that war was an annoyance to war-weary Britain, but not a major impediment to that nation's final drive to victory over the French. If the United States had cause for war with England in 1812, she had had even greater cause five years earlier. Yet war had been avoided then—thanks primarily to the policies of the leading figure of the era, Thomas Jefferson. While his complex and occasionally ambivalent philosophy defies simple analysis, he clearly believed that in this new nation a new ethic could be implemented:

> Never was so much false arithmetic employed on any subject, as that which has been employed to persuade nations that it is their interest to go to war. Were the money which it has cost to gain, at the close of a long war, a little town, or a little territory, the right to cut wood here, or to catch fish there, expended on improving what they already possess, in making roads, opening rivers, building ports, improving the arts, and finding employment for their idle poor, it would render them much stronger, much wealthier and happier. This I hope will be our wisdom.[4]

Jefferson put it into specifically humanitarian terms:

> The evils which of necessity encompass the life of man are sufficiently numerous. Why should we add to them by voluntarily distressing and destroying one another? Peace brothers, is better than war. In a long and bloody war, we lose many friends and gain nothing.[5]

Again he stated: "I hope we shall prove how much happier for men the Quaker policy is."[6] Jefferson the idealist, the political philosopher, could express these sentiments, but it was up to Jefferson the president, the practicing politician, to carry them out. In 1807 he faced a crisis that would have carried lesser men to the more popular expedient of meeting force with military force.

It had all to do with trade, the rights of neutrals, and ultimately, profits. The war in Europe had opened splendid opportunities for merchants flying a neutral flag to trade with all the belligerents. In 1792, the year the European war began, American merchants exported about $20 million worth of goods; by 1801 when Jefferson became president, this figure had risen to nearly $95 million.[7]

Half the latter was the "reexport" trade. Neutral American merchants had found an excellent wartime market in carrying goods to France from her West Indian colonies. However, when the British began seizing these vessels, wily Americans started bringing French West Indian goods to the United States and then "reexporting" them to Europe as American products which, under the loose but generally accepted rules governing trade by neutrals, were not subject to capture.

Jefferson had speculated in 1782 that:

> To remove as much as possible the occasions of making war, it might be better for us to abandon the ocean altogether, that being the element whereon we shall be principally exposed to justle with other nations; to leave to others to bring what we shall want, and to carry what we can spare. This would make us invulnerable to Europe, by offering none of our property to their prize. . . .[8]

But Jefferson the president, facing the demands of a profit-appetized merchant fleet, did not try to intervene. By 1807 the exports had grown to nearly $110 million annually, more than half of them in the reexport trade.[9]

Although the rewards were immense, neutral trade created major controversies relating to the rights of neutrals and the impressment of sailors from American ships. While these issues had long been disputed, they did not become critical until after 1805, when a major naval victory over France established Britain as ruler of the seas. French businessmen became more dependent upon the

American carrying trade, which was all that stood between Britain and a successful blockade of the continent.

So, by court action in 1805 and Orders in Council two years later, Britain declared American reexport trade subject to seizure and established a blockade of the entire French coast. Napoleon, in return, attempted to close to British commerce not only all the ports of Europe but also the overseas colonies of his enemy. All the while, the United States insisted that as a neutral nation, it had the right to trade with anyone.

Closely related to the neutral rights controversy was a manpower problem. The British navy was having trouble getting and keeping recruits—a crisis of major proportions for a nation whose survival in an all-out war depended on domination of the seas. The British navy afforded an extremely unattractive working environment. When recruits proved insufficient to man His Majesty's ships, a highly informal and not very selective service system was used. Captains were allowed to capture sailors in British ports and impress them into service. Sometimes sailors were kidnapped while drunk and never knew they were in the navy until the next morning when they were ready to put out to sea. Captains maintained control through harsh discipline. One contemporary historian of the British navy put it this way:

> No monarch is more despotic, as far as respects the infliction of corporal punishment short of death, than the captain of a ship of war. If a man speaks or even looks to offend, he is ordered to the gangway; and the bloody furrows on his shoulders soon increase, beneath the vigorous arm that lays on the cat-o'-nine-tails.[10]

It is not surprising that the British navy had a desertion problem.

At the same time, Yankee businessmen, unable to fully man their merchant ships with American sailors, capitalized on the problem and contributed to it by encouraging desertions from the British navy. Thousands of sailors abandoned their ships in American ports and signed on the United States merchant vessels. British naval commanders responded by stopping American ships at sea and removing sailors who were believed to be "deserters," returning them to their patriotic duty of shooting Frenchmen. For a British sailor this meant a return to lower pay, much more difficult working conditions, an immense increase in danger, and, very likely, the scourge of the whip or worse to make him an example to other sailors who might be tempted to stray away at the next American port.

Worse still was the plight of the American merchant sailor. The British vessel might stop his ship, come aboard, and declare him to be, apparently, a British subject, and quickly impress him into His Majesty's Navy. True, if he had papers of American citizenship he could apply for release at the next port. But the papers might have been lost or stolen—and the next port might be many months and thousands of miles away.

British captains tended to ignore evidence of United States citizenship, knowing that certificates were often invalid. As rising profits brought the need for increased labor, American merchants often issued fraudulent certificates of citizenship.

Typical of the frauds, according to the British foreign minister, was one practiced by

> an old woman, in one of the seaport towns, who kept a cradle, made for the purpose of rocking full-grown British subjects who were to be converted in a hurry into American citizens, that, when testimony should be called for to prove their birth, she might with a safe conscience swear she had known them from their cradles.[11]

While precise figures are impossible to obtain, one authority estimates that 20,000 British sailors deserted and took service on American merchant vessels. In seeking their return the British impressed at least 10,000 men from American merchant ships, but probably only about 1,000 of them proved to be British subjects. Thus, during a twenty-two-year war, about 9,000 American citizens were impressed into the British navy.[12]

In 1807, the impressment crisis approached critical proportions. On the seventh of March, five British sailors threatened their officer's lives while their sloop was weighing anchor and escaped to the Virginia shore. Thereupon they enlisted in the United States Navy as a part of the crew of the frigate *Chesapeake*. British attempts to have them returned were spurned. Protected by the United States Navy, they remained on board until the *Chesapeake* came down the Potomac. Then all but one, Jenkin Ratford, deserted.

On the morning of June 22 the *Chesapeake* put out to sea. While still within ten miles of shore she was hailed by a British naval vessel, the *Leopard*, with a request to come on board. When the boarding party demanded that the ship be searched for British deserters, Commodore Barron, the commander of the *Chesapeake*, refused permission, because, though merchant vessels were legally subject to search, ships of the United States Navy were totally exempt from such procedures. When Barron refused to allow a search, the *Leopard* opened fire, an act of war against a United States vessel. Three persons were killed and eighteen wounded in a fifteen-minute barrage. A two-hour search turned up four suspects, but three proved to be United States citizens who had previously been impressed into the British navy and had deserted. Only Jenkin Ratford was a certain British citizen. He was courtmartialed, convicted of desertion, and hanged.

After June 22, 1807, American outrage over the *Chesapeake* incident put President Jefferson under tremendous pressure. Had he sought a declaration of war, an enraged public would have been eager to assert its honor. Jefferson lamented that "the world is truly in an awful state. Two nations of overgrown power are endeavoring to establish, the one an universal dominion by sea, the other by land."[13] He called the attack "an outrage not to be borne," which had "produced such a state of exasperation, and that so unanimous, as never has been seen in this country since the battle of Lexington."[14]

The president immediately closed United States ports to all British ships, threatening to keep them out by force if necessary. But he still held to the convictions he had expressed in 1801:

> I do not believe war the most certain means of enforcing principles. Those peaceable coercions which are in the power of every nation, if undertaken in concert and in time of peace, are more likely to produce the desired effect.[15]

Although not a pacifist, Jefferson maintained that war must be only a last resort, when all else had failed.

What were the alternatives? What "peaceable coercions" were available? First, Jefferson tried to use the British government's embarrassment over the *Chesapeake* incident as leverage in an attempt to negotiate "reparation for the past, security for the future,"[16] by which the president meant the restoration of free trade and an end to impressment. The British did apologize for the incident, but reaffirmed their insistence that impressment was necessary as long as British sailors were being "induced to accept letters of naturalization" and were being "taught to believe that, by such letters or certificates, they are discharged from that duty of allegience which, as our natural born subjects, they owe to us."[17]

Twenty-five years earlier, Jefferson, as noted above, had suggested that to avoid war it might be necessary to "abandon the ocean altogether. . . ."[18] Now, in crisis, he acted on this belief in a bold attempt to enact one of those "peaceable coercions" he felt considerably preferable to war. His policy, a total embargo of all trade goods to all nations, passed Congress in December of 1807 by House and Senate votes of 82 to 45 and 22 to 7, respectively. Jefferson hoped the embargo would force Great Britain to repeal her Orders in Council and France's offensive Berlin and Milan decrees, by which Napoleon had blockaded the continent. Jefferson reasoned that each belligerent needed United States trade so much they would both acquiesce to his demands.

The total embargo was in effect for fourteen months before its partial repeal three days before Jefferson left office in March of 1809. During those months neither power repealed its decrees. Bumper crops in England and the opening of trade with a new ally, Spain and her colonies, reduced Britain's need for American products. Nevertheless, the policy would have had an excellent chance to succeed had Americans cooperated more fully. The law was evaded consistently by some merchants who feared extreme financial losses if the embargo were to continue over an extended period, and who were eager to capitalize on the opportunity for immense profits while some of their competitors were obeying the law.

Public opinion was deeply divided. Supporters of the policy argued that a temporary sacrifice would bring a permanent end to Britain's offensive maritime poliices. One newspaper editor listed the advantages:

1. No commerce could be carried on with safety prior to the embargo.
2. We had serious disputes with England that might lead to war.
3. The embargo would bring the British to terms.
4. It would tend to preserve peace.

5. It would prevent the importation of many millions of undesirable foreign goods.
6. It would injure enemies more effectively than war.
7. It would encourage domestic manufacturers.
8. It would discourage "extravagance and expense, in foreign gewgaws."[19]

Another editor contrasted the options of embargo and war:

THE EMBARGO

will produce temporary inconvenience; the loss of a few thousand dollars; and give a little more idle time to the citizens, who do not choose to turn their attention to internal improvements. It will not starve anybody. On the contrary, the staple necessaries of life will be cheaper.

A WAR

will produce the loss of millions of dollars, burning and sacking of towns and cities, rape, theft, murders, streams of blood, weeping widows, helpless orphans, the beggary of thousands, the ruin of agriculture, and an extensive depravation of morals.

Citizens of the United States! Which do you choose?[20]

Some of the embargo's opponents not only evaded the law, but ridiculed it. Cartoonists and newspaper editors had a field day, making the word become "Go Bar Em," "Mob Rage," "Dambargo," and "O Grab Me."[21] One article reflected on a particularly difficult area of enforcement, the border between the United States and Canada:

A PIG CASE

This fag-end of the embargo, goes to prohibit the farmers of Vermont and New Hampshire from driving their swine into Canada for sale. Now suppose a man should drive a herd of hogs close up to the line of the United States, but *not over*, and a Canadian should *accidently* make his appearance just within the boundary of that British colony with a basket of corn in his hand, and should cry Pig—Pig—Pig and the whole drove should run over the line into Canada and voluntarily place themselves under the government of the tyrant of the ocean. Would it or would it not be a breach of the embargo law; and if so, who should be punished, the farmer who drove his hogs so near the despotism, the swine who, regardless of the blessing of a free country, thus ran over the line; or the Canadian who tempted them to this anti-republican act![22]

Historian Fletcher Pratt has colorfully described the dilemma which kept the policy from being enforced fully enough to reap quick results:

> Question—what is the state? Collective citizens, whose collective wisdom, in a democracy, reaches decisions. Collective citizens of America decided that Thomas Jefferson could best speak their will. But did any of them will that his normal mode of life should cease or the market for the labor of his hands be cut off? No. Surely the manifold prohibitions of this embargo were not intended for ME. So the history of the embargo became the history of me and me and me and five million other me's, struggling to win bread for their children from a cosmos beset with difficulties. . . .
>
> At Philadelphia a nameless me found that the embargo permitted coasting vessels to sail as usual. He loaded his ship with flour, took a clearance for Savannah, and out at sea encountered a gale that blew him clear to England before he could turn around. At Boston, another nameless me discovered that whalers and fishermen were exempt. He went to hunt whales in a ship with a most exiguous outfit of tackle and five hundred casks of bacon in her hold (provisions for the crew) and came back from Halifax with one keg of whale oil and four hundred ninety-nine bales of English woolens (clothing for the crew). At Richmond, still another one found river craft were not included. His river boat, loaded with prime Virginia tobacco, had difficulty making Norfolk and sailed to Nassau instead.[23]

Nevertheless, the embargo did damage the belligerents, although it is not easy to distinguish its impact from that of Britain's Orders in Council and Napolean's decrees. Exports from the United States declined from $108 million in 1807 to $22 million in 1808. Those going to Britain were reduced from $19 million to about $4 million; those to France from $9 million to almost nothing in 1808.[24]

A comparison of imports of principal crops into Great Britain from all sources for 1806, 1807, and 1808 is instructive:[25]

	1806	*1807*	*1808*
Corn (in thousands of tons)	814	1,124	146
Sugar	5,206	4,972	5,128
Tea	2,216	1,260	3,568
Raw cotton	2,034	2,610	1,471
Raw wool	382	666	128
Tobacco	228	244	78
Linen yarn	501	325	35

The United States shipped 143,000 bags of cotton to Liverpool in 1807, but only 25,000 in 1808. The average price quotation in England for Uplands (mostly American) cotton in 1807 was 14½ cents per pound, rising to 22 for 1808. Surats (East Indian) cotton rose from an average of 13 to 19½.[26]

Although the embargo damaged both Great Britain and France, the hardships were not great enough, nor permanent enough, to cause immediate repeal of either the Orders in Council or the French decrees. Jefferson left office in 1809 much maligned. His policy had avoided war, but had been extremely unpopular at home.

Jefferson's successor, James Madison, continued a policy of economic coercion, although in a modified form. Trade was reopened with all the world except Great Britain and France; later it was reopened with those two nations, with the provision that if either would drop its offensive decrees, the other would be embargoed. In 1810 Napoleon announced acceptance, so early in 1811 trade with Britain was again discontinued.

In 1811 crops failed in England. With food prices skyrocketing, workers rioting, and factories closing, American trade was desperately needed and British citizens put immense pressure on their government for repeal of the Orders in Council. Finally, on June 16, 1812, the House of Commons repealed the Orders, effective immediately. But repeal came too late. In the absence of a "hot line" between London and Washington, the news did not arrive for several weeks. In the meantime the United States had declared war. Two ships—one carrying news of Britain's repeal, the other of the United States's declaration of war—crossed paths somewhere in the Atlantic, neither knowing of the other's message.

Thomas Jefferson had gambled his presidency on the conviction that peace was possible without bloodshed. Could the Jefferson-Madison policy of economic coercion have succeeded? Had

American merchants obeyed the law, it is very likely Jefferson could have soon negotiated a trade agreement to their general satisfaction. In any case, war would have been avoided—and war, when it did come, damaged the merchants' trade as much as a totally enforced embargo would have done. In retrospect, federal subsidies to offset short-term losses due to the embargo might well have been recommended, but there is no evidence that this was considered.

The policy did force repeal of the Orders in Council. It kept the United States out of war for five years, and peace could have continued indefinitely had Congress so chosen. In the final analysis one has to agree with historian Thomas A. Bailey: "In the end Jefferson's policy triumphed; but America was not patient enough to reap the benefits."[27] Why was the United States too impatient to reap the benefits? What changed the mood of the country and caused it to abandon economic coercion at the very moment of its greatest success? What actually caused the war?

President Madison's war message emphasized maritime problems; many textbooks term it a war for "free trade and sailors' rights." Yet it seems strange that those most supportive of the war were from the interior, and those most opposed were from the commercial Northeast. Maritime problems were clearly less annoying in 1812 than they had been five years earlier. So, while neutral rights and impressment were long-standing, emotion-laden problems for Americans, these issues alone did not bring war. A fruitful field for further inquiry is the collective personality of a group of western congressmen who were elected in 1810.

Commonly termed "War Hawks," these congressmen took office late in 1811 in a militant mood. They vowed to replace the pacific program of Jefferson and Madison with a much more bellicose policy. The War Hawks were mostly young "second generation revolutionaries" inspired by the "spirit of '76" and by the "masculine" frontier atmosphere. Henry Clay of Kentucky, elected Speaker on his first day in the House, made sure hawks would dominate all important committees. One of them, Felix Grundy of Tennessee, threatened: "Rely on one thing, we have War or Honorable peace before we adjourn or certain great personages have produced a state of things which will bring them down from their high places."[28] Clay argued: "What are we to gain by war, has been emphatically asked? In reply . . . what are we not to lose by peace?—commerce, character, a nation's best treasure, honor!"[29]

This theme of national honor permeates the War Hawks' speeches. A further review of some of the rhetoric is instructive. William R. King (North Carolina) lamented: "I find my country degraded by insults unrevenged; almost ruined by her efforts to preserve friendship with nations who feel power and forget right. . . ."[30] David R. Williams (South Carolina) added: "We are going to war for honor; . . . That which is sacred in an individual, cannot be less so in a nation. . . . Shall we, who hold honor dearer than life and all its blessings, consider that of the nation as a bubble?"[31]

Speaker Henry Clay regretted that

> . . . rights which forever ought to be served, are trampled upon and violated. We are called upon to submit to debasement, dishonor, and disgrace. . . . What nation, what individual was ever taught, in the schools of ignominious submission, the patriotic lessons of freedom and independence. . . . You must look for an explanation of Britain's conduct in the jealousies of a rival. She sickens at your prosperity.[32]

Many of their colleagues agreed. Robert Wright (Maryland) argued that violations of commercial rights "are just causes for war. But . . . the impressment of our native seamen is a stroke at the vitals of liberty itself. . . ." Wright thought this issue should bring to the front "patriotic feelings and make (one's) bosom burn with that holy fire that inspired the patriots of the Revolution." He predicted that when any patriotic citizen "reflects on the impressment of our native American seamen languishing under the ignominious scourge, on board the infernal floating castles of Great Britain, he will feel like an American devoted to avenge their wrongs."[33]

Peter B. Porter of New York warned that ". . . if we go on submitting to one indignity after another, it will not be long before we shall see British subjects, not only taking our property in our harbors, but trampling on our persons in the streets of our cities. . . ." Porter was concerned for the nation's dignity: "Our situation is not unlike that of a young man just entering into life, and who, if he tamely submitted to one cool, deliberate, intentional indignity, might safely calculate to be kicked and cuffed for the whole of the remainder of his life."[34] Felix Grundy agreed:

"Sir, I prefer war to submission. . . . I then say it, with humiliation, produced by the degradation of my country, we have submitted."[35]

The nationalistic hyperbole made much of supposed maritime indignities. However, problems in the west also received great attention. The British were accused of insulting the flag of the United States and of inciting frontier Indians to resist encroachment on their land. Britain's monopoly of the fur trade was also deeply resented.[36]

Underlying the rhetoric was the unmistakable assumption that it was in the United States' interest, indeed, it was her Manifest Destiny (although the term was not to be coined for another generation) that the stars and stripes would one day wave over Canada and beyond. "Where is it written in the book of fate" wrote the editor of the *Nashville Clarion* in 1812, "that the American republic shall not stretch her limits from the Capes of the Chesapeake to Nootka sound, from the isthmus of Panama to Hudson bay?"[37] Representative John A. Harper of New Hampshire argued in the House: "To me, sir, it appears that the Author of Nature has marked our limits in the south, by the Gulf of Mexico; and on the north by the regions of eternal frost."[38] Congressman William R. King saw expansion as a natural result of a just war:

> Sire, this will be a war forced upon us; we cannot, under existing circumstances, avoid it. . . . I trust, if our differences with Great Britain are not speedily adjusted (of which indeed, I have no expectation), we shall take Canada, Yes, sir, by force; by valour. . . .[39]

It was a tidy package. American honor had been insulted at sea and in the frontier. It was time to assert national rights and drive Britain from the continent once and for all. A quick victory would bring an end to British insults, the fur trade monopoly, and meddling with the Indians, and would open the door to the West. Concurrently, Canada would be added to United States territory and to complete the program, Florida would be wrested from Britain's ally, Spain.

This ambitious agenda caught the public imagination and put immense pressure on the president. Perhaps wearying of economic coercion and fearing the results of a War Hawk-dominated

Republican party caucus when he sought renomination later that summer, Madison requested war on June 1. The hawkish House answered promptly on June 4, voting for war 79 to 49. A long Senate debate resulted in a 19 to 13 prowar vote. The president signed the declaration on June 18—two days after the House of Commons in London had repealed its Orders in Council.

Americans anticipated a quick victory, but their invasion of Canada proved disastrous. The navy had some successes but numerous failures. By 1814 the allies had defeated Napoleon, and Britain could turn her full attention to the United States. In June the navy blockaded the American coast; in July it raided coastal cities; by September it had sailed up the Potomac and taken Washington.

In December 1814, the war was ended by a treaty which mentioned neither impressment nor neutral rights—the issues over which, presumably, the war had been fought. With the Napoleonic war over, neutral rights was no longer a major issue; furthermore, the military situation gave the United States little bargaining power. Fortunately for the United States, war-weary Britain did not press her advantage nor demand territorial concessions, but allowed the war to end as a stalemate, leaving the prewar status quo in all areas of dispute.

This war may have caused more division than any other in American history. In general, people in the South and West were in favor; those in the Northeast were opposed. Republicans tended to support the war; Federalists almost universally declared their opposition. The religious community was as deeply divided. The younger, more rapidly growing activist denominations, notably Baptist and Methodist, generally applauded the war; the older denominations, notably Congregational, Presbyterian, and Quaker, opposed it.

The Christian prowar rhetoric was filled with patriotic references linking God and country. "Such a war God considers as His own cause, and to help in such a cause is to come to the help of the Lord,"[40] John Stevens averred. Dr. Solomon Froeligh confidently asserted that "The Lord will plead our cause, and execute judgment for us; He will plead our cause . . . in the highway of nations, on the banks of the Wabash, and even before the walls of Quebec."[41] William Plummer asked God to "teach our hands to war and our fingers to fight."[42]

Prowar Christians tended to see revolutionary France, which had destroyed its Catholic church and was fighting Catholic monarchs throughout Europe, as God's agent in a war against the pope, who many thought was the Antichirst. A typical statement proclaimed:

> The overthrow of Antichrist, and the destruction of the seat of the beast . . . is plainly foretold in New Testament prophecy. Our forefathers have made the fulfillment of these prophecies the subject of their prayers in public and private for many centuries. God is fulfilling these prophecies, and answering these prayers, in a surprising manner.[43]

Further, a British victory over France was feared likely to bring an end to religious freedom. Americans were warned against "Blind and subservient attachment to 'the old whore of Babylon,' England."[44] President Madison was applauded in that he had resisted

> . . . the haughty encroachments of Britain, declared war and vindicated the inestimable rights of our own nation against the tyranny and cruelty of that government which may, for the present, be styled the bulwark of national religion; that bane of Christianity, and principle support of Babylon the great, the mother of harlots, and abomination of the earth.[45]

For the most part Christian opposition to the war did not result from pacifism. It came, rather, from the belief that the United States was fighting the wrong enemy. A majority of the dissenters would have applauded a war against France as enthusiastically as the prowar faction supported the one against England. When the Senate voted 19 to 13 to declare war against Britain, it defeated a declaration of war against France by a narrow 18 to 14.

As noted, opposition to the war centered in traditionally pro-British New England, especially among Congregationalists and Presbyterians. Its leaders warned that siding with the French "is of itself sufficient to draw down upon our country the judgments of Heaven."[46] Federalists tended to believe that the French government, "whether Jacobin or Napoleonic, was morally depraved."[47] Deism and radical democracy were seen to have brought revolutionary excesses that were threatening to the interests of the United States. The Francophobia of this faction was little less pronounced than American fear of the Soviet Union and communism in the twentieth century.

In the sermons of the antiwar Protestants the pope began to be less often depicted as the Antichrist; Napoleon quickly gained that honor. A typical speaker declared that "the antichrist foretold, as coming on the earth after the Man of Sin, had literally appeared in the new government of France, having Napoleon Buonaparte for her head."[48] Another decried "a fatal alliance of the United States with Daniel's infidel king, the tyrannical antichrist. Great God forbid it!"[49]

William Gribbin, in a recent thorough analysis of religion during the war period, provides this summary of the arguments expressed in antiwar sermons:

> Napoleonic France was seen as an infidel nation, controlled by the antichrist foretold in the Book of Revelation or by the false prophet of the papal antichrist. Only Britain prevented this beast of Babylon from conquering the world. Britain, moreover, had recently taken the lead in spreading Protestant Christianity over the globe through evangelical societies. No good could come from warring against the enemies of God's enemies, especially in an offensive invasion of Canada, in which no honest Christian would take a willing part. Aggressive war was always contrary to the commands of the Gospel; and this particular war was the instrument of deists, slave holders, Francophiles, and the great anti-Christian league. Americans were to be allied with all of papal Europe against the land of their Protestant fathers. . . . It was little consolation that Napoleon himself had abolished the Spanish Inquisition, [and] that the Pope was his prisoner. . . .[50]

Christian pacifists expressed their dissent less vigorously. Although anyone could be exempted from military service by payment of a special tax, some refused to pay; some also refused to export goods to avoid the war tax imposed on them. One shopkeeper, Isaac Martin, admitted this hurt his business, but believed the testimony "worth suffering for, if thereby the peaceable government of the Messiah may be promoted."[51] Yet the pacifists failed to put much political pressure behind their convictions. While it is probably an exaggeration of potential Quaker strength, the *Federal Republican* charged that had they voted according to their religious beliefs, Pennsylvania Quakers could have kept their congressional delegation from casting 18 votes for war.[52] Had these "yes" votes been "no," the declaration would have lost 67 to 61 and there would have been no war.

This was not a popular war. When the hope for a quick annexation of Canada gave way to the reality of military defeat, support rapidly declined throughout the country. Contraband trade became so common that Congress was forced to pass an embargo even more restrictive than that of Jefferson. The nation's military weakness made it necessary for several states to provide for their own defense. When in 1814 the government put out an urgent call for 95,000 militia to defend Washington, only 7,000 volunteered.[53] After the fall of Washington the army was further decimated by desertions, with replacements scarce.

Late in 1814 the Massachusetts legislature called a convention of New England's dissidents to meet at Hartford, with the prospect of amending the constitution in a manner that would prevent future wars of this kind. Some of the more hot-blooded spoke of secession or a separate peace with England; however, moderates prevailed, and the convention ended with little accomplished.

In many respects the War of 1812 was a fiasco from which the United States was fortunate to escape unscathed. The historian attempting to assess its justice unearths a shocking degree of selfishness and nationalism, leading to the conclusion that the war was justifiable only on a Decatur-like "our country right or wrong" basis—a stance that makes legitimate any war by any country, anytime or anywhere.

When weighed against Augustine's standards for a just war, the war of 1812 is found seriously wanting. His requirement that every attempt must be made to settle the issues nonviolently, although met for five years, was abandoned at the moment of its greatest success. The policy clearly should have been continued. Further, the invasion of Canada hardly met Augustine's requirement that war be fought only in self-defense.

Ironically, the War of 1812 in some ways approaches the medieval church's definition of a holy war. True, this was intended as a justification for the church to wage a holy crusade against the infidel, and separation of church and state makes this theoretically impossible in the United States. Yet the patriotic zeal carried a quasi-religious quality. Some Christians invoked God's blessing on the cause as fervently as did the medieval church in its cooperation with European nations against the infidel.

Moreover, the crusade enthusiasm endured after the war ended. The prowar Christian nationalism continued in the Methodist and Baptist revivals, in the rapidly advancing missionary efforts which linked Christ with American culture, in the white supremacist conquest of the continent, and in the vision of the United States as a chosen nation with a special destiny to establish a secularized version of God's kingdom on earth.

It is remarkable that a war that began with mixed enthusiasm and was pursued with scant vigor could contribute so much to a nation's sense of patriotic purpose. The historian Samuel Eliot Morison has described it as the most unpopular war ever waged by the United States (not even excepting Vietnam), yet the most popular once it was over.[54] It came to be seen in American mythology as a magnificent victory. "The war was just and necessary," one newspaper asserted, "and we have abundant evidence to believe it was a holy war, for the Lord has fought for us the battles, and given us the victories which have been signal and marvelous on water and on land. . . ."[55]

One searches in vain for many "signal and marvelous" victories. Ironically, the most marvelous—Andrew Jackson at New Orleans—occurred two weeks after the war was over, but before the news had been received. Simultaneous word that the United States had won at New Orleans and that peace had been declared caused Americans to assume that one resulted from the other. In spite of numerous defeats, including the temporary loss of the capital, Americans saw themselves as having brought Great Britain, recent victor over Napoleon, to her knees.

"We have not got a stipulation about impressments and Orders in Council nor about idemnity," one patriot named Jonathon Roberts admitted. "But victory perches on our banner and the talisman of invincibility no longer pertains to the tyrants of the oceans. It is the triumph of virtue over vice, of republican principles over the advocates and doctrines of tyranny."[56] The *Niles Weekly Register* triumphantly proclaimed: "The enemy has retired in disgrace from New Orleans, and peace was signed at Ghent on the 24th of December, on honorable terms. .. Who would not be an American? Long live the republic! all hail! last asylum of oppressed humanity!"[57]

Perhaps every nation sees righteousness in its wars and God's purpose in its victories; yet few have practiced more self-deception in eulogizing the past than have Americans. The War of 1812 would be seen by future generations as part of a glorious heritage won by God and guns, an important milestone in the struggle for freedom. Americans would remember the war the way its termination was announced in The *Niles Weekly Register:*

GLORIOUS NEWS

Orleans saved and peace concluded.

"The star spangled banner in triumph shall wave
O'er the land of the free and the home of the brave."[58]

3 RONALD A. WELLS

THE WAR WITH MEXICO

MOST STUDENTS OF WAR, save the dedicated pacifists, would accept the view that war is not an entity unto itself, but is an extension of diplomacy. War itself cannot be said to be unjust or unnecessary; rather, the justice and necessity of war must rest upon a careful analysis of a particular war. Such is the case with the American war with Mexico in 1846.

The Mexican War aroused substantial discord in American society during the years 1846 to 1848. Many Americans viewed the war as unavoidable, or necessary, or even salutary. Others saw it as a blatant act of aggression against a helpless neighbor. The interpretations of historians in the ensuing years reflect the differences that Americans continue to have about that war. Many questions persist, and, as Norman Graebner has noted, "The resulting questions of motivation, alternatives and consequences simply defy any general agreement."[1]

Most historians have viewed the causes and consequences of the Mexican War within a nationalistic framework.[2] Even working within this framework, however, there has not been historiographical agreement: some argue that the war came "as logically as a thunderstorm" that cleared the air; others blame American aggression. The present work proceeds within a framework formed not by a nation but by ideology. In seeking an answer to the question of whether or not the war with Mexico in 1846 was a legitimate extension of diplomacy, this study frames its analysis using the Christian assumptions outlined in the introduction of this book. In asking whether or not the Mexican War was a "just war," one must ask questions about justice that transcend the more limited scope of a nationalist consciousness.

David M. Pletcher has enriched our understanding of the Mexican War by producing the first "international" study of the diplomacy of annexation based on multiarchival research. His intent is to avoid accusations and recriminations against President James K. Polk and his policies. Pletcher tries to be objective. In doing so, he asks to be granted an assumption:

> Let us start with the assumption that the duty of those who determine or carry out foreign policy is to secure their country's best interests in the most efficient and safest manner available to them—by peaceful means if at all possible, since wars are costly and dangerous, but by war if it cannot be avoided. Further, if they can, it is their duty to use honorable means, as this term is understood by their generation.[3]

I am reluctant to grant that assumption for reasons both of ideology and methodology. Ideologically, I am diffident toward the fortunes of the United States and its diplomatic policies. In my view, duty obtains in the pursuit of human rights, not of national interest. Whether or not American policies secure the interest of the nation is a matter of secondary concern when viewed from the perspective of the justice required by God in his creation. Indeed, as Robert L. DeVries has argued, it may be that the entire question of "national interest" ought to be revalued to include human rights. In such a revaluing, a statesman might pursue goals of international justice that are in the long-run interest of the people but against the interest of the nation in the short run. Surely "national interests" are not worth preserving if they do violence to justice, upon which a Christian view of the state puts a prior commitment.[4]

Methodologically, I am reluctant to grant that assumption, because "objectivity"—a laudable goal—is virtually impossible to achieve. That all history is written from some perspective has become an accepted principle in the historical profession, the advocates of "objective-scientific" history having conceded the debate. It is clear that the presuppositions of the historian inform his methodology both in the questions he sees as important to ask and in the field of vision to which he limits himself. One stops short of saying that every man is his own historian, because one is duty bound to approximate through rules of evidence "reality as it actually was." Interpretations—the context into which one places "facts"—follow from presuppositions. Many historians may not agree with a given set of assumptions and presuppositions; that disagreement, however, must be argued in another place. The Christian assumptions with which we work here offer no unique or special revelation, no talisman of historical understanding. What they offer is the opportunity to analyze an important aspect of American history—specifically the justice of the Mexican War—liberated from the confines of a nationalistic consciousness and a specious objectivity.

For more than half a century, students—both graduates who prepared bibliographies for qualifying exams and undergraduates who have pursued "suggestions for further reading" in textbooks—learned that the "standard work" on the Mexican War was the two-volume work by Justin Smith, *The War with Mexico*, published in 1919. In 1964, Peter Harstad and Richard Resh stated that Smith's work, despite its age, remained the only full-length, scholarly history of the war; thus an analysis of the war must still begin with Smith.[5] In 1971, Seymour V. Connor and Odie B. Faulk appended a nearly exhaustive bibliography to their history of the Mexican War. They maintained that Smith's history remained "a monument of historical scholarship." When they departed from Smith's interpretive framework they did so with great caution. Historians who seek to revise Smith's interpretation are often said to be "blinded by bias."[6] In 1974, K. Jack Bauer, contributing the Mexican War volume to the highly respected Wars of the United States series, apologized slightly for trespassing on Smith's domain. Further, the justification for his volume was based not so much on new research, but the truism that "every generation must reinterpret history in the light of its own experience."[7]

David Pletcher accurately notes that Smith's *The War with Mexico* is a "classic example" of a genre of historical work that holds a low opinion of Mexicans and a high, patriotic view of American expansion. It is a genre that reaffirmed "the case of Polk's Democrats and used scholarly evidence to demonstrate that Mexico was really the aggressor and that the American victory had served the cause of humanity."[8] Stout defenders of the Smith interpretation such as Connor and Faulk realize that there is another view of the war; they call it the "New England interpretation" (although it is curious that Justin Smith of New Hampshire did not agree with it).[9] By the New England interpretation, I take it they mean a view of the war that does not take at face value the self-justification of the Polk administration. While the view to follow may agree in part with a so-called New England interpretation, one would judge it is not worthwhile merely to exchange a "national" interpretation for a "regional" one. Ideology is more important than nation or region.

What was Smith's basic orientation? It is revealed with utter candor in his preface:

> As a particular consequence of this full inquiry, an episode that has been regarded both in the United States and abroad as discreditable to us, appears now to wear quite a different complexion. Such a result, it may be presumed, will gratify patriotic Americans, but the author must candidly admit that he began with no purpose or even thought of reaching it.[10]

If Smith's work would "gratify patriotic Americans," his later defenders, Connor and Faulk, worry that historians have sometimes taken an alternative view and have "denigrated the American role in the conflict."[11] If the present essay has any value, it is neither in gratifying or denigrating American attitudes per se, but in subjecting the ideology of war to analysis in the context of the 1846 war against Mexico.

The ideology of expansion sprang from the logic of European settlement in the New World. The desire for a continental empire may even predate the existence of the American republic, but after the establishment of the new nation, the possession of most or all of the continent seemed to be both its birthright and its mission.[12] The ideology of American expansion existed for a long time before expansion began again in earnest in the 1840s, but during and after that decade, it grew to proportions that stretched credulity. In seeking to justify expansion, both in their own eyes and in those of the world, Americans accepted in varying degrees a diverse body of doctrines. The classic study of the ideology notes the major themes:

> It comprises metaphysical dogmas of a providential mission and quasi-scientific "laws" of national development, conceptions of national right and ideals of social duty, legal rationalizations and appeals to "the higher Law," aims of extending freedom and designs of extending benevolent absolutism.[13]

The term "Manifest Destiny" was new to the 1840s, and it reflected the immediate needs of the times, especially in relation to Texas, Oregon, and California. The notion, of course, was not new, which is why "Manifest Destiny" was so widely and so quickly accepted as the logical conclusion of ideas that Americans had believed about themselves for some time. Although latter-day cynics might believe that the creed was a propagandist's attempt to cover undiluted aggression, in fact the ideas involved in "Manifest Destiny" were not those of mere land-grabbing expansionism. Rather, they proceeded from a fundamental conviction that the United States was, in Frederick Merk's phrase, "the temple of freedom." American expansion offered all the diverse peoples of North America the opportunity for self-realization, that is, admission to the temple of freedom. As Merk writes in characterizing the expansionist's creed.

> Any hurried admission would be a contradiction in terms, unthinkable, revolting. But a duty lay on the people of the United States to admit all qualified applicants freely. The doors to the temple must be wide open to peoples who were panting for freedom. Any shrinking from admitting them, out of selfish disinclination to share with others the blessings of American freedom, would be disgraceful.[14]

Even if one were to agree with Merk that most American people, in advocating expansion, did so out of the "higher" motivations of "mission" rather than the "baser ones of imperialistic aggression," one would nevertheless ask if the basic conviction that Americans had about "the temple of freedom" was in fact realistic or pretentious.

The term "Manifest Destiny" was apparently used in public for the first time in 1845, by John L. O'Sullivan, in an essay on the Texas issue in his literary journal *Democratic Review*. O'Sullivan, who was also the editor of the *New York Morning News*, was an important figure in American history as the theoretician of the doctrine of Manifest Destiny.[15] Just because Americans could not define precisely the nature and extent of their obvious destiny did not mean that they were unsure of it. To the contrary, the genius of the notion of a national destiny was that it, like beauty, was in the eye of the beholder. There were, however, certain elements of the ideology that achieved widespread acceptance. The continental domain of the United States—from sea to shining sea—would be a free society in every sense: free from the restraint of a powerful central government, of a class system of the European type, or of an established church. It would be a democratic society in every sense: its citizens would be equal in opportunity under the law, in ownership of land, and in economic pursuits generally, especially in developing the blessings of the natural resources with which the continent was so amply endowed.

In discussing the relative merits of claims to lands not yet under American control, O'Sullivan dismissed claims based on discovery or settlement. In his essay "The True Title," the claim to Oregon and Texas "is by the right of our manifest destiny to overspread and to possess the whole of the continent which Providence has given us for the development of the great experiment of liberty and federative self government entrusted to us."[16] That God was involved in the process of American expansion was often claimed by Americans. A congressman spoke perhaps for many when he said:

> Long may our country prove itself the asylum of the oppressed. Let its institutions and its people be extended far and wide, and when the waters of depotism shall have inundated other portions of the globe, and the votary of liberty be compelled to betake himself to his ark, let this government be the Ararat on which it shall rest.[17]

In practical political terms, the annexation of Texas in March 1845 provided the pattern that the United States was urged to follow elsewhere. The propagandists of Manifest Destiny were quick to pick up the pattern: Americans should populate a region, then revolt from the "illegitimate" authorities, and then, in the fulness of time, the region could be admitted to the Union. O'Sullivan raised the question in the summer after the Texas annexation: "Texas, we repeat, is secure; and so now, as the Razor Strop Man says, 'Who's the next customer?' Shall it be California or Canada?"[18] It might be added that New Mexico and Oregon were also presumed to be ripe for American dominion. With the Texas pattern firmly in place, the task of future governments was as obvious and manifest as the destiny they were to fulfill.

When President Polk assumed office in March 1845 there was no doubt that he was committed to implementing the territorial implications of Manifest Destiny. Polk had a "continental vision," and he was determined that during his term in office, California would follow the Texas pattern.[19] The matter that occupied the Polk cabinet was the method of implementation. Moderates in the cabinet, especially James Buchanan, argued a line in private that O'Sullivan argued in public. If one truly believed in Manifest Destiny, one believed that force need not be resorted to in obtaining the destined territory; such territory would come into the Union when the time was right. Militants in the cabinet, especially Robert Walker, advocated a more active policy, in which the American government would pursue with greater keenness the ultimate destiny of the nation. At first Polk was enough convinced of his continental vision to ally himself with the moderates; in due course of time, he moved toward the militants. With the Texas question settled by President Tyler on the eve of Polk's coming to office, the only campaign issue that remained for Polk to resolve was the dispute over Oregon. In the end, that matter was settled peacefully, but only after Polk had gone to (what later generations would call) "the brink" of war with Britain. The policy of public brinkmanship had won Polk a major victory in Oregon. That victory may have seduced him into believing that a similar policy of brinkmanship toward Mexico would similarly bring the desired result of a border redrawn between the United States and Mexico—one that had California safely on the American side.[20]

The concern that fanned the fires of hostility between the United States and Mexico was the continued disagreement over the location of the boundary between the two nations on the southern Texas border. In the treaty with Spain in 1819, the United States had agreed to the Sabine River as the boundary between Louisiana (the United States) and Texas (Mexico). Many Democrats were angry with John Quincy Adams for agreeing to that boundary because of their conviction that the Rio Grande had been the western boundary of the Louisiana Purchase. Mexico asked repeatedly that the boundary on the Sabine be marked, but the United States delayed. Finally in 1828, President John Quincy Adam's administration did officially mark the boundary at the Sabine. Democratic leaders such as Thomas Hart Benton accused Adams of having "despoiled" the rightful inheritance of the United States of its "natural" border on the Rio Grande.[21]

The southern boundary of Texas really should have caused little difficulty. The Nueces River had been the traditional boundary between Texas and Tamaulipas, and it appeared as such on all reliable maps of the period. Indeed, many American leaders accepted that boundary, including Stephen Austin, Andrew Jackson, Martin Van Buren, and John Calhoun.[22]

After the Mexican defeat at San Jacinto in 1836 by Texans under Sam Houston, Texas claimed the Rio Grande as its southern boundary. Santa Anna, the Mexican president, was captured at San Jacinto, and as a condition of his release as a prisoner of war, he signed an undertaking that in a later treaty the boundary of Texas would be the Rio Grande. The Mexican congress immediately repudiated Santa Anna's actions, but most Texans and some Americans claimed that Santa Anna's signature made the Rio Grande the "true" boundary of Texas.

The claim was important for the later actions of the Polk administration. When Polk ordered General Zachary Taylor to move his troops south of the Nueces, the Mexican government warned the Americans that they were on Mexican soil. Mexican forces later attacked the Americans. Polk's war message claimed that war existed between the two countries because of the actions of Mexico: "After reiterated menaces, Mexico has passed the boundary of the United States, has invaded our territory, and shed American blood on American soil." Polk's war message to Congress was unique and contentious: unique because it said that war already existed on May 11, 1846, whereas the Constitution provides that war cannot exist unless and until Congress declares it; contentious because it insisted that Mexico was the aggressor.

Even Justin Smith, historian of the "classic" work on the Mexican War, who views the United States in the most favorable light possible in this war, admits that Polk had gone too far in claiming the disputed territory as "American soil." Smith suggests that Polk would have done better to say that the United States had an as-yet-unsubstantiated claim to the territory between the Nueces River and the Rio Grande. But even here, where Polk's position is nearly untenable, Justin Smith excuses the overstatement, noting that Polk's assertion about "American soil" was contained in a war message and that "in a trumpet-call to arms, qualifications would have appeared out of place."[23] Later historians have followed Smith's lead on this matter, and their footnotes reveal a heavy dependence on Smith's work. For example, William H. Goetzmann wrote that Taylor did not "seize" territory south of the Nueces; "he merely stationed his troops there. The Mexican army was free to do the same since the status of that territory had not yet been determined."[24]

A war hawk congressman, William H. Brockenbough of Florida, added a preamble to the war message that was equally explicit about Mexican aggression as the cause of the war. Whig opponents denounced the message and especially the preamble. They believed that the war was an aggressive war, and that it was an outrageous lie to claim that it was a defensive war. The enabling bill was hurried through Congress, and debate was severely limited by the Democratic majority to two hours in the House and to one day in the Senate. Dissent in the House was led by John Quincy Adams, but since congressmen were not allowed to read the documents accompanying the president's message, the House was stampeded into accepting war by a vote of 174 to 14. The Senate voted the next day, and the tactics of stampede again produced an administration victory. Calhoun asked if a local skirmish between fragments of armies by a river constituted war between two nations. But, as Calhoun concluded, Polk seemed determined to have war and war it would be, the facts of the incidents in southern Texas and northern Mexico notwithstanding. The bill passed the Senate 40 to 2, with Calhoun not voting and Webster absent.[25]

Antislavery, Whig-oriented newspapers in New England echoed the criticism in Congress. Charles Francis Adams, writing in the *Boston Whig*, attacked the preamble to the war bill as "one of the grossest national lies that was ever deliberately told." Other Whig newspapers, especially the *New York Tribune* and the (Washington) *National Intelligencer* used similar language, and accused the congressmen who voted for the bill of signing their names to the "national lie" and of covering their hands with the blood of a helpless neighbor. In 1847, Congressman Abraham Lincoln demanded that the president show the Congress and the American people the exact spot where American blood had been shed on American soil. It was Lincoln's contention that the Polk administration had deceived the American people and continued in a "cover-up" of the truth. Lincoln maintained that of course Mexicans had fired on Americans, but in whose country? If both nations claimed the territory one had to go behind the claims to determine actual ownership. In Lincoln's view, Mexico had clear title to the land south of the Nueces, because neither Texas nor the United States had ever engaged in civil rule of the area. Lincoln concluded that Polk's attempts to place the blame on Mexico was the "half insane mumbling of a fever-dream," the product of "a bewildered, confounded and miserably perplexed man."[26] The Polk administration never answered the question of "spotty" Lincoln.

Since both the political parties were divided over the war, and over whether or not the war was traceable to a desire to expand slavery into new territories, the question remains as to why both Whigs and Democrats in Congress voted so overwhelmingly for the war. Frederick Merk believes that the Polk administration converted a momentary public hysteria into a stampede, using a supposed "attack on the flag" as the occasion to begin the stampede. This took place despite the provisions of the Constitution that the founding fathers had hoped would prevent such actions. The fathers had hoped that by dispersing power in the several branches of government, the Congress, in this case, might check the desires of a war-minded president. The safeguards did not work during the crisis of May 11 and 12, 1846, because antiwar elements in both parties failed to act: antiwar Whigs failed to act because they realized that a majority of Americans believed in Manifest Destiny, and to oppose so broad a public feeling was to court the electoral disaster that had befallen Federalism; antiwar Democrats failed to act because, while not wanting war with Mexico, they nevertheless shared Polk's desire for Texas and especially for California.[27]

It is by now accepted by most historians that the 1846 war between Mexico and the United States was not about the mere possession of the bit of territory between the Nueces River and the Rio Grande, but about the meaning of that possession, and the perception of that meaning in the two nations. In fact, the two nations had strikingly similar perceptions of the meaning of such possession: both Americans and Mexicans shared the opinion that if the American desire for a redrawn boundary were fulfilled, it would mean much more territorially than whether one river or the other was the appropriate border between the two nations. Rather, it would mean that much more of northwest Mexico would have to become southwest United States. The import of the "Texas pattern," founded upon a more general notion of Manifest Destiny, was not lost on either Americans or Mexicans.

America's desire for California was long-standing. For at least a generation prior to the Mexican War, Americans had given many indications of their desire for California. But that desire was not so much solely for land as for the maritime commercial possibilities of California. Norman A. Graebner contributed an important insight to the general discussion of American expansion by suggesting that the initial American interest in acquiring California focused not so much on land but on ports, especially San Francisco. The entire understanding of Manifest Destiny must be weaned away from an exclusive focus on the acquisition of land. Americans, especially in the Northeast, had long been aware of the commercial possibilities that a presence on the Pacific Ocean would afford. Interest in California was due as much to its maritime potential as to the land it offered for settlement.[28]

This broadened focus of Manifest Destiny allows us readily to exonerate the Polk administration of one of the charges leveled against it during the war — that the war was prosecuted by a Democratic administration in which southerners were dominant. This view, held mostly by northern Whigs and abolitionists, was founded on their fear of a conspiracy by the southern planters to expand the territory to slavery. However, most leaders in the South realized that lands in the far West would never be appropriate for the large-scale migration of the South's "peculiar institution." As Frederick Merk has shown, the South was the region of the nation least attracted by the ideology of Manifest Destiny. Perhaps because of its own ideas about race and nationality, the South was less than enthusiastic about adding Indians and Mexicans to the population of the United States.[29] James K. Polk was not the archconspirator, the tool of slavocracy. He may have been duplicitous toward Mexico, but with respect to the American people, he stood openly as their agent, pointing the course of American dominion westward to the sea, in fulfillment of the ideology of Manifest Destiny, which enjoyed a national consensus. On the particulars of the boundary question Polk may be accused of a "national lie," but on the general matter of American acceptance of the territorial logic of Manifest Destiny, Polk spoke for a majority of the American people, in all sections of the nation.

California, the western jewel of the continent, was a prize that the Polk administration and the American people wanted, and Polk's attempts to coerce Mexico into ceding it to the United States must be regarded as the major cause for the Mexican War. Polk wanted to minimize hostilities in California itself, because bloodshed there would surely antagonize the *californios*, who were "destined" soon to become Americans. The Polk-Buchanan policy toward California and the *californios* was one of "peaceful persuasion."[30] That policy had been laid down clearly by Secretary of State Buchanan in a message (October 17, 1845) to Thomas A. Larkin, the American consul in Monterey. Larkin was appointed a special and secret agent of the State Department, and was instructed to encourage the *californios* to avoid an alliance with any European state, especially Britain. At the same time he was told that "the President will make no effort and use no influence to induce California to become one of the Union, yet if the people should desire to unite their destiny with ours, they would be received as brethren, whenever this can be done without affording Mexico just cause of complaint."[31] Polk, such a true believer in Manifest Destiny, apparently believe as late as the autumn of 1845 that California could come into the Union peacefully, and without "complaint" from Mexico. Of course, Mexico did "complain" about the potential loss of California, and within a year hostilities erupted in both northern Mexico and California.[32]

The "standard" interpretation (Justin Smith, et al.) had it that Mexico lacked "realism" in her dealings with the United States. First, Mexico was "unrealistic" to be upset by "the loss" of Texas to the United States. Further, Mexican fears and anxieties about future American designs on its territory were "exaggerated," and as the patronizing Justin Smith noted, "such talk was largely for effect."[33] But were Mexican fears of the United States "unrealistic" or "exaggerated"? As noted above, the Texas pattern had become as clear in the minds of many Mexicans as it had for many Americans. The question that Mexicans asked themselves in 1845 and 1846 was whether or not they were condemned to the continual dismemberment of their nation. They believed that they had reason to fear the aggressive desires of the United States, and with the advent of Manifest Destiny in the Polk administration, Mexican leaders wondered if Mexican sovereignty could survive, or if Mexico might only hitherto exist as a client state of the

United States. The potential "loss" of California was a realistic assessment by Mexican leaders in 1845 and 1846, and they saw America's wish for negotiations on borders as the first step toward that loss.[34]

Mexican fears were also fed by the American press, whose views were widely quoted in Mexican newspapers. Many American newspapers took note of the continued immigration into Mexican territory, especially California. A comment in an American newspaper by Congressman Thomas Gilmer was typical of the comments that were repeatedly reprinted in the Mexican press: "our population is invading the Pacific in an irresistible manner," and expansion was as inevitable "as the current of the Mississippi."[35] The *Diario del Gobierno*, official paper of the Mexican Executive, noted in 1845 the full potential of American immigration in California:

> The emigration which the United States is practicing toward the Californios is inconceivable; entire caravans are discovered on route, with only the purpose of establishing colonies; and they even carry pieces of artillery to defend themselves and the land that is *theirs by right*. Who supports that right? Is this not the beginning of a new usurpation?[36]

By late 1845, many Mexicans were convinced of the appropriateness of the analogy between Texas and California. Texas had already been taken by the aggressive sister republic to the north. If California fell to the Americans so soon after Texas, little of the northern half of Mexico could be preserved.

Mexican anxiety toward the United States was engendered not only by the loss of territory but also by American treatment of Mexico regarding the Texas question. Mexicans believed that they were being given supercilious treatment by the government and people of the United States, and that they were regarded by their northern neighbors as not meriting respect, mostly because they had no right to the land for which Americans had "the true title."[37] American diplomatic representatives in Mexico were "ugly Americans," so much so that historian Gene Brack wonders (with perhaps a retrospective tongue in cheek) if "the United States selected its diplomatic representatives to Mexico by calculating their potential offensiveness to Mexico," so bluntly offensive and insulting was their manner of communication.[38]

Patronizing and insulting attitudes are, alas, not confined to the American diplomatic representatives of the 1840s, but have been transferred into the historiography of the Mexican War. Justin Smith's nationally ethnocentric version of the war is still deferred to by many scholars, yet it contains many indications of a deprecatory attitude toward Mexicans. Describing Mexican attitudes on the eve of the war, Smith wrote that Mexicans were "vain and superficial, they did not realize their weakness."[39] To the contrary, highly placed Mexicans, even Presidents Santa Anna and Herrera, realized that their forces would be defeated by the better-prepared and stronger Americans. Herrera's dilemma on the eve of war was that Mexico was a "nation in no condition to wage war and in no mood to preserve peace at the price of concessions."[40] Smith's treatment of Mexican attitudes focuses on violent anti-Americanism, which was certainly present in segments of the press and of then-out-of-power political factions. But this is to create a false picture of Mexican bellicosity on the eve of war.

Perhaps the greatest insult to Mexico by the Polk administration was the belief suggested by the American negotiating position that Mexico might sell national territory and national honor for money. No American president would exchange honor and land for cash, but Polk believed that by applying military pressure a Mexican president would. This suggests Polk's very low opinion of Mexicans, and he was surprised that they responded by accepting war, even with dim prospects of success, rather than further territorial concessions. Polk assumed that Mexico would not fight, because of his military assessment—quite correct, be it said—that it could not fight a successful war against the United States. By applying pressure on President Paredes, he joined the opposite pressure being applied on the Mexican president by political opposition and the popular press within Mexico.

Anti-Americanism in Mexico surely was important in pushing Mexico into refusing further territorial losses to the United States. The question, however, to be asked by historians is whether or not Mexicans were justified in their anger and anxiety toward the United States. Gene Brack suggests a provisional answer:

> Over the years Mexicans had become increasingly aware that many Americans . . . looked upon Mexicans as inferior beings. This had frightening implications, for Americans had respect for neither the rights nor the culture of those whom they con-

> sidered inferior. They had been merciless in their treatment of the Indian and had reduced blacks to a brutal form of servitude. Mexicans were perceptive enough to recognize that a similar fate threatened them should they fall under American domination.[41]

American racism cannot be said to be the primary cause for the Mexican War, but no historian can be unaware of the important role played by race in Manifest Destiny. Manifest Destiny was supremely ethnocentric, as is the nationalistic historiography that accepts Polk's version of things.

Another question that historians of the Mexican War must answer is: did Polk have freedom of choice, or were events forced upon him by circumstances beyond his control? Polk's policy was what post-Vietnam era historians would call "escalation." As David Pletcher suggests, the policy maker has many options open at the beginning of the process, but as the process unfolds and violence or the threat of it becomes more real, the range of choices for the policy maker is narrowed, until in the end, he has only two choices. Through his blundering brinkmanship, Polk lost most of the options open to him through conventional diplomacy.[42] On the other hand, Shomer Zwelling has correctly noted that the mission of James Slidell to Mexico in late 1845 is a key to understanding Polk's diplomacy. The minimum American demand was that in exchange for assuming Mexico's debt to certain American citizens the Mexican government would recognize Texas as part of the United States and would cede additional territory to the United States. As Zwelling notes:

> This *sine qua non* reveals either shocking naiveté or devious scheming. . . . Given Mexico's inability to reconcile herself to the loss of Texas, one wonders if Polk actually expected her to accept this. . . . The burden of the decision and responsibility for the consequences were shrewdly placed on Mexico. Once again, by yielding the initiative, Polk improved his tactical position.[43]

It is agreed that the acquisition of California was fundamental to Polk's policy. But what other acquisitions were involved in his determination to implement the territorial implications of Manifest Destiny? During the war, a "Movement for the Acquisition of All Mexico" emerged among some of the true believers in the ideology of Manifest Destiny.[44] Whatever support there was for the movement outside the Polk administration, it does not appear to have enjoyed much, if any, support inside the administration. Polk's cabinet discussed future American territorial desires in a regular cabinet meeting about six weeks after the onset of war. Although agreed on expansion and the "need" to include California and New Mexico in any future settlement with Mexico, the cabinet was divided on how far American claims should go. The "hawk" faction in the cabinet was led by Robert Walker, secretary of the treasury. He seems to have been the only one with an interest in the "All Mexico" movement. The "dove" faction was led by James Buchanan, secretary of state. Buchanan argued that the United States should claim a line along thirty-two degrees north latitude as the future boundary, while Walker argued for at least a line to the Pacific drawn along the twenty-six degrees north latitude. Polk was more accepting of Walker's view than Buchanan's, but was willing to be "flexible" within the agreed-to confines of certainty about the acquisition of California and New Mexico.[45]

In the end, Polk sided with Buchanan, and the Treaty of Guadalupe Hidalgo took less than "All Mexico." The moderation of territorial demands can be linked to domestic political realities. In the congressional elections of 1846, the Whigs gained control of the House, and this in the midst of a supposedly popular war conducted by a Democratic president. Frederick Merk believes that the swing to the Whigs in the country "was a clear measure of the moral protest which had developed against the war."[46] For Polk, a popular president prosecuting a popular war, this was humiliating. His defensiveness about this apparent public rebuke can be seen in his annual message to Congress, written about a month after the election. He devoted about two-thirds of his message to a defense of his version of the origin of the war. He insisted that the boundary was the Rio Grande, and that by crossing it Mexico had invaded American soil and had shed American blood there. As to the Whig charge that he was the aggressor, Polk repudiated it, and countercharged the Whigs with the next thing to treason. Despite the president's fulminations to the contrary, he abandoned his tentative affiliation with the movement that desired more or all of Mexican territory. There may have been a majority in the country for acquiring California, but not for all or most of Mexico.

The antiwar movement was able to moderate the provisions of the treaty by exposing the dangers in a Manifest Destiny that was too all-embracing. Without dissent, the United States may have demanded more than "merely" the one-third of Mexico for which the treaty provided.[47]

The responses and attitudes of American churches to the Mexican War is a long and complicated story, which can only be told fully in a denomination by denomination analysis. However, some predictable responses can be noted in general.[48] Many churches took no official position on the war, and the few that did condemned it. The clergy, and the constituencies of most denominations, were generally prowar. Methodists, Baptists, and Old School Presbyterians provided the Polk administration with its most ardent support. Episcopalians, Lutherans, and the ethnically oriented Reformed churches (Dutch and German) were either silent or yielded only a few clergy either in favor or in opposition to the war. Northern Baptists and New School Presbyterians were substantially divided, but provided eloquent spokespersons for both sides in the conflict. Wholehearted opposition came from Congregationalists, Unitarians, and Quakers. In general, support for the war came from churches where evangelical priorities caused them to approve of Manifest Destiny's "mission of civilization," or churches with a territorial stake in the southwest. Opposition to the war came from churches whose philosophies opposed war principally or from those whose membership was concentrated in areas of the country far from the conflict.

Justin Smith thought that the history of the Mexican War would "gratify patriotic Americans." Yet, even by so ethnocentric a standard, the war cannot be praised. The bitterness of conflict and dissent generated by the war left behind secretarial strains that sped the process of breaking the bonds of union, especially by replacing political parties with sectional parties. In the fierce national debate over how to organize the Mexican Cession, the fugitive slave law emerged as a part of "the compromise of 1850," and became in itself one of the most potent agents in dissolving the bonds of union. The divisiveness begun over the Mexican War opened a road that led to the Civil War. As Frederick Merk has concluded, the results of the Mexican War "illuminate an old truth: that moral issues are not easily quieted when they are as basic as those raised by Polk in 1846. They remain in the earth like dragon's teeth to grow into future armed conflict."[49]

At the beginning of this essay we noted that an analysis of the "justice" of the Mexican War could not proceed in general but in particular, not from a fixed view on war itself, but from inquiring into the issues of the Mexican War to see if they could be reconciled with a "just war" theory. This case, like many others, proceeds from definitions. If one were to accept the ideology of Manifest Destiny and were to cast one's historical inquiries in a context set by a nationalist consciousness, then it would follow that the Mexican War need not be regarded as having brought dishonor to Americans. However, if one views (as the present writer does) the ideology of Manifest Destiny as a major example of arrogant American ethnocentrism, and if one's historical consciousness is set by Christian ideology rather than the nation-state, one cannot approve of the Mexican War. The twin requirements of a just war are the restoration of justice and the preservation of peace; the Mexican War failed to conform on either score.

Richard E. Stenberg was a historian who contributed a great deal of venom to the historiography of the Mexican War. With the bombast typical of his writings, he pointed an accusing finger at Polk, saying that "Polk was the grasping hand of a nation infected by the expansionist urge; the Americans' adolescent greed and land hunger . . . led finally, after many years of craving, to the taking of New Mexico and California."[50] Few historians would have used such language today, but Stenberg's basic idea rings with truth. When confronted with such a truth, some historians defend a nationalist consciousness by asking if the alternative is to return the ceded territory to Mexico. Arthur M. Schlesinger, Sr., in reporting his poll on "presidential greatness," addressed the relatively high placement of Polk: "Though Polk's conduct toward Mexico violated international ethics, it is noteworthy that his critics, neither then nor later, have ever proposed that the conquests be returned."[51] Surprisingly, David M. Pletcher, in his otherwise laudable study, repeats this nonsensical comment.[52] It would be pretense for any historian to recommend that Mexico be given back its northern territories taken as the spoils of war by the United States. Nevertheless, in the last third of the twentieth century, as many Mexicans—"illegal aliens," it is said—are coming across the border into New Mexico and California, one must wonder whether they are so illegal or alien after all.

Many historians in the 1960s and 1970s, when viewing with alarm the rise of a "new left" historiography, have expressed their concern about the validity of making moral judgments about the past. This concern is important, and one should not judge the past by the standards of the present lest we "play tricks on the dead."[53] Of equal importance, however, is the need to ensure that our historical studies do not play tricks on the living. An important part of the American myth—the approving manner in which Americans selectively remember their own past—is that the United States has always been "the innocent combatant" when it has gone to war. In the context of the Mexican War, this myth has been discussed by Glenn Price.[54] Citing William H. McNeill's *The Rise of the West*, Price notes that Western civilization has had a history of "extra-ordinary pugnacity, of the unrestrained use of force." But this pugnacity is contrary to the dominant cultural strain of the Christian heritage in which humility and love for one's enemies are cardinal virtues. The tension of this contradiction is great enough to compel the governments of the Christian West, when they are going to war, to paint the cause of the war in colors of self-justification. Hence, most declarations of war contain the following: our cause is just and our motives pure, thus making the final victory sure. This had had a profound effect on the writing of American military history, inclining many historians to see the war the way the government saw it. As suggested earlier in this essay, the dominant strain in the historiography of the Mexican War—beginning with Justin Smith—has been one which is largely celebrative of American actions, and of "the winning of the West."

An alternative view, one which will not accept that the United States was the innocent combatant in the Mexican War, was suggested nearly a century ago by Josiah Royce, who wrote one of the earliest histories of California. Although remembered more for his work in philosophy, as principal antagonist of William James at Harvard,[55] Royce's historical work is still worthy of note.

> The American as conqueror is unwilling to appear in public as a pure aggressor; he dare not seize a California as Russia had seized so much land in Asia. The American wants to persuade not only the world, but himself, that he is doing God service

> in a peaceable Spirit, even when he violently takes what he has determined to get. His conscience is sensitive, and hostile aggression, practiced against any but Indians, shocks this conscience, unused as it is to such scenes.[56]

Royce's philosophical life was an attempt to cast ethical choices in terms of what he called "The Absolute." For Royce the historian, the confession of sin was the beginning of wisdom. He concluded his history by saying that he was "glad to be able to suggest what I have found, plain and simple as it is, to any fellow Californian who may perchance note in himself the faults of which I make confession."[57]

The version of the Mexican War given in this essay is by no means the only possible version. The conclusion that the war was both unjust and unnecessary proceeds from certain attitudes that this historian has about justice, about war, and about history. Some historians, however, arguing a different view are unwilling to accept any interpretation other than their own. Such are two well-known historians, Odie B. Faulk and Seymour V. Connor, whose work has been cited frequently in this essay. In April, 1972, the *Journal of the West* was given over entirely to the Mexican War, under the guest editorship of Odie Faulk. There were thirteen articles, mostly from Faulk's graduate students at Oklahoma State University or those of Seymour Connor at Texas Tech University.

Faulk had had his graduate seminar study the Mexican War because, to his astonishment, many of his students shared the view of some textbooks: that the United States provoked the war with Mexico in order to acquire California and the Southwest. When the seminar was completed, Faulk reported, the students no longer accepted such a view of the war. Further, he could not "answer the question why so many American historians and students of his find it necessary to denigrate the American role in this conflict. . . ." Faulk went on to challenge "any historian to hold a serious seminar on this topic, one that uses creditable sources, one that includes both Mexican and American imprints, one that investigates for truth, and come [*sic*] radically different conclusion than did the students who wrote these papers."[58] The intent of the present paper is serious, one that would "investigate for truth," but that comes to a substantially different conclusion than the Faulk-Connor-Smith interpretation. No one questions

Justin Smith's scholarship. What is questionable about the nationalist interpretation, however, is that a historian like Justin Smith or Odie Faulk has presuppositions that lead him to make conclusions that are unacceptable to another historian who brings other presuppositions to the same facts. While one may remain grateful to Justin Smith for providing us most of the facts through his great research, one need not necessarily follow his judgments.

In concluding that issue of the *Journal of the West*, Seymour Connor, who collaborated with Faulk on *North America Divided*, repeated that credulity was stretched in trying to explain why so many historians "denigrate" the American conduct of the war, and why some historians allege that "a sense of guilt about this war is the legacy of every American."[59] Why do many historians not accept Polk's version of the war, a version now enshrined in nationalist historiography? Connor concludes: "The objective historian cannot answer this question. Perhaps it is a challenge that demands the attention of psychologists."[60] If Josiah Royce be any guide, the "objective historian" might do well to avoid the counsel of a psychologist and seek the solace of the confessional.

As noted above, when human rights and international justice are at odds with national interest, the Christian is constrained by his commitment to choose the former. This Christian historian is similarly constrained to interpret the Mexican War in a way that does not necessarily denigrate the American people, but that establishes a critical and ironic distance between his ideology and the ideology that led to that war.

4 RONALD D. RIETVELD

THE AMERICAN CIVIL WAR: Millennial Hope, Political Chaos, and a Two-Sided "Just War"

"FONDLY DO WE HOPE—FERVENTLY DO WE PRAY—that this mighty scourge of war may speedily pass away. Yet if God wills that it continue," intoned a war-weary president in the final days of the nation's bloodiest war, "so let it be said 'the judgments of the Lord, are true and righteous altogether.' " In the severe language of Scripture, Abraham Lincoln and many of his contemporaries held the United States under judgment. God's divine wrath would serve a purpose in the reformation of his people, but the nation must become aware of his hand in the visitation of war. The renewal of the nation newly dedicated to the increase of freedom must be understood as a correlative of the emphasis upon judgment; it was the renewal that made the Civil War just.[1]

To most Americans, the notion that this nation would descend to fratricidal strife was unthinkable. "There must be no war" had been a familiar refrain in both North and South. But fratricidal war had come with a shattering result. Seemingly, divine favor had been withdrawn from God's "Almost Chosen People," as it had been withdrawn from Judah of old. Had the great experiment failed? No longer would Americans be able to picture themselves as an example to the nations of the world, nor could national leadership blame the disaster upon external circumstances. The responsibility rested with the American people themselves. They alone were involved; no other nation interfered or precipitated the tragedy. Had not God himself "designed this continent to be the asylum of liberty" and selected the United States to be an example to the nations of the world? This conviction of millennial hope had given Americans a sense of common nationality. But this unity evaporated in shot, shell, and blood. The nation's God had seemingly become partisan. How then could this war be just? It became increasingly clear to many Americans during the Civil War, and especially to the Northern president, that the war itself must be brought within the scope of a much larger design if this country were to be reunited.[2]

The Civil War etched itself more deeply upon the American consciousness than any other conflict in which the United States has been engaged. The steady stream of books and articles about this war is in part attributable to the fact that it has the poignant qualities of a tragic romance. It attracts novelists because it supplies unlimited potential for plot and for character analysis. It attracts historians because they comprehend the crucial significance of this conflict in the whole of the American experience. "Though less of a watershed, perhaps, than has sometimes been claimed," writes Dennis Welland in *The United States: A Companion to American Studies*, "it was nevertheless an event of the most profound significance for the whole future of the United States and, indeed, for the world." The war settled much that previously had been in doubt and determined many areas of national life in which the nation would develop. But this great interest in the Civil War has not been matched by a comparable effort to comprehend its significance.[3]

The generation that experienced the war soon sketched out all the major lines of interpretation that gave shape to a hundred years of explanations of this crucial episode. In the 1950s, Professor Thomas J. Pressly summarized and classified the interpretations of a host of statemen, historians, publicists, and other commentators. Concerned with investigating periods of consensus in America's past experience, Pressly found three schools of thought among those whose lives were touched by the war: some called it the "war of rebellion," others the "war between the states," and still others "the needless war." The interpretations that lasted through the years "sought to place personal guilt for the conflict upon . . . foes" and have "generally pictured the struggle in black and white lines, with little or no intermediate shading: their side was absolutely right, their opponents absolutely wrong." Pressly concluded "that individuals suggested in the 1860's and 1870's most of the major factors which were later to be singled out as the causes of the Civil War," so that "at least the seeds of most of the later explanations, and sometimes the full-blown explanations themselves, are to be found in the 1860's and 1870's." Until recently, students of the Civil War have generally agreed with Pressly.[4]

In 1960, as Americans prepared to observe the centennial of the Civil War, David Donald, one of the foremost historians of the conflict, published a brief article entitled "American Historians and the Causes of the Civil War."[5] Rather than develop a survey of the changing course of Civil War interpretation, Donald announced that as a subject of serious historical analysis, Civil War causation was "dead." Two decades later, we find the field of inquiry, if it had been truly "dead," having now experienced a resurrection to new life. In the 1950s, Pressly and his fellow historians were concerned with investigating periods of consensus in America's past. But in the 1960s and 1970s, renewed attention to civil strife came about as historians wrestled anew with the issues of race and war. The issue of slavery, for example, was no longer viewed outside of the nation's development but as a matter absolutely central to the American experience.[6] This virtual flood of studies on slavery, abolitionism, and the race issue does not seem to have brought historians any nearer to a concensus on the causes of the war than they had twenty years ago. The late historian David Potter pointed out the irony of these disagreements persisting when we have a greatly increased body of historical knowledge.[7] The Civil War has raised many still unresolved issues. Historian Eric Foner believes there is another reason for these continued disagreements. In spite of the fact that historians' methodologies and value judgments have changed considerably over the past twenty years, the questions historians have continued to ask of their data have remained "static." "Historians of the Civil War era," declares Foner, "seem to be in greater need of new models of interpretation and new questions than of an additional accumulation of data."[8]

In the past twenty years there have been attempts to develop entirely new ways of looking at antebellum America and the origins of the Civil War. The "new political historians" have attempted to recast our understanding of prewar political alignments. These historians have deemphasized the "national issues like the tariff and slavery, and have substituted ethno-cultural conflicts between Protestants and Roman Catholics, or between pietistic and ritualistic religious groups, as the major determinants of antebellum political culture." Truly, these works have broadened our understanding of American antebellum political culture. Professor Foner believes these works have "demonstrated the inevitable failure of any 'monistic interpretation' of political conflict. . . . And they should force historians to abandon whatever economic determinism still persists in the writing of political history."[9] These works view men and women as a part of a complex network of social and cultural relationships.[10]

The "new political history" involves a new methodology—the statistical analysis of quantitative data—and a distinctive model of historical explanation. However, these new methodological tools have come under criticism for their tendency to reduce basic concepts to the most easily quantifiable elements.[11]

Rejecting the economic determinism used by progressive scholars in tracing the coming of the war, the new political history poses a sharp distinction between real and unreal issues. Some aver that these historians have simply substituted an equally one-dimensional "religious man" for the "economic man" of the progressives. The new mode of explanation has been challenged as "fundamentally ahistorical," its "key variables" existing independent of historical context. Foner holds that "religion and ethnicity are generally treated as uni-dimensional concepts, without reference to time, place, rate of acculturation, or individual personality." He makes a valid point that all historical variables are interrelated and continue to change as society develops. He believes that taking one key variable—religious belief—and abstracting it from its social context and the processes of historical change distorts and fractures "historical reality." But religious belief need not be abstracted from its social context, and thus need not distort the reality of the historical moment.[12]

The moral issue of slavery became the one issue with religious overtones that, in the context of a given time and place, initiated and integrated the new Republican movement. This newly formed political party soon endangered the Union. Without question, the word "slavery" took on many meanings, a complex set of collateral values, ambitions, and interests. Various issues that had been torn from their natural contexts were fused with the difficult problem of Negro slavery. Historian Don E. Fehrenbacher aptly declares: "Only the steady growth of a Northern consensus on the moral unacceptability of slavery explains either the rise of Republicanism or its brillant success in contrast with the disintegration of Whiggery, the failure of Know-Nothingism, and the disruption of Democracy."

The moral issue of slavery became an abstract as well as a concrete factor in the developing sectional conflict of the 1850s. This does not mean, however, that the moral crusade against the institution of slavery was either incidental or artificial. The power of this very issue upon the hearts and minds of the American people, both North and South, is revealed in the fact that nearly all public controversy fell into alignment with the slavery issue in the years preceding the war. The symbolic importance of the slavery issue may be seen in the various reactions to the culminating event of this decade of moral fervor, the election of Abraham Lincoln to the presidency.

The "new political historians" present arguments that do indeed have some profound implications for the question of Civil War causation. For example, Joel Silbey's 1964 article "The Civil War Synthesis" chided historians for writing the history of the 1850s solely from the vantage point of the slavery issue while ignoring the nativist question, which seemed to have little to do with the coming of the war. Silbey's position contained the new outlook, but made too much of the supposed split existing between Northern political elites and the mass of voters. In the religious setting of the day the same public that deliberated on Oberlin perfectionism, Congregational independency, Presbyterian principles, and nativism also discussed the issues in the Lincoln-Douglas debates, secession, and war.[13]

The weaving of secular and religious motifs into one holy history became commonplace. Many Americans believed that the advance of God's kingdom on the earth was intimately connected with the progress of democracy, and that both were best exemplified in the United States. America was leading the world toward a "millennium of republicanism."[14] The conviction of a great work to be done prompted exertion of great religious zeal. There emerged the so-called evangelical united front in the first quarter of the nineteenth century. A vast network of tract, Bible, temperance, missionary, and other benevolent societies operated on behalf of a great effort. Protestants, for the most part, employed these tools to build a Christian America, and they were hopeful that the kingdom of God was coming. The idea of Union had become invested with religious and cultural expectations:

> Our government will be the grand center of this mighty influence. . . . The beneficial and harmonious operation of our institutions will be seen, and similar ones adopted. Christianity must speedily follow them; and we shall behold the grand spectacle of a whole world, civilized, republican, and Christian. Then will wrong and injustice be forever banished. Every yoke shall be broken, and the oppressed go free. Wars will cease from the earth. Men "shall beat their swords into plough shares, and their spears into pruning-hooks. Nation shall not lift up sword against nation; neither shall they learn war any more;" for each man shall feel that every other man is his neighbor—his brother. Then shall come to pass the millennium, when "they shall teach no more every man his neighbor, and every man his brother, saying Know ye the Lord; for all shall know him, from the least of them unto the greatest."[15]

The evanglical reform movements of the 1830s and 1840s—abolitionism, prison reform, temperance, the emancipation of women, and many others—expressed the Puritan impulse for salvation. Salvation could be achieved in this world, in this dispensation. In practice, sin could be ultimately expelled by man's own endeavor rather than by God's grace alone, if, indeed, it was still possible to distinguish between the two.[16]

This was the age of postmillennialism, the technical term designating the belief that Jesus Christ will return to earth after the millennium—a humanly established millennium. Jonathan Edwards had been one of the first prominent Americans to espouse this point of view, and by 1859 it was asserted that the postmillennial theory was "the commonly received doctrine" in the United States.[17] In the mid-nineteenth century, this idea meant that the present labors of the church on the earth would usher in the millennial age. This ultimate promise of success gave impetus to every good work, and made kingdom work of such endeavors as social reform, home and world missions, science, the arts, and the American democratic experiment. George Marsden rightly declares: "The differences between the millennial views in the pre-Civil War era appear to have been less important than the similarities of the militant apocalyptic imagery shared by most American Protestants."[18] Aided by God, man could establish the millennial kingdom by his own initiative in ridding the world of manifested sin.[19]

This strange sense of expectancy was not limited to those chiliastic sects that had proclaimed God's forthcoming wrath upon a world of sin, for a more pervasive millennialism existed that looked upon America's future as the fulfillment of God's promises. The millenarian concept for America had both a secular as well as a religious basis.

The ideals of the Declaration of Independence were combined with the preachings of God's servants to promote a vision of national perfection. The natural law of the Declaration of Independence and the moral law of Christian tradition made up the primary doctrine, the fundamental law not made by man that underlay society and made human association possible. A second important doctrine in this era was that of the free and responsible individual. The citizen was responsible to the fundamental law before which all men are equal.[20] America had become a new Israel, a new witness to the world; Lincoln called Americans "the Almost Chosen People." While American Protestants were moving outward to establish missions on the frontier and in non-Christian nations, the doctrine of a national mission to stand before the world as a witness for democracy was being born and ultimately found its codification in the ideas and utterances of President Abraham Lincoln.

There was a darker side of the Apocalypse emerging by the middle of the century. Responsible millennialists, like Timothy Dwight, had warned that a chosen people would be subjected to more severe tests than other peoples. While assuring his countrymen in 1801 that God had in all respects treated Americans as his chosen, Dwight warned that the nation's future must not be taken for granted: "We may be scourged, for we merit it, but I trust we shall not be forsaken; we may *be cast down*, but we shall not be destroyed."[21] There were warnings that national sins would bring wrath on the day of the Lord and that the nation could become a fearful example of retribution unless there were repentance. "For the power of Antichrist was still apparent in the slave market, even in the nation's capital itself, and the apocalyptic angel would surely have to pour out the vial of wrath to its fullest on this peculiar people if they failed to reform speedily," writes Ernest Tuveson in the *Redeemer Nation*.[22] In 1844 Robert Baird declared in his classic *Religion in America* that men "must first acquiesce with submission in the government of God before they can yield a willing obedience to the requirements of human government."[23] The secret of American greatness, according to Philip Schaff, lay in the fact that "the impulse towards freedom and the sense of law and order are inseparably united, and both rest on a moral basis."[24]

Many believed that nothing stood in the way of America's divine witness but the burden of our inherited institutions, such as government, authoritarian religious bodies, and archaic forms of social and economic life, among which was the institution of slavery. All institutions, however, were at the mercy of public opinion, especially those media of communication that influence public opinion: the pulpit, the newspaper, and the politician.

Throughout the decade of the 1850s, the Northern clergy, in the religious editorial chair and in the pulpit, divided over the interpretation of Christ's words, "Render therefore unto Caesar the things which are Caesar's; and unto God the things that are God's." The crucial issue was whether or not the Christian gospel was to deal directly with the problems of secular government and society. As the *Chicago Western Citizen* declared: "Men's conduct in the political relations is no less moral and accountable, than is any relation of life. And the gospel of our Lord Jesus Christ would be a failure in part, if it did not reach and regulate it."[25]

Should sermons preached in Christian pulpits deal with political, economic, and social affairs? The moment the minister spoke from the pulpit "of the corruption of government and political parties, their departures from the great rules of right and law of love—the gospel course of Christians concerning them," some cried with horror, "*Politics in the Pulpit*. Horrible!"[26] The disposition of several denominations "to interfere with the laws of government" was viewed by some as "the most alarming manifestation of the times."[27]

Long before Stephen A. Douglas introduced the Kansas-Nebraska bill in 1854, an action that raised a moral outburst among Northerners, some segments of American Protestantism had demonstrated an interest in the slavery controversy. Many American churches, North and South, had defined slavery clearly as morally wrong and had expressed their sentiment in favor of its ultimate abolition. Those early *pronunciamentos* had been nonsectarian. But as early as the 1830s, churches were drawn into the conflict and began to divide regionally over the issue. From the 1830s on, the principal carriers of antislavery sentiment were the major Protestant denominations of the North, which attempted to inject moralistic and higly religious sentiment into the public issues of the day. Baptist associations, Methodist conferences, and other denominational organizations passed strong antislavery resolutions. In the late 1840s and 1850s the slavery question was the most important link between religion and politics.[28]

As the agitation continued, it was most effectively felt by those very denominations that had a nationwide membership. Denominations discussed the expediency and debated the morality of the issue. By 1845, most of the major bodies had split into Northern and Southern churches. The new churches had differences in policy and administration, but the most divisive issue clearly was slavery. Writing in April 1845, Henry Clay of Kentucky noted: "Scarcely any public occurrence has happened for a long time that gave me so much real concern and pain as the menaced separation of the Church, by a line throwing all the Free States on one side, and all the Slave States on the other." Such an example, he warned, would be fraught with imminent danger, and together with other national problems, would dangerously affect the stability of the Union. Lincoln expressed the same concern some thirteen years later when he noted that slavery was not "confined to politics alone. Presbyterian assemblies, Methodist conferences, Unitarian gatherings, and single churches to an indefinite extent, are wrangling, and cracking, and going to pieces on the same question. Has any thing ever threatened the existence of this Union save and except this very institution of slavery."[29]

Sharing Henry Clay's fears for the safety of the Union was the leading Southern statesman, John C. Calhoun. In his speech to Congess during the debates on Clay's compromise proposals on March 4, 1850, Calhoun said that the states were bound together by many different cords. These national cords were political and social as well as spiritual: "The strongest of those of a spiritual and ecclesiastical nature, consisted in the unity of the great denominations, all of which originally embraced the whole Union." Calhoun was dismayed that these ties, which had formed a strong cord to hold the Union together, had "not been able to resist the explosive effect of slavery agitation."[30] He recounted the facts that the Methodist and Baptist churches had each split into two hostile bodies, and observed that while the Presbyterian cord had not entirely snapped, the strands were frayed. "If the agitation goes on," warned Calhoun, "the same force, acting with increased intensity, as has been shown, will finally snap every cord, when nothing will be left to hold the States together except force."[31]

Just a few weeks before his death in 1852, Henry Clay reinforced Calhoun's fears for the Union in an interview with the Reverend Doctor W. W. Hill, editor of the *Presbyterian Herald* of Louisville, Kentucky. Clay told him: "I tell you this sundering of the religious ties which have hitherto bound our people together, I consider the greatest source of danger to our country." "If our religious men cannot live together in peace," he explained, "what can be expected of us politicians, very few of whom profess to be governed by the subject of slavery." Clay believed there would be nothing left to bind the people together but trade and commerce. Although they formed a powerful bond, the Kentuckian perceived that "when the people of these states become thoroughly alienated from each other, and get their passions aroused, they are not apt to stop and consider what is to their interest." If the preachers would only keep the churches from "running into excesses and fanaticism," Clay thought the politicians could control the masses. But he admonished the reverend gentleman that "yours is the harder task; and if you do not perform it, we will not be able to do our part." Then Clay concluded: "That I consider to be the greater source of danger to our country."[32]

The disruptive effect of this growing agitation was accentuated because it was appearing at a time when the equally aggressive proslavery movement was developing. During the first third of the nineteenth century, there were many southerners who had been as critical of the institution as anyone in the North, but by the 1830s, and certainly by the 1840s, this sentiment declined and highly vocal champions of the Southern "peculiar institution" dominated the opinion of the South. Writing in his diary, former president John Quincy Adams said: "It is also to be considered that at this time the most dangerous of all subjects for public contention is the slavery question. In the South it is a perfect agony of conscious guilt and terror, attempting to disguise itself with sophistical argumentation and braggart menaces." If this were true, then how much more acute the situation became after twenty years of agitation.[33] Historian Don E. Fehrenbacher declares:

> Of particular significance was the interpenetration of religion and politics throughout the decade. It is well known that much of the original impetus and moral fervor of the antislavery movement came from evangelistic Protestantism; and that the slavery question divided several of the major church organizations before it disrupted the national parties and government.[34]

The crisis of the apocalyptic drama had begun. As the confidence in the American ideal of the new chosen people reached its peak in the years before 1860, the impending confrontation also came to a head. Slavery had been an integral part of southern life for nearly two hundred years. Southerners had often viewed it as a misfortune but never as a sin, accursed of God. Southern ministers and laymen had defended it, and the Bible had been a favorite source of justification, particularly the Old Testament scriptures. By 1860 the Southern people were unwilling to confess moral inferiority. To hear a United States senator speak of "the whole slave-holding class as a combination of ruffianism and bluster, whisky-drinking and tobacco-chewing," and to be "held up to the gaze of an eager world as slave-drivers lost to humanity and accursed of God" infuriated Southern people. Senator Charles Sumner's attack on the South contradicted Abraham Lincoln's repeated declarations and those of conservative and moderate Republicans that Southerners had nothing to fear from Republican success in the 1860 election.[35]

The Republican movement was not only an outgrowth and manifestation of the reforming spirit; it was also the climax of antebellum reform. By 1860 the party had become conservative enough to win a presidential election and yet provocative enough to light the fuse of a major national explosion. The essence of the early Republican party was revealed in Abraham Lincoln's 1860 campaign, and his election to the presidency proved to be that circumstantial link between causes and effects that led to the Civil War in the United States.[36]

On November 6, 1860, Abraham Lincoln was elected the sixteenth president of the United States. "Your selection is a revolution in itself, your administration, if successful, will mark a turning point in our history," wrote the German leader Carl Schurz to the new president-elect. Across the nation, the press and the pulpit were announcing to northern people that a great crisis had been reached and passed in American history. "When it was announced that the people of the United States in the legitimate way had designated ABRAHAM LINCOLN as their next President," declared the *New York Independent*, "the crisis was over—the most critical point in the struggle between Freedom and Slavery, since the adoption of the Federal Constitution, was passed, *safely, decisively, finally* passed." The substance of the revolution for "freedom" was yet to be tested in civil war.[37] Men might, as always, dispute the meaning of the election of 1860. Its central import, however, was plain—slavery must be circumscribed and contained. Lincoln's 1,866,000 followers wished to contain slavery within limits by congressional action. A large portion of Stephen A. Douglas's 1,375,000 supporters sought its containment by means of local option. Thus, Lincoln's election had a deep significance that went beyond compromise; it signified the end of slavery's advance as a national institution. Slavery was to be "denationalized," and then would follow the "demand of Christendom for the abolition of the system."[38]

For Southerners, who had been persuaded increasingly through the preceding decade that slavery was righteous, blessed, and a Christianizing force, resistance to the newly elected administration became a responsibility—a moral responsibility. "The salvation of the whole country" depended on "united and determined resistance." Southerners were persuaded that "in saving ourselves we shall save the North from the ruin she is drawing madly upon her own head." If the South "has grace given her to know her hour she will save herself and the country, and the world."[39]

For Northerners who believed slavery to be wrong, a curse, an evil, and a sin in the sight of God and man, Lincoln's election was another occasion of moral significance in the history of the world. The well-known preacher Henry Ward Beecher believed "the sixth of November, 1860 will hereafter rank with the landing of the Pilgrims and with the Declaration of Independence. They are links in the chain of gold by which God is measuring time, and fixing eras of moral development in this world." The antislavery preacher averred that "we have entered upon a new day."[40] Little did Beecher or thousands of other antislavery citizens realize that the "new day" would occasion war. Moral persuasion had been their means, not force.

Even such a competent observer as the European Count Agenor de Gasparin noted that "the election of Mr. Lincoln is a painful but salutary crisis; it is the first effort of a great people rising." The vital force in this moral crusade was the fundamental antagonism of the gospel and slavery.[41] The slavery question was certainly the most important link between religion and politics in the 1850s and aided the national drift toward confrontation by arms.

Many people in the North as well as a few European observers celebrated Lincoln's election, some heralding the event as "one of the great dates of American history" and as an "initial victory of a great moral principle." Yet, at the same time, ominous threats of civil war hung over the land like a pall. For most Northern Protestants the issue was no longer focused alone on whether a local institution, though sinful, should be endured, but whether the nation could endure having Southern iniquity pressed upon the entire country. Charles Hodge wrote: "There are occasions when political questions rise into the sphere of morals and religion; when the rule for action is to be sought not in consideration of state policy, but the law of God." The existing crisis was just such an occasion. The *New York Independent* fathomed the workings of the Almighty in the affairs of the dividing nation:

> God, who controls the destiny of nations, is opening a new chapter in the history of the world's wickedness. He has permitted the apostasy of Southern Christianity and the incendiary sophistry of Southern politics to work out their results. He has permitted that revolutionary frenzy to sweep over so many states. *Quis vult perdere, dementat*. It is for us to accept the fact. Those states must be permitted to work out their own destruction under the retributive Providence which is ordering their dreadful destiny.[42]

By April 1861, the Union had to be preserved, because it was perceived as containing the hopes of all people, not just of Americans alone. The preservation of the Union was a sacred trust and a holy cause for the benefit of all humanity.

God was going to battle in America, sustaining the hopes and justifying the righteous indignation of both North and South. Even though the war was waged over a great moral issue, this was more than just another war about moral issues; it had become *the* crisis affecting all of mankind, or so the rhetoric seemed to indicate. One Pennsylvanian wrote:

> This war is but the work of the Lord. He has this nation in the crucible of affliction, to burn up the dross. If I was ever thankful for anything, it is for this; and my prayer is, that the fires may not cease to burn until the gold of this nation shine in righteousness, clear and bright, reflecting the image of our Saviour.[43]

Addressing a farewell service for departing recruits in Rhode Island, an Episcopal bishop declared, "Your country has called for your service and you are ready." "It is a holy and righteous cause in which you enlist," he averred. "God is with us; . . . the Lord of hosts is on our side." Closing in prayer, the bishop told God that these men were "now going forth to aid in saving our land from the ravages of sedition, conspiracy and rebellion."[44]

Without question, however, Southerners were as certain as their former Northern brethren that God was on their side to defend liberty, hearth, and altar. In Louisiana, another Episcopal bishop, soon to be a Confederate major general, wrote a friend: "I believe most solemnly that it is for constitutional liberty, which seems to have fled to us for refuge, for our hearth-stones, and our altars that we strike." Needing providential support for the task ahead, he declared, "I hope I shall be supported in the work and have grace to do my duty."[45] Four years of fratricidal strife would not dim the conviction that Southern arms were doing battle for a Holy God.

In linking the positions of the South with the cause of God and religion, the most effective apologists were two Presbyterian theologians, J. H. Thornwell and Robert Lewis Dabney. Thornwell declared that "the Scriptures not only fail to condemn slavery, they as distinctly sanction it as any other social condition of man." Northerners who called slavery "sinful" were simply rejecting the Bible. Dabney wrote: "Our policy . . . [must be] to push the Bible argument continually" and thus force the enemies of slavery to reveal their infidel colors. Baptists, Methodists, and Episcopalians also defended Southern slavery and therefore the Southern military effort on biblical grounds.[46]

Thus, on both sides of the Mason-Dixon line, brothers in theology and piety offered contradictory prayers, as the apologists in both camps justified the resort to arms.

As soon as the first guns had fired, Northern Protestants began to reevaluate their conception of national destiny. "Drawing upon the Puritan tradition of pulpit jeremiads," writes James H. Moorhead in *American Apocalypse*, "the clergy suggested that the nation's hope had gone away because the people had sinned." Since the time of the nation's revolutionary ancestors, virtue and piety had fallen short of their glorious example. It was argued, therefore, that a just God demanded expiation in blood. The clergy preached that apocalyptic woes applied even in the United States. "Here, too, the Kingdom could come only through travail and the clash of arms," declares Moorhead. "God was violently overturning the old, corrupt order and was bringing the disparate forces of history to a climactic revolution in one place and time." Americans were fighting the definitive battle that would ensure the future happiness of the *United* States and the world. "The Armageddon of the Republic had begun."[47]

War had come to the nation for sins that all the people had committed. Therefore, the North was as much the object of divine wrath as was the South. God was scourging both for their sins, using the two parties in the conflict as rods. But this chastisement of God was moving the nation toward a final victory. Great eras are marked by great judgments. The Civil War was to be a watershed between an old and a new America.

With disunion a reality, the churches, already divided, functioned as separate bodies in separate nations and professed the most loyal sentiments for their respective governments. Bereft of its Southern synods, the General Synod of the Lutheran church in 1862 appointed a special committe to assure President Lincoln of their wholehearted support and characterized the rebellion as most wicked, unjustifiable, unnatural, inhuman, oppressive, and "destructive in its results to the highest interests of morality and religion." In 1862, Southern Presbyterians expressed a deep conviction "that this struggle is not alone for civil rights and property and home, but also for religion, for the church, for the gospel, for existence itself." Virtually every church held the same position.[48]

Churches North and South attested their loyalty to their respective governments and armies through memorials, prayers, and sermons. During the war, various charitable organizations were formed with the encouragement of churchmen to minister to the needs of the soldiers. One of the most important of these efforts was the United States Christian Commission, which became a vast interdenominational organization. The commission's five thousand unpaid delegates offered spiritual counsel to the distressed, distributed tracts, wrote letters for the wounded, nursed the sick, operated lending libraries, and ran soup kitchens supplementing the soldiers' diet.

With astounding success, Christian Commission delegates and military chaplains presided at prayer meetings and revival meetings in camp. The United States War Department authorized one ordained and denominationally certified chaplain per regiment, and eventually placed chaplains in the hospitals as well. The Confederacy made similar arrangements. The number of chaplains who volunteered was remarkably high.

During the war great revivals swept through the armies of both the North and the south. Estimates of conversions within the military during the Civil War range from one to one hundred thousand. Writing of the "Great Revival" in the Southern armies, John B. McFerrin, a Southern Methodist chaplain, noted:

> The result was that thousands were happily converted and were prepared for the future that awaited them. Officers and men alike were brought under religious influence. In all my life, perhaps, I never witnessed more displays of God's power in the awakening and conversion of sinners than in these protracted meetings during the winter and spring of 1863–64.[49]

After the Union army left the bloody Gettysburg battlefield in July 1863, it experienced one of the greatest revivals in the war, the "revival on the Rapidan." The Union armies had become responsive to revival fires spreading among both officers and men. One Christian Commission officer reported that Union general O. O. Howard "spoke of the Saviour, his love for Him and his peace in His service, as freely and simply as he could have spoken in his own family circle." General Howard reported visiting a hospital the night after the battle of Resaca, where he found a "fair-faced boy who could not live till morning." The Union general knelt down on the boy's blanket and asked if he could do anything for the dying lad. "Yes," said the boy, "I want somebody to tell me how to find the Saviour." "I never felt my ignorance so much before," said General Howard. "Here was a mind ready now to hear and act on the truth. What if I should give him wrong directions? How I wished I had a minister's training." Then he related what directions he had given the boy, the prayer he spoke, and the boy's smile and newfound peace.[50]

Pious experience was recounted by men on both sides, for both sides experienced revivals. According to American church historian Sydney Ahlstrom, the soldier's sense of duty, on both sides, was deepened, morale improved, and loyalty intensified. "More cynical commanders and more despairing men might have been less sure that the Almighty was with them and that victory must surely come," writes Ahlstrom. It is possible that they might have felt a stronger impulse not to compromise. "Perhaps piety lengthened the war," he declares. "Certainly it deepened the tragedy and made the entire experience a more enduring scar on the national memory."[51]

The Civil War raised the deepest questions of national meaning. If the United States would ultimately be the instrument of a millennial reign, it would seem to be inevitable that in the hour of great trial, when God's judgment was poured out, the redeeming nation should have a leader of millennial stature, a redeemer-president. Ernest Lee Tuveson writes: "The fact that, in the crucial hour, there was elected a President who did indeed have qualities expected of such a figure was further proof that the millennial mission was no dream." The man who not only formulated but in his own person embodied the national meaning in the conflict for Americans was Abraham Lincoln. "With the Civil War, a new theme of death, sacrifice, and rebirth enters the civil religion," writes Robert N. Bellah in *Civil Religion in America*. "It is symbolized in the life and death of Lincoln."[52]

When the national bond that united North and South was being utilized by apologists in both camps to justify the resort to arms, it became clear that the war itself must somehow be brought within the scope of God's greater sovereign design if the United States were to be reunited. Abraham Lincoln struggled throughout the bloody years of war to find a larger and deeper meaning to civil strife than that suggested by a simple alliance of Providence with either the North or the South. Lincoln never questioned the ultimate justice of God. But he struggled, like every Christian historian, to read "the signs of the times," to learn what God's will actually demanded in the conflicting events of his own day. The president believed that God was involved in the day-to-day process of history but that men were still personally responsible. He warned:

> Fellow-citizens, we cannot escape history. We of this Congress and this administration, will be remembered in spite of ourselves. No personal significance, or unsignificance, can spare one or another of us. The fiery trial through which we pass, will light us down, in honor or dishonor, to the latest generations. . . . The way is plain, peaceful, generous, just—a way which, if followed, the world will forever bless.[53]

Lincoln questioned how to know the divine will in those day-to-day responsibilities of the nation that was at war with itself. He wished to avoid the futility and rebellion of opposing God's purposes in history. Many times he told callers that his greatest concern was not to get God on his side, but to be sure that he and the nation were on God's side. In June 1862, an Iowa delegation led by Congressman James Wilson interviewed the president at the executive mansion. One member of the delegation pressed the president for more resolute action, saying, "Slavery must be stricken down wherever it exists. If we do not do right I believe God will let us go our own way to our ruin. But if we do right, I believe He will lead us safely out of this wilderness, crown our arms with victory, and restore our now dissevered Union." Lincoln agreed about the judgment of the God of history but added, with a sparkle in his eyes and with his right arm outstretched toward the speaker:

> My faith is greater than yours. . . . I also believe He will compel us to do right in order that He may do these things, not so much because we desire them as that they accord with His plans of dealing with this nation, in the midst of which He means to establish justice. I think He means that he shall do

> more than we have yet done in furtherance of His plans, and He will open the way for our doing it. I have felt His hand upon me in great trials and submitted to His guidance, and I trust that as He shall further open the way I will be ready to walk therein, relying on His help and trusting in His goodness and wisdom.

Lincoln believed that military reverses were to be expected: "Sometimes it seems necessary that we should be confronted with perils which threaten us with disaster in order that we may not get puffed up and forget Him who has much work for us yet to do."[54]

Among the president's papers after his death was discovered an undated document that he never intended for others to see, according to his secretaries, John Nicolay and John Hay. The document may have been associated with Lincoln's despair following the second battle of Bull Run. He wrote that "it is quite possible that God's purpose is something different from the purpose of either party; and yet the human instrumentalities, working just as they do, are of the best adaptation to effect his purpose. I am almost ready to say that this is probably true; that God wills this contest, and wills that it shall not end yet."[55] Such were his private thoughts.

During the last year of his life, President Lincoln came to understand that the suffering of war was God's judgment upon the evil of slavery and a divine punishment to bring about its removal. But his public declaration on sanguinary judgment, delivered only weeks before his own martyrdom, must be juxtaposed with a call for reconciliation and mutual forgiveness. The destruction of slavery, although accomplished in God's appointed time by a bloody war, is now almost finished. Judgment, about to be terminated, must yield to forgiveness. Feeling this keenly, Lincoln himself wrote in a letter: "I am a patient man—always willing to forgive on the Christian terms of repentance; and also to give ample *time* for repentance." Writing to another correspondent, he declared, "I shall do nothing in malice. What I deal with is too vast for malicious dealing."[56]

Steeped in a biblical understanding of God, man, and history, Lincoln observed in his second inaugural address that God's judgment had fallen upon both sides, for slavery was a national, not a sectional sin. "Both parties deprecated war," declared the president, "but one of them would *make* war rather than let the nation survive; and the other would *accept* war rather than let it perish. And the war came."

Illuminating the finiteness of man, Lincoln noted that sincere men embraced opposite courses of action under the conviction that they were responding to God's will: "Both read the same Bible, and pray to the same God; and each invokes His aid against the other." A sincere intention to do God's will does not guarantee that what one does sincerely is therefore the will of God. Both sides could not be right: "The prayers of both could not be answered; that of neither has been fully." Each side could be partly right and partly wrong and God's purpose might be to use both sides as His instruments to effect a result that neither had foreseen. "The Almighty has His own purpose," he observed. Then the president declared that judgment on an offense can be expected to be equal to the offense itself:

> "Woe unto the world because of offenses! For it must needs be that offenses come; but woe to that man by whom the offense cometh!" If we shall suppose that American Slavery is one of those offenses which, in the providence of God, must needs come, but which, having continued through His appointed time, He now wills to remove, and that He gives to both North and South, this terrible war, as the woe due to those by whom the offense came, shall we discern therein any departure from those divine attributes which the believers in a Living God always ascribe to Him?

Indeed, judgment had fallen on both sides. Northern factories had prospered from the cheap raw materials that Southern slave labor had fed into them during the past decades. Northern merchants and bankers, as on New York's Wall Street, had prospered greatly from Southern loans and other financial endeavors. It seemed possible to Lincoln that a just God might allow the war to continue "until all the wealth piled by the bond-man's two hundred and fifty years of unrequited toil shall be sunk." Using the severe language of Scripture, Lincoln held the entire nation under judgment: "the judgments of the Lord are true and righteous altogether." And then breathing a prayer, he declared: "Fondly, do we hope—fervently do we pray—that this mighty scourge of war may speedily pass away."

If the judgments of God have as their purpose the reformation of his people, then the end of the war implied that renewal was just around the corner. In an almost scriptural paraphrase of Christ's summary of the law, President Lincoln concluded his public expression on the occasion of his second inauguration:

> With malice toward none; with charity for all; with firmness in the right, as God gives us to see the right, let us strive on to finish the work we are in; to bind up the nation's wounds; to care for him who shall have borne the battle, and for his widow, and his orphan—to do all which may achieve and cherish a just, and lasting peace, among ourselves, and with all nations.[57]

A just God was in the process of using the judgment of war to bring about a "just peace" through the efforts of men. This just peace was for all Americans as well as for the whole world. The God of history was seen to work out his apocalyptic program under his sovereign power.

Lincoln, who had refused to compromise on the moral issue of slavery and slavery's extension in the territories, had also refused to accept the disruption of the Union, and thus had turned to war. The man who preached reason and peace had also grasped the sword. "Only God can claim it," he once said. The president had not merely spoken to but had in fact preached to the nation at war with itself, knowing his words would not be "immediately popular." "Men are not flattered by being shown that there has been a difference of purpose between the Almighty and them," he wrote to Thurlow Weed. "To deny it, however, in this case, is to deny that there is a God governing the world." Lincoln believed "it is a truth which I thought needed to be told."[58]

By the time Robert E. Lee had surrendered to U. S. Grant on April 9, 1865, at Appomatox, Virginia, the brutal slaughter had reached staggering proportions. Some questioned even then, as others have questioned since, the justification for such bloodshed. What could possibly be the benefits of such a war? Out of the tragedies, and there were many, were there any triumphs—triumphs impossible without war? What possible spoil of war could justify such slaughter? By the end of the war, the Union dead approximated 360,000, and Confederate deaths almost equaled that figure; the Union counted 275,175 wounded, with perhaps an equal number of rebels wounded. The numbers are overwhelming. We must bear in mind that these casualties are not just numbers—they represent husbands, fathers, sons, and brothers. In addition, we should recognize the anguish of millions of survivors, a grief that is incalculable in human terms. Furthermore, these dead cost the nation, not just the families, all the future inventions, solutions, or alternatives that they might well have contributed.[59]

In the atmosphere of urban riots, assassinations, and the violent Democratic National Convention of 1968, a young graduate student at Stanford University, John S. Rosenberg, wrote an article that was published in the Spring 1969 issue of the *American Scholar*. Rosenberg asserted it was time to move "toward a new Civil War Revisionism." While admitting that his opinions were influenced by contemporary problems in America, he urged historians to recognize that over one hundred years after Appomatox, blacks still had not achieved full freedom. Furthermore, he suggested that the evils of this country's Vietnam involvement might give new insight into discussions of the merits of the Civil War. Rosenberg insisted that, in the light of such current realities, the Civil War had achieved little of lasting merit. Of the Civil War's two achievements, emancipation and union, the first had been hollow, and the second dubious. Therefore, concluded the young historian, the 600,000 dead in the war had died in vain.[60]

Challenging Rosenberg's thesis, Phillip S. Paludan avowed that "historians as sensitive human beings can hardly escape making moral judgments about the events of their time." But even as historians opposed to both war and racism, they have a responsibility to describe and assess events not just with compassion or outrage but with their critical moral intelligence. Paludan criticizes Rosenberg for being an historian among those who "warp the past to suit their present hopes" and who are guilty of "a poorly executed presentism." Certainly history can serve as a tool for understanding contemporary crises, but it cannot do so if we do not tell the harshest truths about our past. "It cannot do so if we persist in shaping the past to satisfy our fondest hopes for the present or to verify our outrage against current national misdeeds," declares Paludan.[61]

There were triumphs that would have been impossible without the Civil War. The death of slavery was a result of the war. "The peculiar institution's grip on the South," posits Paludan, "tragically, was too tight to be loosened except by the imposition of outside force." Slavery was still adaptable to mining, industry, and agriculture. It served as the means of control of the feared slave population, and served profound social and psychological needs as well. Of course, freedom for blacks was not equality, but it was not slavery either.[62]

Another benefit out of this war was the preservation of the Union. But does this fact justify the great number of Civil War dead? Paludan believes that twentieth-century historians are ill equipped to answer. "The meaning of the Union," he writes, "does not have for us the meaning it had in the nineteenth century. We presently take for granted the nation they died to preserve." In addition, the predominant historiography of the Civil War era impedes our understanding. The deemphasis of, or lack of interest in, the unionism of the past results from the faulty parallels between the revolution of 1776 and the secession of 1860, from recollections of the bloodbath of the war, and from improper assessments of Reconstruction as a mistake. More historians, for example, devote their attention to the meaning of emancipation than to the meaning of the Union. Therefore, historians have yielded to the temptation to "trivialize the saving of the Union." Paludan concludes that "we must accept the war as the necessary instrument of order, strength, wealth and liberty." As the preacher in Ecclesiastes would put it, there is an appointed time for everything—even "a time for war."[63]

To acknowledge that there were benefits from the American Civil War is not to argue the blessings of war itself:

> It is to recognize that we cannot always pay cheap prices for things that are precious; that we cannot undo the evils of centuries without enduring the wrenchings and tearings of our enormous efforts, that while we must measure our efforts at liberty in terms of our dreams, we should measure our progress in terms of what was possible lest we lost faith in our ability to make progress at all.

It is still possible, then, to speak in terms of a just war with a just cause. To encourage perseverence in such a cause, Lincoln wrote General U. S. Grant, "And now with a brave Army, and a just cause, may God sustain you."[64]

As a result of the Civil War, this nation experienced a "new birth of freedom." The process of birth, however, was accompanied by great pain and agony. In the last months of the war, the president expressed it succinctly:

> The purposes of the Almighty are perfect and must prevail, though we erring mortals may fail to accurately perceive them in advance. We hoped for a happy termination of this terrible war long before this; but God knows best, and has ruled otherwise. We shall yet acknowledge His wisdom and our own error therein. Meanwhile we must work earnestly in the best light He gives us, trusting that so working still conduces to the great ends He ordains. Surely He intends some great good to follow this mighty convulsion, which no mortal could make, and no mortal could stay.[65]

With the agony of war behind it, a reunited nation emerged out of fratricidal strife. The American people, North and South, were once again free to pursue the future, confident that "some great good" would follow the "mighty convulsion."

5 AUGUSTUS CERILLO, JR.

THE SPANISH-AMERICAN WAR

THE "SPLENDID LITTLE WAR" OF 1898, as John Hay called it at the time, is hardly splendid when viewed from a Christian perspective. Instead, America's armed intervention in Cuba's rebellion against Spanish colonial misrule offers striking illustrations of the ironic contrasts and contradictions between our pretentious views of the purity and innocence of our national motives, actions, and goals and the actual harsh consequences of the exercise of our power. One of the major ironies of the Spanish-American conflict was that what began ostensibly as a popular American crusade to liberate freedom-seeking Cubans from Spanish imperialism quickly became a war of American conquest. By the time the three-month skirmish with the Catholic monarchy was over, the United States had granted Cuba a drastically limited independence and had acquired Puerto Rico, Guam, and, against the wishes of the islanders, the Philippines. A further ironic twist was that the United States, so morally revulsed by Spain's treatment of her colonial subjects, was forced to suppress in brutal fashion a Filipino rebellion against American imperial rule. It is additionally ironic that William McKinley, the man presiding over the American quest for empire, should have stated in his first inaugural address as president in 1897, "We want no wars of conquest; we must avoid the temptations of territorial aggression."[1]

One source for our understanding of the causes, consequences, and ironies of the war of 1898 is America's foreign policy in the late nineteenth century. The war with Spain belongs in the category of those events and ideas that, after the 1880s, increasingly combined to convince a number of Americans that their nation, now a great power, needed to open its doors to world affairs and extend its influence abroad. Actually, the late 1880s and 1890s were difficult years for the United States. A century of urban and economic growth needed to be accommodated. Many Americans, Robert Wiebe writes, "sensed something fundamental was happening to their lives"; many were less sure than they had been about the quality of the nation's institutions and the future promise of American life.[2]

There were a number of developments that contributed to the growing sense of anxiety. Not only was the country's population growing, but its ethnic mix was changing drastically as millions of culturally different Jewish, Eastern Orthodox, and Roman Catholic immigrants from southern and eastern Europe were pouring into a nation earlier settled primarily by Protestant people of northern European stock. Further contributing to the uneasy feeling was the fact that thousands of these "uprooted" immigrants from abroad were joining a stream of city-bound rural Americans to swell the size and change the internal structure of American cities. The older walking, commercial city increasingly was giving way to the industrial metropolis. Most cities experienced common problems related to chaotic growth, municipal corruption and inadequate government, poor housing and health, and insufficient utility services. For many Americans, the cities seemed to represent the failure, not the hope, of democracy.

Industrialization, with its accompanying growth of giant bureaucratic corporations, joined immigration and urbanization to form a trinity of developments that rapidly were transforming the country from a decentralized, agrarian nation into an increasingly integrated and urban society. Scores of old-fashioned independent artisans, middle-class local entrepreneurs, and professionals, along with countless workers and farmers, came to believe that individual opportunity was becoming more and more constricted; the American dream was becoming, if not a nightmare, a less sure guide into the real future. Dreams and reality, which even in the best of times are always in partial antithesis, now seemed hopelessly separated into two very different orders of existence.

The last decade of the century witnessed a group of events that further intensified the nation's sense of crisis. The nineties saw the so-called closing of the frontier; a devastating economic depression; millions jobless, some of whom were organized into "industrial armies" of which Coxey's was only the most famous; countless labor strikes, such as at Homestead and Pullman; a growing bitterness on the farms, which gave rise to populism and the crusade for free silver; and the advocacy of all sorts of utopian, radical, and socialistic panaceas for solving the nation's ills. No wonder many respectable Americans genuinely feared the nation faced growing social disorder, perhaps even revolution. "We have been steadily, but inevitably, forced out of our old conditions of exceptional well-being, which came from our possession of a virgin continent," one writer gloomily reported.[3]

A frustrated people, possibly undergoing what Richard Hofstadter called a "psychic crisis," seemed ready to reexamine old ideas and policies and entertain new approaches both in domestic as well as in foreign affairs.[4] For some businessmen and politicians, as well as farmers and workers, the answer to at least the nation's economic crisis and waning business prospects rested in aggressively finding new markets abroad—particularly in Latin America, Cuba, and East Asia. The possessors of large amounts of capital also sought new opportunities for investments in foreign mines, railroads, and manufacturing plants. More than in the past, however, these "profit-oriented" capitalists expected systematic help from Washington. The need for government-as-partner in overseas economic expansion, especially in Asia, seemed critical by the mid-nineties: Russia, Japan, Germany, France, Great Britain, themselves lusting after the Asian market, began carving China and Manchuria into spheres of influence. To avert economic disaster, many believed, the United States somehow had to keep the door open to China.

Other Washington officials and opinion molders who advocated what Henry Cabot Lodge called a "large policy" blended economic considerations with a sense of American mission, social Darwinism, Anglo-Saxon racism, and concern for national security in rationalizing expansion and a greater exertion of American power throughout the world. More than likely, as Ernest R. May points out, these apologists for an enlarged foreign policy were influenced by the similar justifications for imperialism that were becoming fashionable in England and Europe by the last decades of the century.[5]

By viewing the world in Darwinian terms, these influential shapers of foreign policy believed that the nation, if it were to survive and progress, had no choice but to compete aggressively in the quest for wealth, power, and glory. Moreover, a great many Americans found in this evolutionary theory seeming scientific sanction for their long-standing belief that the world was composed of superior civilized people and inferior barbarians. The lesser breeds, who primarily inhabited Latin America, Asia, and Africa, were the obvious losers in life's struggle and were thus fit subjects for European and American imperialism. In the minds of many Americans, the purest of all the world's people were the Anglo-Saxons. Inherently superior, occupying the highest rung on the evolutionary ladder, their mission was to spread their superior language, political institutions, and culture around the world and thereby uplift the darker, backward peoples. The Anglo-Saxon race, "having developed peculiarly aggressive traits calculated to impress its institutions upon mankind, will spread itself over the earth," wrote Congregational clergyman Josiah Strong in his missionary tract, *Our Country*. It "will move down upon Mexico, down upon Central and South America, out upon the islands of the sea, over upon Africa and beyond. And can any one doubt that the result of this competition will be the 'survival of the fittest'?"

The newly acquired evolutionary version of "Manifest Destiny," combined with a traditional American predisposition to view even Europe as decadent and tired next to the virile, young Republic, provided further impetus behind United States expansion. Navy Captain Mahan worked out the grand strategy by which the United States could become predominant. In several books and articles he aggressively publicized a program of commercial, naval, and territorial expansion that he believed would bring the nation power and prosperity. He called for the building of a strong navy, an Isthmian canal, Caribbean bases to protect the canal, the annexation of Hawaii, and the expansion of markets in Latin America and Asia.

Protestant churchmen contributed in other ways to the expansionist mood of the late nineteenth century. Their stress on the role of American Christians in redeeming the world expanded the horizons of countless citizens and no doubt predisposed many to a greater acceptance of a larger world role for their Christian nation even in more secular matters. More specifically, the intensified emphasis on world evangelization during the Gilded Age stimulated a surge in American foreign missions. Millions of Protestants first learned about far away China, Japan, Africa, and other remote places around the globe from the written and oral reports of the missionaries. Even the State Department sometimes viewed conditions in foreign lands through the eyes of Christ's messengers. "In short," Milton Plesur comments, "missionaries broadened American contacts with the wider world."[6]

From today's religious perspective there was much about expansionist thought and activity that was morally reprehensible and exerted a negative influence on the nation's decision makers. America's efforts to expand trade and investment abroad were free from the constraints of the biblical norms of equity, justice, and preference for the poor. Thus the nation's trade arrangements sought to maximize American economic gain, often at the expense of impoverished indigenous workers or small entrepreneurs and a balanced economy in the less industrialized trading partner—as seems to have been the case in Hawaii, Cuba, and Latin America generally. A form of economic imperialism, this type of trade sowed the seeds of future anti-American violence and revolution among underdeveloped countries.[7] Along with goods and services, Americans sought to export what they believed were their superior political and economic institutions and religious and cultural ideas. To the extent such ideological imperialism was motivated by racist assumptions, it ultimately stemmed from the same biblically condemned sin of self-pride and hatred of others that had shaped domestic attitudes and policies toward Indians, blacks, Orientals, and "new" immigrant groups.

More generally, the American quest for power, wealth, and strategic advantage belied the nation's belief that it was, in Niebuhr's classic phrase, "the most innocent nation on earth." National ambition in the late nineteenth century both highlighted and encouraged the deeply embedded tendencies within American society toward economic cupidity, territorial aggrandizement, national selfishness, and idolatrous self-worship—the tendencies of any great power that seeks to master the world. America's innocent illusions about itself, its history, and its international reputation, although incongruous with the realities of its historical experience and projected goals, served as powerful vindicators of its political actions. Against such pagan and ultimately morally and spiritually destructive national and personal characteristics the prophets of Israel came preaching judgment. It was to replace such human values that Jesus came preaching the kingdom of God.

In the Gilded Age few evangelicals wore the mantle of Amos, Micah, or Isaiah; many could more easily identify with Peter's sword than Jesus' cross. Sadly, the unbiblical and misguided understanding of the nation's history and place in the world led too many Christians to contribute to the growing expansionist sentiment. Early in the nineteenth century, historian John Higham tells us, evangelical Protestants had identified "the Kingdom of God with the American Republic," marrying evangelical Christianity to liberal democracy to produce what Ralph Henry Gabriel called "The American Democratic Faith." When linked with a view that "God had assigned to America the leading role in the enterprise of redeeming mankind," this fusion of Protestant Christianity and secular political sentiment became a powerful ideological force—Manifest Destiny—behind the nation's continental expansion.[8]

During the post–Civil War years many Protestant Christians were confident that an American brand of Christianity—a combination of what Josiah Strong called "spiritual Christianity" and "civil liberty"—would come to dominate the world in their generation. The Christian of today can sympathize with the biblically informed intentions of the hundreds of spirit-filled men and women, especially the young, who went to the ends of the earth to preach the gospel. But fidelity to the Scriptures also forces us to condemn that evangelical generation's willingness to define the Christian life narrowly in terms of American, even Anglo-Saxon, civilization.

These American evangelicals, by encasing the gospel too rigidly in Western cultural, technological, and economic terms, unwittingly sowed the seeds of future trouble for the Christian message when indigenous anti-Western movements arose in the non-Western world. Moreover, by becoming ambassadors for the American way of life as well as for the church of Jesus Christ, American missionaries unconsciously became advance agents for Western penetration. Walter LaFeber points out that the missionaries dispensed "Western food, clothes, and customs, as well as spiritual values." Sometimes they sought American military protection; at times they sought to influence the political life of their host country. Many missionaries along with their stateside supporters were prone to assume that commerce, material progress, civilization, and Christianity went hand in hand across the waters. "God means that the type of religion and civilization attained by the Anglo-Saxon race shall have, for the present at least, the predominating influence in moulding the civilization of the world," declared missionary Sidney Gulick in 1897.[9]

By fusing the gospel, racism, and nationalism, evangelical leaders at home contributed to the inordinate amount of national pride that pervaded American thought by giving to it a sort of priestly blessing. Moreover, Protestantism's penchant for military metaphors—soldiers, battles, conquests—to describe the American evangelization of the world further inflamed the "crusading" mindset stimulated by militant, war-happy jingoists and humanitarians wanting to "free Cuba." It was but a short and easy step to accept a war between "Christian America" and reactionary Catholic Spain as a righteous conflict. American evangelicals failed to question sufficiently the motives and goals of the expansionists in terms of God's requirements for justice, righteousness, mercy, peace, honesty, selflessness, and the other fruits of Christian life.

Historians by no means agree on which ideas, developments, or interest groups most directly influenced foreign policy and caused the war with Spain.[10] There is no simple one-to-one correspondence between any aspect of this larger social context and President McKinley's response to the Cuban crisis or his decision on colonies. One thing we are fairly certain of is that some time around 1890, a fragmented grouping of Americans, with a rudimentary interest in foreign policy, wanted an extension of the nation's commitments abroad, a government more continuously involved around the world, and, for some, American control of foreign pieces of territory.

President McKinley came of age politically during the emergence of this expansionist era in American foreign policy. It would be historically inaccurate to suggest that he was out of step with his times and politically unrealistic to think that he formulated foreign policy in an intellectual and social vacuum, his claim of divine help in deciding to keep the Philippines notwithstanding. Yet we must keep in mind that the various publics, including Congress, that the president faced sometimes changed views and certainly sent diverse signals to the White House. Moreover, actual circumstances in the world continually changed: no exclusive focus on the domestic sources of foreign policy can adequately account for the *Maine* disaster, or the Filipino insurrection.

When Republican William McKinley entered the White House after his decisive victory in 1896 over the Democratic and Populist candidate William Jennings Bryan he faced what today would be called a war of national liberation by Cuban insurgents against a decaying yet brutal Spanish imperial administration. However, this rebellion by independence-seeking Cubans, begun in 1895, was just the most recent in a long series of insurrections against Spanish authority. Moreover, American interest in Cuba dated at least from the founding of the nation. Throughout the nineteenth century many Americans, mindful of their own recent revolution and their creation of a democratic nation, were sensitive to and encouraged Cuban demands for national freedom or at least a greater measure of self-rule. American humanitarian instincts frequently were touched by the heavy-handedness of Spain's colonial administration.

But even more powerful, more earthy considerations and motives—greed, covetousness, fear—shaped American responses toward Cuba. Private citizens as well as public officials lusted after the "Pearl of the Antilles" both for its economic potential and for its strategic location, especially in relation to a future Isthmian canal. Early in the history of the Republic a succession of administrations protested, on behalf of enterprising Yankee merchants and businessmen, Spain's colonial infringement on a Cuban commercial and financial "open door." In 1827 John Quincy Adams warned that the United States would consider the transfer of Cuba from Spanish control to another European power inimical to the nation's security. He and others during the first quarter of the nineteenth century also shared the view that in the short run Spanish rule in Cuba was preferable to a revolution or even independence because of the threat of possible English intervention. Southerners had still other reasons for disliking the prospects of an independent Cuba: they feared the impact on American slavery of a free black republic so close to American southern shores.

Whatever their motives, expansionist-minded Americans in the antebellum years blandly assumed that Cuba, only ninety miles from Florida, would someday become part of the Union. Manifest Destiny, Frederick Merk remarks, "became, in the fifties, Caribbeanized." Presidents Polk, Pierce, and Buchanan tried various schemes, from purchase to abetting internal revolution, to pry loose Cuba from Madrid's grasp, all to no avail. After the interruption of the American Civil War, Secretary of State William H. Seward expressed the hope that the island might be annexed, although with Spain's consent. Thus from the founding of the nation to the 1860s, an American Cuban policy had been shaped not so much by American concern for the welfare and desires of the Cuban people, but primarily by self-serving considerations of strategic and economic power.[11]

A ten-year civil war broke out in Cuba in 1868. It ended in the defeat of the rebels and promises by the victorious Spanish government to reform the island. While the carnage was in progress the Grant administration, under intense prodding by Secretary of State Hamilton Fish, restrained those pushing Washington either to grant belligerent status to the rebels, intervene militarily, or recognize Cuba's independence. Basically what Fish wanted in Cuba was what American leaders had always preferred, short of outright annexation: order, stability, peace, and an open door for United States trade and investments. The problem he faced was how to achieve these ends short of war with Spain.

Fish quickly overruled formal recognition of the belligerents as unjustified according to the standards of international law and potentially damaging to the government's case against Great Britain for recognizing the Confederacy in 1861. Grant's secretary of state also was certain American recognition of the rebels would mean war with Spain and the probable incorporation into the nation of a people he "regarded as totally unsuitable for a place in the American union." The aristocratic Fish also intensely disliked Spanish rule and slavery in Cuba, but, at the same time, as Lester Langley contends, did not believe the Cuban revolutionaries—a "*poutpourri* of Indian, Negro and Spaniard"—capable of guiding "the island towards stable self-rule."[12]

Secretary Fish's management of the nation's response to the Spanish-Cuban war was shaped by the interplay of his own attitudes and biases, events in Spain and Cuba over which he had little control or leverage, pressures from Congress and an American public demanding some kind of action, and the occurrence of unforeseen and largely fortuitous events arising out of the violence of the conflict. Over the length of the war, the administration's diplomatic tactics varied from friendly persuasion to offers of mediation to threats of future intervention. Convinced that Spain could not quash the revolt through military power alone, Fish at times proposed that Spain grant its colonial possession independence, at other times that Spain grant the Cubans economic and political reforms, including the emancipation of the island's slaves. In either case, what Fish wanted was a Cuba of "peace, prosperity and stability"—a situation consistent with America's commercial and strategic interests.

To his credit, Fish refused to push for the annexation of Cuba, and he kept the United States out of the war. A mixture of motives—economic, strategic, racial, and humanitarian—combined to shape the American government's diplomatic response. Robert Beisner, however, puts the secretary of state's legacy in perspective: "The United States did not have so much a Cuban 'policy' as a Fish policy, which could be altered 180 degrees in a twinkling."[13] A generation later similar circumstances in Cuba and a similar mixture of motives supported American armed intervention.

Between the ten years' war and 1895 things were relatively calm in Cuba. The United States continued its economic penetration of the island: trade increased and several Americans replaced Cubans and Spaniards as owners of sugar plantations and mining operations. A growing American taste for sugar encouraged American capital to introduce new technology and centralized corporate management and business techniques into the island's sugar-producing industry. This Americanization of the sugar industry effectively eliminated many small proprietors and relegated scores of Cuban sugar workers to a tenantlike status.

Madrid, failing to follow through on promised reforms, did little to improve its reputation among the Cuban people. The rebels bided their time—many of them as exiles in the United States—dreaming of another day. In 1892 exiled poet and patriot José Martí organized in the United States a Cuban Revolutionary Party committed to the struggle for a free and independent Cuba. Three years later, the Cuban economy devasted by the American reimposition of duties on foreign sugar, Martí and his revolutionary associates, inside and outside Cuba, launched another revolution against Spanish colonial administration.[14]

Once again Cuba was plunged into violent upheaval. Quickly the guerrilla-style warfare on the "ever faithful isle" fulfilled all too well what Jacques Ellul calls "The Law of Violence."[15] In an ongoing reciprocal relationship, the violence and cruelty of one side's strategy and tactics elicited equally violent and cruel military measures on the other. The hatred of one party was matched by the hatred of the other.

Both sides "engaged in a struggle of devastation" and "disregarded recognized laws of combat." Cuban armed revolutionaries, numbering at the most about 54,000, deliberately engaged in scorched earth practices, putting to the torch even American-owned plantations and sugar mills. Their strategy, according to Marxist historian Philip S. Foner, was to make the island "useless to the Spaniards by destroying every possible source of revenue." The Spaniards were to outdo the rebels in the work of destruction. Together the Spanish colonialists and Cuban revolutionaries brought about the collapse of the Cuban economy, causing hundreds to go homeless, hungry, and without work. Millions of dollars of American investments and trade alone were destroyed.

The cruelest action of the war was born of Spanish frustration over fighting against elusive guerrillas who successfully lived off the countryside. In 1896, General Valeriano Weyler, aptly nicknamed the "Butcher" for his brutality in putting down the rebels in the ten years' war, replaced the unsuccessful General Martinez Campos and took command of the Spanish troops. Weyler lost no time in living up to his reputation. He initiated a "reconcentration" policy, herding noncombatant Cuban peasants, including women and children, into fortified towns and cities, the purpose of which was to prevent the rural peasants, most of whom were sympathetic to the revolution, from giving food, clothing, and intelligence information to the rebels. The towns were unprepared in terms of sanitation, housing, and food supply for the influx of these uprooted *reconcentrados*. By the thousands they died of disease and starvation.[16]

The violence, bloodshed, and devastation in Cuba warranted in the name of humanity—and certainly of the Christianity so many Americans in the nineteenth century professed—some protest from the United States government and our government's use of whatever diplomatic and moral leverage it possessed to bring the fighting to a halt. The men who were chiefly responsible for fashioning Washington's initial response to the Cuban revolution were President Grover Cleveland and his secretary of state, Richard Olney. Neither man doubted their nation's right or ability to interpose its will and desires in the conflict between Cuba and Spain.

According to historians Grenville and Young the key to understanding Cleveland's Cuban policy is to recognize that the cautious president believed the security of the United States was threatened more by Cuban independence than by some type of continued although more moderate and humane Spanish control over the island. Like administrations before his, Cleveland's also was suspicious that other European powers, especially Germany, might try to gain control over Cuba should Spain lose the ability to hold onto the island. In seeking to bring about a negotiated settlement of the Cuban war on American and not Spanish or Cuban terms, Cleveland was following the precedent established by Grant and Fish. Such a self-serving approach to hemispheric diplomacy, however, was consistent with Secretary Olney's boast to Great Britain in July 1895—with respect to American interest in the Venezuelan boundary dispute—that "the United States is practically sovereign on this continent, and its fiat is law upon the subjects to which it confines its interposition."[17]

Cleveland and Olney were forced to take control over the formulation of a Cuban policy from a restive Congress backed by a militantly anti-Spanish public opinion. According to historian Ernest May, what began in 1895 as carefully contrived rallies and demonstrations, attended mainly by Cuban-Americans, union workers, and patriotic middle-class Protestant Americans, had become by 1896 a broad-based national crusade in support of the Cuban revolutionaries. "It seemed," May writes, "as if the mass of the people from coast to coast were in the clutch of feverish emotion." Numerous Protestant clergy served as the evangelists for the crusade, perhaps outdone in their enthusiasm for the rebel cause only by the nation's press, which unabashedly fed the public a steady stream of anti-Spanish, prorebel stories—some true, many fabricated. After Cleveland was to give up the White House to McKinley, the press, led by "yellow journalists" William Randolph Hearst and Joseph Pulitzer, even outdid its earlier sensationalism and in a shocking disregard for truth or the cause of peace gleefully fanned the flames of war—building their circulations in the process. Although scholars today no longer believe that the "yellow press" caused the United States to enter the war in 1898, it is plausible to contend that the press conditioned the American public to accept armed intervention as a morally justifiable and strategically necessary exertion of American power on behalf of a Caribbean neighbor.

It is difficult if not impossible to know with assurance what, in 1895 and 1896, motivated the countless Americans who attended the rallies on behalf of the Cuban rebels or precisely what they expected of the American government. More than likely most had mixed motives. No doubt, as May suggests, some saw in the revolution another hemispheric nation striving for an American-style freedom. Some Protestants jumped on the Cuban bandwagon in order to regain influence with the working masses who were sympathetic to the Cuban struggle. Both Republican and Democratic politicos sought to exploit the popularity of the Cuban crisis for partisan ends. This early popular outpouring of sentiment on behalf of the Cuban fighters gave rise to general calls for Cuban independence, an occasional request for annexation, and, in some highly emotional meetings, a plea for military volunteers. Such activities probably had little direct impact on the policy makers in the Cleveland White House. Public sympathy for Cuban independence did, however, provide a popular base for repeated Congressional moves to nudge the Cleveland administration toward more active support of the Cuban revolution.

Against this congressional pressure the cautious president, ever alert to keep control of foreign affairs in his own hands, stood firm. On June 12, 1895, he proclaimed the nation's neutrality and did his best to see that it was enforced. In his December message to Congress, Cleveland reiterated his call for American impartiality in the conflict. Not only did Cleveland fear that recognition of the revolutionaries would mean war with Spain, he also was influenced by those Americans with investments in Cuba who feared such a move would "free Spain from the responsibility of protecting American property," a matter of great urgency. Unlike their fellow citizens who at mass rallies gave emotional support to Cuban national aspirations but who failed to translate such sentiment into specific requests of the government, Americans whose property in Cuba was being destroyed bombarded the State Department with complaints and pushed for specific American commitments to protect their interests. Although Secretary Olney was unsure the government could do much in the situation, he dutifully lodged protests with Madrid, requested restitution for property loss, and generally asked that the personal rights and safety of American citizens in Cuba be protected by the civil authorities on the island. Against the Cuban insurgents he had little leverage, except enforcing the neutrality laws and withholding the granting of belligerent status.

As 1896 approached, Olney searched for a more positive American-Cuban policy. He was concerned about the damage to American commerce with Cuba and investments on the island. Congressional initiatives forced him to find ways to keep control of the situation in executive hands. And he became increasingly convinced that Spain was unable to suppress the revolution. He still was unwilling, however, to grant the rebels belligerent status and risk war with Spain. Instead, taking a cue from the old Grant-Fish policy, Olney forwarded to Spain in April 1896 what might reasonably be called a plan to save Cuba for America.

In Olney's famous diplomatic note, he, of course, cited the standard ideological, humanitarian, and economic reasons for Washington's concern about the fate of Spain's colony. The Americans, he wrote, naturally supported any struggle for "freer political institutions"; they wanted to see ended the suffering, violence, and tragedy of the war; and they deplored the economic devastation of Cuba and injury to American commerce. Robert Beisner adds that unmentioned concerns were the safeguarding of America's canal prospects and the possibility of European intervention in the Cuban-Spanish war.

Olney's specific suggestions for the resolution of the conflict and his statements of American goals for Cuba were more revealing of the American position than his explanation of American concern. The secretary rejected both Cuban independence and American annexation. Instead he urged Spain to pacify the island "on such a plan as, leaving Spain her rights of sovereignty, shall yet secure to the people of the Island all such rights and powers of local self-government as they can reasonably ask." He suggested Washington would help Spain in the pacification effort and see that the terms satisfied "the reasonable demands and aspirations of Cuba." Such a program of reform and autonomy, he argued, would speedily bring about the "termination of hostilities, and the restitution of peace and order to the island." It would further have the advantage of preventing "a war of races" between black and white Cubans should Spain, because of exhaustion, be forced to abandon the island. Moreover, the plan would deflate popular support in the United States for the rebellion. Olney's "peace plan" also contained an implied threat of future American intervention. "The United States," he wrote, "cannot contemplate with complacency another ten years of Cuban insurrection."

After a two-month delay, Spain formally rejected Olney's offer of United States mediation. From that time until the end of Cleveland's term both the president and his secretary continued to seek a solution to the Cuban rebellion on their own terms. Against congressional sentiment for Cuban independence, Cleveland urged patience and restraint; against Spain's intransigence he warned that time for a reasonable solution was running out; against the independence-seeking Cuban junta and guerrillas in the field, he offered only the promise of reform and autonomy under Spanish rule. In his last message to Congress the president repeated all of his concerns and proposals, if in a slightly more militant tone, and further added the threat of future American intervention. That decision was to await his successor in the oval office.

Cleveland's handling of the Cuban crisis had profound significance for the events of 1898. On the one hand he had maintained the peace, but on the other he had assumed certain rights for the United States in regard to Cuba that violated Spanish and Cuban national integrity, and set the United States on an increasingly escalating interventionist course. The administration's diplomatic responses to the Cuban tragedy were informed by the conviction, expressed in Olney's note, that "American interests were deeply involved in the rebellion and that the United States would be forced to protect those interests." Olney's note with its offer of mediation was a form of American intervention in the struggle short of military action. In his December message Cleveland pushed the logic of American interests further when he announced, according to LaFeber, that the United States had the unquestioned right to intervene in order to end the fighting and chaos and protect American interests. The president thus "provided a rationale for the right to use force" to protect his country's interests. From there to actual armed intervention was a short step.

Unfortunately for the future of United States-Latin American relationships, the powerful American republic did not define its interests in terms of the nationalist aspirations and economic well-being of the Cuban people, but according to a calculus of economic and strategic gain for the United States. This led both Cleveland and Olney to the morally dubious position that they, and not the fighting Cubans, knew what was a reasonable and just solution to the Cuban civil war. Neither man seemed to understand the notion, later stated by Reinhold Niebuhr, "that power cannot be wielded without guilt since it is never transcendent over interest." The triumph of American imperialism occurred before the first Yankee troops engaged the hated Spaniard ninety miles from Florida's shore.[18]

The self-reliant, determined, and politically shrewd William McKinley and a strong, cohesive Republican party committed to national economic development and overseas expansion inherited the Cuban crisis from Cleveland and the Democrats. Although the bitter, hard-fought, and highly emotional presidential contest in 1896 between McKinley and William Jennings Bryan focused on domestic issues, especially the nature of the currency, the Republican platform had called for, among other expansionist objectives, the independence of Cuba. A skillful manager of men, the new president was not to be bound unduly by the party's platform. He firmly exercised control over his party and Congress with the help of a loyal group of congressional leaders. And from the White House he shaped his administration's foreign policy with the aid of Assistant Secretary of State William R. Day.[19]

The president's primary goal was to bring the Spanish-Cuban conflict to a speedy conclusion. Toward that end he firmly resisted a jingo press and belligerent Congress clamoring for early American involvement in the war. He showed great restraint in the face of fortuitous crises in Spanish-American diplomatic relations: the unexpected publication of the deLome letter, the blowing up of the battleship *Maine*. Yet in retrospect McKinley's views about Spain's conduct of the war, his assumptions about a proper and justifiable role for the United States, and the policies he actually formulated seemed designed to guarantee that the war would fester and that at some point American intervention would appear morally necessary and militarily inevitable. No less an astute observer of the ironies of American history than the brilliant Reinhold Niebuhr has observed that McKinley's statements of policy "are a perfect mine for the cynic."[20]

Initially McKinley followed a cautious approach toward Spain and the Cuban crisis, recognizing that the proud and sensitive monarchy, pressed by its own peoples' anti-Americanism, needed time. So too did the United States, if it were to recover completely from the lingering economic depression of 1893. More positively, McKinley was pledged to cooperate with business in getting the economy moving by stimulating production, bringing about financial stability, and increasing the nation's world trade. Not only was the Cuban war destroying a lucrative American trade with the island, costing the United States government millions of dollars to enforce neutrality, it also was diverting the government's time and energy away from the efforts to keep the door open for American business in Asia, especially China. The German seizure of Kiaochow on the China coast in 1897 seemed an ominous portent of worse to come.

Economic concerns were not the only ones to plague the new chief executive. The Cuban crisis was "a constant irritation" in American public life. Many Americans believed some kind of intervention was a moral necessity in a righteous cause; certainly McKinley was moved deeply by the Cuban suffering. In fact, he persuaded Congress to appropriate $50,000 for a relief fund for Americans in Cuba and personally contributed $5,000 to the cause. A devout church-going man, the president no doubt was influenced by these humanitarian considerations. But like most Christians then and later, McKinley, in Ernest May's words, was "neither a Levite nor a prophet, nor was he any more experienced in applied ethics than in diplomacy." "The chances are," May perceptively writes, "that McKinley's conscience did not tell him very clearly what he ought to do." If not a social ethicist, the president was an astute politician. Whatever his ultimate response to the Spanish-Cuban crisis, its impact on Republican unity and the party's chances of keeping control of the government would be weighed carefully.[21]

Toward the latter half of 1897 McKinley worked out his Cuban policy. It was a curious blend of forbearance and impatience, pacific encouragement and hostile threats toward Spain, and good will and distrust toward the Cuban patriots. In his notes to Spain and other messages, McKinley stressed that a continuation of the war was inimical to American economic interests on the island, upsetting to the general political, social, and economic peace of the United States, and irritating to America's moral sensitivity over the wanton destruction of human life. Much like Cleveland, therefore, he wanted Spain to pacify the island with or without American mediation; but unlike his predecessor, McKinley refused to accept Spain's right to use in her pacification efforts what he considered inhumane and uncivilized methods of warfare. The "cruel policy" of reconcentration, he contended, "was not civilized warfare"; "it was extermination."

McKinley's policy contrasted with that of Cleveland and Olney in yet another way, according to Grenville and Young. Whereas Cleveland was prepared to sacrifice Cuban desires for a quick Spanish-American settlement, McKinley seemed genuinely sympathetic to the Cuban cause and reluctant to accept a solution that was unacceptable to the rebels. No doubt, though, he thought he could convince the Cubans of what was a reasonable and just solution. This was to be extremely difficult, however, for two reasons. First, the insurrectionists, after fighting for two years, were less interested in reform and autonomy under Spanish sovereignty than in independence. Yet no Spanish government, liberal or conservative, would relinquish all control over the New World colony. Second, for its part, the McKinley administration seemed unsure of what it ultimately wanted for Cuba.[22]

By the end of the year the president was encouraged by the coming to power in Spain of the new liberal regime headed by Praxedes Mateo Sagasta. Sagasta removed the notorious General Weyler, released American prisoners held in Cuban jails, and promised to introduce comprehensive reforms in Cuba, including an autonomy plan. In light of these "hopeful changes" in Spain's policy toward Cuba, McKinley told Congress in his annual message of December 1897 that Spain should "be given a reasonable chance to realize her expectations and to prove the asserted efficacy of the new order of things to which she stands irrevocably committed." If this implied ultimatum to Madrid was unclear, the president continued:

> The near future will demonstrate whether the indispensable condition of a righteous peace, just alike to the Cubans and to Spain as well as equitable to all our interests so intimately involved in the welfare of Cuba, is likely to be attained. If not, the exigency of further and other action by the United States will remain to be taken.

This message by the president made the following crystal clear: the president assumed first the right to judge Spain's conduct and the speed with which she made progress in resolving the Cuban crisis; and second, the right to intervene should Spain, or for that matter the Cubans, not live up to McKinley's expectation of "a righteous peace." He rationalized this rather arrogant assertion of national will and power by claiming, in Niebuhr's words, "general and universally valid objectives for the nation." "If it shall hereafter appear to be a duty imposed by our obligations to ourselves, to civilization and humanity to intervene with force," the president declared, "it shall be without fault on our part and only because the necessity for such action will be so clear as to command the support and approval of the civilized world."[23]

The "near future," the closest McKinley came to setting a time limit on American patience with Spain's handling of her colonial crisis, turned out to be approximately four months. From January to mid-April 1898, the president was faced with Madrid's continuing failure to bring peace to Cuba and a series of diplomatic crises and disasters that rocked the nation and intensified the war fervor among large portions of the American public, press, and Congress. War came, however, not because McKinley was pushed into it by this growing public hysteria, but because the logic of his own Cuban policy impelled him toward a showdown with Spain. Such a denouement took on the air of inevitability when Spain in February formally and rather testily responded to McKinley's message of the previous December. Madrid in effect told the American government to mind its own business. "Spanish government does not admit the right of neighboring country to limit duration of struggle," the royal government's note in translation read. "Aspirations for peace and friendly observations are justified. Foreign intrusion and interferences are never and in no way justified. These might lead to the intervention which every country that respects itself must repel with force."[24]

The Catholic monarchy shrewdly pierced the pretentiousness of America's position, but failed to acknowledge the morally legitimate concern of the United States for peace in Cuba, or the hypocrisy of its own supposedly conciliatory gestures toward the Cuban rebels in the light of its unfulfilled promises of reform. Ironically, the day before the Spanish note arrived in Washington, the *New York Journal* gleefully printed a private letter by Spanish minister Dupuy deLome in which the proud Spaniard referred to McKinley as "weak," "a bidder for the admiration of the crowd," "a would be politician." DeLome's personal attack on the president's character was shocking enough, but of larger significance was the minister's confession that Spain was not serious in her efforts to reform Cuba and would only be satisfied with a complete military victory. The publication of deLome's letter "had the effect of deepening the public's disgust with Spanish failure in Cuba and solidifying the conviction that the Spanish were perfidious scoundrels."[25]

Evidence of such apparent Spanish duplicity further reinforced the McKinley administration's growing skepticism about the probability of Spain's success in ending the war in Cuba. The month before, loyalist-led antiautonomy riots, supported by the Spanish army, had erupted in Havana. McKinley had responded to this sign of Spain's inability to control Cuba and protect American life and property by sending to Havana the second-class battleship *Maine*. Ostensibly on a friendly visit, the ship had hardly reached its destination before the deLome letter made the headlines. Seven days later the American vessel was destroyed by an explosion in the Havana harbor with the loss of 260 lives.[26]

The American public, already outraged over the deLome letter and whipped up by the yellow press, demanded vengeance for the *Maine*. A minority of clergymen called for war. One Episcopal priest in Terre Haute, Indiana, promised to do all he could "to make Spanish the prevailing language of hell"; on a more lofty plane, Methodist Bishop Charles C. McCabe declared before a ministerial association in St. Louis: "There are many things worse than war. It may be that the United States is to become the Knight Errant of the world. War with Spain may put her in a position to demand civil and religious liberty for the oppressed of every nation and of every clime."[27]

Initially, cooler heads among the clergy and business community called for restraint, at least until McKinley's naval court of inquiry would report on the disaster. The president did not believe the country was ready for war and refused to give in to a Congress screaming for action. Publicly McKinley appeared to be doing nothing and thus became the target of public anger. At this critical juncture in Spanish-American relations, H. Wayne Morgan suggests, the president failed to "use whatever moderate strength remained to support him, and to repudiate the jingoes publicly."

If McKinley did not openly provide positive leadership in the cause of peace, neither did he lose control over the situation. The chief executive pursued a course of action that included tightening the "diplomatic screw" on Spain. Through American minister Woodford he let Spain know he considered her reform and military efforts in Cuba a failure. He "stunned" Madrid and encouraged the insurgents by easily getting from Congress on March 8 a fifty-million-dollar military appropriation. Secretary of the Navy John D. Long began buying vessels abroad and beefing up the fleet in the Caribbean. Then on March 17, McKinley's friend, the conservative senator from Vermont, Redfield Proctor, recently returned from a trip to Cuba, shocked the upper house with a several-hour dispassionate speech that severely indicted Spanish rule and military conduct on the island. He ended his speech with a call for intervention. Several of his colleagues and many in the press were convinced the speech meant war. Four days later the American naval board of inquiry reported that the *Maine* had been sunk by an external submarine mine.

By late March McKinley's patience with Spain was nearly exhausted. He had little hope either for the Sagasta reform program or in Spain's ability to govern effectively in Cuba; the naval board's conclusion that a submarine mine caused the *Maine*'s explosion was sure to inflame public and congressional opinion further; there were reports that Republican voters were threatening to abandon the party if he did not soon deal more forcibly with the Cuban situation; and he had mounting evidence that several in the business community, many persuaded by Senator Proctor's speech, were shifting from opposition to support of war, if only to end the suspense and uncertainty. Likewise the vocal and influential Protestant clergy were abandoning their earlier restraint and calling for a righteous crusade against Spain on behalf of humanity, "democracy and Chistian progress" in Cuba. Against this background, McKinley, between March 20 and March 27, sent to Madrid a last group of proposals to solve the Cuban crisis on American terms.[28]

In effect an ultimatum, the heart of what McKinley demanded was that "Spain end reconcentration, proclaim an armistice *and* acknowledge that she would make Cuba independent if the president deemed it necessary."[29] All had been suggested before except the hint of Cuba's independence. Historian Charles S. Campbell faults the administration for not more explicitly informing Madrid "of this *sine qua non* of independence." Inept diplomacy or not, the Spanish government, knowing it could not stay in power and accede to the American demands, refused to capitulate. It did, however, revoke the reconcentration order, agree to arbitrate the *Maine* incident, and promise reform and an armistice if the rebels asked for one. Although from Spain's point of view these were significant concessions, they did not meet McKinley's demands. The president began preparing a message to Congress, which after some delay in order to allow American citizens to leave Havana, was sent to Congress on April 11. The message was Congress's cue to declare war.

Two days before, on April 9, Spain agreed unilaterally to suspend hostilities "in order to arrange and facilitate peace on the island." Woodford in Madrid advised that in his view the armistice would bring peace in Cuba. No one in Washington, including McKinley, took the offer seriously or had faith it would lead to a long-term settlement. The president merely appended the information to the end of his already prepared message.[30] "I have exhausted every effort to relieve the intolerable condition of affairs which is at our doors," he told the Congress.

In the name of humanity, civilization, and American interests, President McKinley asked the Congress for the authority to take whatever measures he thought necessary to stop the war in Cuba, to "secure in the island the establishment of a stable government," and to use the military and naval forces as he saw fit. He justified American intervention on the following four grounds: first, to end "the barbarities, bloodshed, starvation, and horrible miseries" existing there; second, to protect the life and property of American citizens residing in Cuba; third, to prevent the continuing "serious injury" to American trade, business and property; and fourth, to remove the threat to the peace of the United States and the huge financial burden entailed in maintaining neutrality.

McKinley strongly urged against recognizing Cuban independence, specifically "the so-called Cuban Republic." He did not consider the insurgents yet worthy of recognition. "Such recognition," he stated,

> is not necessary in order to enable the United States to intervene and pacify the island. To commit this country now to the recognition of any particular government in Cuba might subject us to embarrassing conditions of international obligation toward the organization so recognized. In case of intervention our conduct would be subject to the approval or disapproval of such government. We would be required to submit to its direction and to assume to it the mere relation of a friendly ally.

The president argued for complete freedom of action in Cuba, for intervention, as he put it, as "an impartial neutral" who could impose "a rational compromise between contestants."[31]

For several days a number of congressmen — a combination "of idealistic jingoes, suspicious Populists, and political rivals" — tried to have included in the joint resolution authorizing the president to use the armed forces a resolution recognizing the insurgents as the government of Cuba. But after much political maneuvering McKinley was able to defeat such a proposal and retain control over foreign policy. On April 19 a joint resolution emerged from Congress that stated "the people of the island of Cuba are, and of right ought to be, free and independent." It further declared the end of Spanish rule in Cuba, empowered McKinley to use the military forces, and, in the famous Teller amendment, renounced any intention by the United States to annex Cuba. On April 25 Congress formally declared that a state of war had existed since the twenty-first.[32]

McKinley's war message did not contain an exhaustive justification for the nation's decision to war against Spain, but it did point to the mixed motives that underlay the administration's and people's desire to end the Cuban rebellion. It also revealed how little concerned the United States was with the desires of Cuba's fighters, ostensibly on whose behalf the nation was going to war. The groundswell of national support for a crusade to free Cuba derived in large measure from the public's genuine moral aversion to the brutal nature of the insurrection, especially the death and misery accompanying the Spanish reconcentration policy. But as this essay suggests, there were other specific reasons for going to war: to stop the destruction of American investments and trade with Cuba; to pacify the Caribbean area thought vital to American security; to clear the way for a more concentrated effort to expand American trade in the Far East; to eliminate a divisive political issue within the Republican party and between the Republicans and Democrats.

President McKinley was not content to rest his administration's case on specific grievances and war aims, but claimed the nation was fighting for humanity and civilization. By hitching the national interest to more universally valid objectives, the president sought to place his decision for war within the boundaries of morally permissible intervention in the affairs of neighboring states established by international law and sanctioned by just war theory. Nonpacifist Christians generally accept the morality of armed intervention for humanitarian reasons, that is, to redress grievous wrongs and to restore justice, as, for example, to eliminate "massive violations of human rights."[33]

If we were to give the highest priority to the humanitarian motive, as several historians do, we still face a problem beyond that of mixed motives in evaluating the ethics of American intervention in Cuba. America's humanitarian concern itself derived not from altruism alone, but from a mixture of sentiments, some less than noble. The American desire to intervene on behalf of the exploited Cubans stemmed in part from national pride. Superior Anglo-Saxon Protestant Americans, by replacing the decadent Spanish as the dominant influence in Cuba, would introduce on the island better government and political institutions, purer religion, free trade, and more rapid economic development. In other words, McKinley wanted more than an end to hostilities in Cuba; he sought the opportunity to remake Cuba in the American political and economic image.

From this imperialistic outlook flowed a number of consequences. First, it doomed serious, long-range diplomatic give-and-take with Spain. At best such prolonged diplomatic sparring would have led to an end of hostilities, and more than likely, to a lengthy unsettled state of affairs in Cuba. American political, economic, and strategic concerns required a more clearly defined final settlement.

Second, it led McKinley arbitrarily to demand of Spain the right to decide the ultimate political fate of her island possession. It was thus not specific reforms that the president was really after. Therefore Spain's concessions, even the last minute one to suspend hostilities unilaterally, failed to deter McKinley from pursuing a showdown with Spain. He would have preferred Spain's diplomatic surrender; but he was willing to procure surrender by force of arms. If all McKinley wanted was for Spain to treat her Cuban subjects more humanely, he could have given more serious attention to Spain's final concessions, offered more America aid to the Cuban people, and continued to exert moral pressure on Madrid, perhaps even through the European powers that at the last moment tried to talk McKinley out of war. In any event, the president seems not to have exhausted every effort to bring about a peaceful solution to the tragedy in Cuba. American participation in the war was not quite a last resort.

Third, McKinley's covetous attitude toward Cuba partially answers historian H. Wayne Morgan's complaint that the president failed to provide imaginative leadership. He "sought peace by the only means available, threatening war," Morgan writes. "The basic problem was a lack of alternatives to intervention." The significant point about this is not, as Morgan suggests, that McKinley's mind was too pedestrian to "cut through the tedium of diplomacy with a striking idea to move ahead of both the Spanish and the Cuban rebels." The point is that the president knew exactly what he was doing and firmly controlled his administration's foreign policy. Given proud Spain's inability to let go a centuries-old possession and the Cubans' unwillingness to accept anything less than independence, McKinley could only get what he wanted—the removal of Spain from the hemisphere and an increase in American influence in Cuba—either by Madrid's diplomatic capitulation or war. Spain ruled out the first alternative; McKinley accepted the second. In the president's judgment, what he did was consistent with his administration's rational pursuit of American interests in the Caribbean.

A fourth consequence of America's low view of Cuban capabilities was the president's refusal to recognize the insurgents as the legitimate government in the island. Even if one was to concede that McKinley had the fine points of international law on his side in not recognizing the rebel government, and by no means is this clearly the case, such a legalistic approach begged the question of who had a legal right to speak for the Cuban people; it further served to conceal the administration's view that the Cuban rebels were as incapable of properly managing the island as were the Spanish. By casting the Catholic monarchy in the image of a tyranical beast worthy of the Apocalypse, a self-proclaimed innocent America could in good conscience wage a righteous war against Spain. By defining the revolutionaries as politically incapable, if not ethnically and culturally inferior, a nation sure of the virtues of its own political and economic institutions, sure of the purity of its motives, and sure of its God-given vocation to remake the world in its image, could justify establishing, once Spanish power was removed, a protectorate over a "freed" Cuba.[34]

The nation may have gone to war "in a holiday mood," as one historian has suggested, but unlike the nation's capability in the Great Crusade of 1917, the United States of McKinley's era could not efficiently mobilize for war. The ideological commitments to federal supervision of the entire economy, the entire military, and the entire society, and the bureaucratic means to accomplish such a task, lay in the Progressive future. Fortunately for the republic, Spain was even less inclined toward or prepared for a prolonged conflict. By late July, having suffered military defeats in Cuba and naval disasters in Cuban and Philippine waters, Spain was ready to quit the fight.

By prior agreement, McKinley's administration had approved the Navy Department's plan that in the event of war Commodore Dewey, stationed at Hong Kong, would move against Spain's Philippines colonies. An easy naval victory on May 1 against outclassed Spanish vessels, followed up a couple of months later by American troops taking Manila, left the United States with a small grip on the Philippines when the war ended. The fruits of victory were too enticing to relinquish.

In the peace treaty that followed the end of the war Spain gave up Cuba, the island to be occupied by the United States for an unspecified time. The "Rising American Empire" also got from Spain Puerto Rico in the Caribbean, Guam in the Mariannas, and all of the Philippines, for which Washington paid Madrid $20 million. Furthermore, Dewey's victory at Manila was the catalyst behind congressional approval in the summer of 1898 for the long-sought annexation of Hawaii. The United States now had a formal empire in the Pacific and informal control over the island of Cuba.[35]

The content of the peace treaty suggests that the question of the moral legitimacy of American intervention in Cuba cannot be settled solely by examining the nation's initial motives for war. We must also look at the consequences, for the war created its own opportunities and temptations. From 1898 to 1902 the United States military occupied Cuba, deriving its authority from American treaty commitments to Spain and the law of conquest. At no time were the Cuban revolutionaries seriously consulted regarding the future of their homeland. In fact, American military personnel on the island had contempt for the Cubans and distrusted the insurgents' nationalism. Shortly after taking office, General Leonard Wood, as second military governor of the island, wrote McKinley that "we are dealing with a race that has steadily been going down for a hundred years and into which we have got to infuse new life, new principles and new methods of doing things."[36] Such a paternalistic attitude, shared also by Wood's predecessor General John Brooke, reinforced the administration's racist assumption about the unfitness of the natives to govern themselves.

The American victory and occupation had humane effects. It ended the long years of fighting and bloodshed; it brought food and other relief to thousands of starving and destitute people. The military government created a free public school system, overhauled the judiciary, reformed municipal government and administration, and built and repaired roads, hospitals, and other public works. In cooperation with Cuban doctors, American medical personnel successfully attacked and contained tropical diseases, including the dreaded yellow fever. Unfortunately, the practical good of these material benefits was tarnished by General Wood's arbitrary methods and the American occupation government's insensitivity to Cuban culture and ways of doing things.

Such humanitarian, although paternalistic, benevolence was accompanied by a growing United States political and economic stranglehold on Cuba. For one thing, General Wood and Secretary of War Elihu Root established a restrictive suffrage (limited by literacy, property, and military requirements) to disfranchise the illiterate and nationalistic masses and the working class in hopes of strengthening the political power of Cuba's conservative and largely white upper classes, many of whom favored ultimate annexation to the United States. For another thing, the United States only ended military rule after a newly established Cuban Republic reluctantly accepted the Platt Amendment, which severely limited its freedom.

The new Cuban government was forced to continue the American-initiated sanitary and health projects. It could not make any treaty that would impair its independence or allow a foreign power to control any portion of its territory. It could not encur public debt beyond its ability to service such a debt out of ordinary revenue. The Cubans had no choice but to sell or lease to the United States territory for coaling or naval stations. Most important of all, the Cuban government was required to grant to the United States "the right to intervene for the preservation of Cuban independence" and "the maintenance of a government adequate for the protection of life, property, and individual liberty." Such an infringement on the sovereignty of Cuba was designed to safeguard American interests on the island and secure stability in the Caribbean. For years it became the basis for American interference in Cuban affairs. Lester Langley points out that the Platt Amendment "spiritually violated" the pledge of the Teller Amendment, which had morally obligated the United States to seek Cuban independence; it was a "symbol of colonialism." Langley further states, "The United States merely replaced Spain as the arbiter of Cuba's destiny."

Paralleling the extension of American political control over Cuba after 1898 was the growth of the American economic presence on the island. Large amounts of United States capital was invested in the Cuban sugar and tobacco industries and in banking facilities. By 1902 American investment in Cuba was more than double what it had been before 1898. In addition, General Wood facilitated American investment in Cuban railroads, mining operations, and land. To tie the island's economy, especially its principal export crop, sugar, more tightly to the American economy, the United States Congress in 1903 passed a tariff reciprocity treaty. "By tying the basis of the Cuban economy to the U.S. market," suggests John Robert Benjamin, "the treaty rendered true Cuban independence 'irrational' in that only by faithfully fulfilling her dependent position as a raw-material supplier could she hope to benefit completely from reciprocity." In the years beyond 1902 giant American companies came to dominate all sectors of the Cuban economy, creating what Benjamin calls "an agro-industrial-commercial complex," which transformed much of Cuba into company-owned metropolitan centers and stunted the growth of an industrial and agricultural middle class.[37]

The history of American intervention in Cuba from the invasion to liberate Cuba from Spanish misrule to the creation of a political and economic protectorate easily opens the United States to Niebuhr's charge that "the Spanish-American War offers some of the most striking illustrations of the hypocrisy of governments," and, according to Michael Walzer, should make us skeptical of America's "professions of humane concern." "The entire course of action, from 1898 to 1902, might be taken as an example of benevolent imperialism," Walzer concludes, "but it is not an example of humanitarian intervention."[38]

In his *Just and Unjust Wars*, Walzer presents an intriguing approach to evaluating humanitarian intervention, including the American effort in Cuba. The problem of mixed motives, raised earlier in this essay, does not trouble him, for he doubts there has ever been a pure humanitarian intervention. Nor is he concerned about benevolent consequences. Humanitarian intervention on behalf of oppressed people, the only legitimate kind, he writes, requires "that the intervening state enter, to some degree, into the purposes of those people." It may not achieve those purposes, but "it also cannot stand in the way of their achievement." "One cannot intervene on their behalf," he writes, "and against their ends." Furthermore, Walzer suggests, respect for the purposes and goals of the oppressed must be matched by a respect for "local autonomy." The intervening state cannot "rightly claim any political prerogatives for itself." If it does, as the United States did in Cuba, it is highly likely, Walzer suggests, that from the start the intervention was for the purpose of gaining political power.[39]

The American decision to annex the Philippines as a prize of the war ostensibly begun to free Cuba was not without its own ironies as the United States sought to rationalize this naked aggression by appeals to God-given duty, destiny, and benign intentions. The historians' debate about exactly when President McKinley decided to take the entire Philippines need not concern us, except to note that the exigencies of war certainly provided the proximate cause for Washington's plucking of the archipelago from Madrid's grasp. McKinley's decision to allow Dewey's fleet to stay in the Philippines, his decision, even before knowing of Dewey's victory, to send American troops to capture Manila, and his decision to ignore the wishes of the Filipino insurgents who hoped for American aid to establish an independent republic, all suggest that, if not before, at least after Dewey's success the president had territorial designs on the Pacific colonies. McKinley's subsequent decision to exclude the Filipino insurgents from any share in the capture of Manila and his executive order of December 21, 1898, proclaiming American sovereignty throughout the Philippines islands further lent an air of inevitability to his decision to annex a colony in the Pacific and to reject the political claims of Filipino nationalist Emilio Aguinaldo and his supporters.

Although it was McKinley's decision to take the entire archipelago, he was influenced both by political and diplomatic considerations and the views of various expansionist groups. He feared that the major powers would scramble for parts of the Philippines should he not annex all of Spain's Pacific possession. A seasoned politician, the president saw political gains for his administration and party in colonialism. In addition, naval officers saw in the Philippines the answer to their quest for a Pacific base.[40] Businessmen saw in the Philippines a source of customers and raw materials and more importantly a "commercial stepping stone and a political-military lever" to the Orient's potential market. "Had we no interest in China," declared the secretary of the American Asiatic Association, "the possession of the Philippines would be meaningless."[41] Numerous Protestant clergymen and missionaries, hitching the cross to the flag, saw foreign colonization and foreign missions as practically synonymous. "We cannot ignore the fact that God has given into our hands — that is, into the hands of American Christians, the Philippine Islands, and thus opened a wide door and effectual to their populations, and has by the very guns of our battleships summoned us to go up and possess the land," declared the Presbyterian Board of Foreign Missions. "Civil and religious liberty will be enjoyed in Cuba, in the Carolines, . . . and Philippine Islands," preached Robert S. MacArthur of New York's Calvary Baptist Church.[42]

In his own oft-quoted words to a group of Methodist ministers, McKinley testified to how the themes of duty, destiny, and missionary and commercial opportunity came together in his decision to keep all of the Philippines:

> I walked the floor of the White House night after night until midnight; and I am not ashamed to tell you, gentlemen, that I went down on my knees and prayed Almighty God for light and guidance more than one night. And one night late it came to me this way—I don't know how it was, but it came: (1) That we could not give them back to Spain—that would be cowardly and dishonorable; (2) that we could not turn them over to France or Germany—our commercial rivals in the Orient—that would be bad business and discreditable; (3) that we could not leave them to themselves—they were unfit for self-government—and they would soon have anarchy and misrule over there worse than Spain's was; and (4) that there was nothing left for us to do but to take them all, and to educate the Filipinos, and uplift and civilize and Christianize them, and by God's grace do the very best we could by them, as our fellow-men for whom Christ also died. And then I went to bed, and went to sleep, and slept soundly.[43]

McKinley failed to mention that at the end of the war the United States did not possess most of the Philippines. Other than Manila, the rest of the archipelago was under the "moderately effective control" of Aguinaldo's insurgents and their supporters, who like their Cuban counterparts were fighting to establish an independent republic. The president also did not explain that his low opinion of the political capabilities of the Filipino nationalists derived in part from ignorance of the situation across the Pacific and in part from the racially prejudiced opinions of American and English observers. How the island's eight million inhabitants felt hardly mattered to McKinley. "Once it had been determined what was the safest policy politically, the most intelligent policy economically, and the wisest policy strategically *for America*," writes Richard E. Welch, Jr., "then the 'little brown men' must necessarily accept its implementation."[44]

At home McKinley successfully combated various anti-imperialist foes—Republicans, Democrats, Independents, businessmen, intellectuals, and reformers—who hurled an assortment of pragmatic, moral, constitutional, and racist arguments against the Republic's forcible annexation of a culturally different colony. Over the course of the months-long debate in the United States

Senate, where the Treaty of Paris ending the war with Spain had to be approved, the president's spokesmen countered anti-imperialist arguments by stressing the commercial, strategic, and diplomatic value of the islands. They further pressed the president's conviction that the nation had a God-given responsibility to civilize the backward and politically incapable Filipinos. Some administration spokesmen bolstered their arguments for American political rule over subject peoples by likening the "barbaric" Filipinos to America's dependent Indians. These arguments, plus the fact that McKinley had already declared America sovereign throughout the Philippines, kept all but two Republicans in line behind the treaty. With the assistance of sixteen Democrats and independents, several of whom were followers of William Jennings Bryan, McKinley on February 6, 1899, got Senate approval by a vote of 57 to 27, one vote more than the needed two-thirds.[45]

The evangelical Bryan, the Democratic standard-bearer in 1896, had supported American intervention in Cuba on humanitarian grounds, and had even volunteered for duty during the war. An ardent anti-imperialist, Bryan opposed the acquisition of the Philippines and pled that what began as a war for humanity not degenerate into a war of conquest. Yet he supported Senate approval of the treaty of Paris as the quickest way to end the bloody fighting. His unexpected support of McKinley's treaty made it easier for those Democrats who voted for the historic measure. Bryan's strategy called for the United States to take the Philippines from Spain in order to grant the islands independence by congressional resolution. When this did not happen, Bryan reluctantly made imperialism the major issue of the election of 1900. But in the midst of McKinley prosperity, a united Republican party, and a divided Democracy, the great commoner and his anti-imperialist supporters failed to arouse great public enthusiasm for reversing the decision on colonies. McKinley defeated Bryan by almost one million popular votes.[46]

Ironically, two days before the Senate voted for the treaty, a Philippine-American war had begun. Unconvinced by Washington's denigration of their political skills, and unenamored of America's assumption of the right to decide unilaterally on the fate of their country, Aguinaldo and his "little brown men" determined to throw off the yoke of American rule and establish a Philippine republic. It took the United States forty-one months, over 4,000 lives, more than 2,800 wounded, and an expenditure of $40 million to pacify the islands. The Filipinos lost in battle between 16,000 to 20,000 men; possibly another 200,000 people died from famine, disease, and war-related activity. American soldiers spent the last three years of the war bogged down in a guerrilla war against Aguinaldo's men. The fighting was increasingly marked by racial hatred, brutality, torture, indiscrimate killing, and the devastation of crops and uncooperative villages. In what must be considered a double irony, before the war was over democratic "christian" America felt forced to allow its army to fight the guerrillas in at least one province by herding civilians into camps, a pacification program not unlike "Butcher" Weyler's reconcentration method used a few years earlier in Cuba. Such a strategy proved effective, and by April 1902 the insurrection came practically to an end. "The islanders had been conquered in every sense of the word," comments Leon Wolf in his sensitive and descriptive narrative of the Philippine-American war.

In July 1902 the United States government terminated formal military control over the Philippines. Under the Civil Government Act of that same year, Washington inaugurated a highly centralized American dominated civilian control. Over the years Filipino participation in the governing process was gradually expanded; however, the pace of increased self-government was determined by the American government. Not until 1933 and largely due to domestic American considerations, did Congress formally enact legislation granting Spain's former colony independence. Its actual consummation was not to occur until 1946.

Whether one sees McKinley's grabbing of the Philippines as part of a previously planned grand design or simply as a rationally calculated decision made necessary by the victories of war, the inescapable conclusion is the same. Regardless of the specific motives—duty, destiny, evangelism, economics, strategy—the United States seized from a vanquished foe a foreign colony that only indirectly had anything to do with the supposed causes of the war. Moreover, the United States acquired the Philippines against the wishes of a fairly well-organized indigenous independence movement. No amount of presidential casuistry can hide the fact that the nation sought to impose by force of arms its sovereignty "on millions of ethnic aliens."

McKinley bears much of the blame for what can only be judged an unnecessary and unjust war against the Filipinos. The president refused to offer the Filipinos future self-government or even seriously consider a limited and temporary American protectorate over the islands, a pragmatic compromise between American colonialism and Filipino nationalism that even Aguinaldo seemed ready to accept before the outbreak of hostilities. Historian Richard E. Welch plausibly suggests that war might have been averted had the United States "proclaimed its willingness to recognize the independence of the islands, provide naval protection for a specified time, and assist the Filipinos in the establishment of their government during a transitional period terminable at the decision of the Filipinos." McKinley, however, adamantly refused to place any limits on American sovereignty or restrictions on the nation's future freedom of action. Moreover, he did not believe the "little brown men" were capable of effectively governing themselves, and he did not take seriously their nationalistic revolution. Given the clash, then, between the American goal of exclusive control over all of the islands and the Filipino nationalists' goal of an independent republic, war was inevitable. In this showdown, the United States was the aggressor.[47]

McKinley and a host of Americans may have viewed their nation as an instrument of God or Anglo-Saxon civilization chosen to bring order, justice, and peace to the Philippines. In contrast, Aguinaldo and his supporters saw the United States as a Great Babylon or Beast, a source of persecution and injustice. The Filipino leader did not consider the American takeover as a gift of civilization, but as a "violent and aggressive seizure" of his people's land. This was being done, he noted, "by a nation which has arrogated to itself the title: champion of oppressed nations." After unmasking the hypocrisy of American imperial rhetoric, Aguinaldo shrewdly appealed his nation's case to "the conscience of mankind," a tribunal familiar to the American president.[48] The fact that the other major powers engaged in the same aggressive behavior or even that some of them welcomed the American takeover of the Philippines in no way justifies the United States's violation of its own democratic tradition of self-government and the requirements of biblical morality for governments to do good.

The goals of the Philippines-American war — the imposition of colonial rule — were unjust. On balance, the results and benefits of the conflict probably were insufficient to justify the evils of the war itself: thousands were killed in battle and through disease and famine, scores of villages were destroyed, hundreds of animals were slaughtered, and a large amount of land was devastated. Probably such damage would not have been matched even under the most incompetent independent Philippine government. "The loss of life and resources," Welch writes, "weakened the potential of the islands for economic viability over the next generation." In addition, the long-range benefits of American occupation—the schools and hospitals built, the public health measure introduced, the legal reforms instituted, the increased measure of political influence granted the Filipinos—bore the price of a stifling American paternalism and cultural coercion and Filipino economic dependence. By 1934, when the Commonwealth Government was established, the United States, according to Welch, had not established in the Philippines "a viable economy, a democratic social structure, or broad-based popular government."[49]

The Philippine-American war stemmed from the United States's annexation of the Pacific archipelago, which itself was a by-product of the Spanish-American war. Interconnected, these events of 1898 emerged with other forces to accelerate the growth of the role of the United States in world affairs and the emergence of foreign policy. For Christians today, the significance of the Spanish-American war lies not so much in its specific long-range consequences for subsequent foreign and domestic policies, an issue still debated by historians. Rather, the war, like all wars, tears "the veil off reality for a moment"; it offers us a vivid look into the darker side of American life at the end of the last century.[50] The war and its attendant imperialism help us see, as this essay has shown, just how much like other world powers we really were, how much our behavior toward others, our foreign policy, was shaped not by the biblical standards of justice, righteousness, and peace, but by a quest for national power, wealth, and security. In the contrast between our assumed national goodness, innocence, and uniqueness and the historical realities of our actions lies the key to unraveling the many ironic elements of the Spanish-American war.

6 ROBERT BOLT

AMERICAN INVOLVEMENT IN WORLD WAR I

ON AUGUST 4, 1914, AS DUSK FELL OVER LONDON, British Foreign Secretary Sir Edward Grey stood at the windows of his room in the Foreign Office watching the lamplighters in St. James Park. As he gazed out at the scene below and thought of the war rapidly enveloping Europe, he remarked to a friend, "The lamps are going out all over Europe; we shall not see them lit again in our lifetime."[1] And so Europe stumbled into war during that fateful summer and in time the lamps flickered and then went out over much of the world.

Robert Palmer and Joel Colton write that "When a traveler has wandered off his course, it is easy for him, if he has a good map and if the country is well marked with road signs, to retrace his steps, find the point where he went astray, and resume the route to his destination." These writers point out it would be more difficult if the traveler had "no map, if there were no signs," and if one "could never under any circumstances go backward." They compare the lost traveler with a 1914 Europe that "went off its course" and "stumbled in 1914 into a disaster" because "history is not as exact as a map, its road signs are read differently by different people—and the traveler can never go backward."[2]

The analogy demonstrates that most men had not intended war in 1914. Even though many Christians accept that wars and rumors of war haunt mankind until the end of time, many individuals, including some theologians, were confident that man had progressed to a point where he could settle disputes without resort to violence. Thus, there was bitter disappointment when the war came.

Although many Americans were among those dismayed, most were confident that the United States could and should remain free of the conflict raging in Europe. Statements like "peace-loving citizens of this country will now rise up and tender a hearty vote of thanks to Columbus for having discovered America" or "we never appreciated so keenly as now the foresight exercised by our forefathers in emigrating from Europe" reflect this stance.[3] Many of those sentiments indicated that Americans rather selfishly wanted no part of the war because it would not profit their nation or because foreigners had brought it on themselves and should not expect the Americans to rescue them from the morass.

Using a Christian perspective to analyze America's involvement in the First World War, this essay examines the motives that prompted President Woodrow Wilson to keep his nation from becoming militarily involved. Unlike many of his fellow citizens, Wilson was motivated by a concern for the nations that were at war. He believed that he and his nation were their brother's keepers and thus their backs could not be turned on those in need. Therefore, he attempted repeatedly to mediate, believing that the United States could better serve the belligerent nations and the cause of peace in this way than by joining the fighting. Wilson, hoping to avoid war, also was more sensitive than many leaders to war's evil effects on the human spirit or soul, and for that reason as well he hoped to spare his countrymen from war's affliction.

The Scriptures enjoin men to walk uprightly. President Wilson did that in attempting to maintain American neutrality. Wilson's injunction to be neutral in thought and action, however, appears to be unrealistic. The president himself could not live up to this completely, but his behavior does reveal a genuine desire to remain truly neutral. To be an effective conciliator, Wilson realized that he would need the confidence of both sides, and that he therefore could not be a partisan. Wilson took sides only after he became convinced that he would not be able to bring the war to an end through mediation.

We need to be more critical of President Wilson for his ultimate request for a declaration of war. Christ teaches his followers humility, a characteristic that appeared to be lacking when the

Americans joined the fray. In the rhetoric of the time, America seemed to be free of the sins that afflicted both its enemies and allies. A Christian who studies the First World War stands appalled at the hatred generated by the war. In spite of Wilson's idealism, the American government did its part in manufacturing enmity—enmity that did not immediately subside with the cessation of hostilities. The role of the church during this wartime must also be examined. With some chagrin, one discovers that Christ's institution here on earth often violated the teachings of its founder.

Christ taught his followers that even enemies must be loved, and in the end President Wilson did not forget this command. At the time of the November 1918 armistice and again at the Paris Peace Conference, Wilson sought justice for both sides, demonstrating as he did so some compassion for the defeated foe.

Finally, this essay maintains that the formation of the League of Nations was an attempt to achieve a more lasting peace for the world. It seems obvious that Christians should support efforts to lessen killing and promote understanding between people. President Wilson believed that the United States should assume some responsibility in that undertaking. Ironically, because Americans, including Woodrow Wilson, did not understand each other, the United States failed to join the very league that the American president had proposed.

While he was president, Woodrow Wilson said, "My life would not be worth living if it were not for the driving power of religion, for faith, pure and simple."[4] The year before he was elected he asserted, "He alone can rule his own spirit who puts himself under the command of the Spirit of God, revealed in His Son, Jesus Christ, our Savior. He is the captain of our souls, he is the man from whose suggestions and from whose life comes the light that guideth every man that ever came into the world."[5] The life of Woodrow Wilson affords little doubt that the Christian religion played an important role in his thought and action.

In his early days, Wilson believed that it was the church's duty to save souls.[6] He believed that Christianity should be concerned with redeeming the individual and be less involved in the transformation of this world and human society. However, about five years before he became president, Wilson's thinking on this subject began to change significantly. Arthur Link writes, "Wilson's political thought first began to show signs of changing about 1907, and the first sign of this metamorphosis was a significant shift in his thinking about the role that Christians and the church would play in the world at large."[7] About that time we hear Wilson saying,

> If men cannot lift their fellowmen in the process of saving themselves, I do not see that it is very important that they should save themselves. . . . Christianity came into the world to save the world as well as to save individual men, and individual men can afford in conscience to be saved only as part of the process by which the world itself is regenerated.[8]

Wilson came to understand that the Christian religion requires more than the attainment of personal salvation. Christ's followers are expected to be active in this world, combating evil and transforming the world into something more in accord with the way God would have it. Thus, Wilson began to promote social reform at home. Abroad, this meant that while he was president, he could not ignore evil. It was the obligation of the United States, as Harley Notter puts it,

> . . . to realize an ideal of liberty, provide a model of democracy, vindicate moral principles, give examples of action and ideals of government and righteousness to an interdependent world, uphold the rights of man, work for humanity and the happiness of men everywhere, lead the thinking of the world, promote peace—in sum, to serve mankind and progress.[9]

With religious tenets that stressed duty and service, it is not surprising that Wilson "hoped and prayed since the first week of hostilities that he might lead the warring nations to peace." Thus, early in 1915 he sent his top aide, Edward House, to Europe on an exploratory mission. Wilson hoped the warring nations could be brought together with the help of the American government. House discovered instead that each side hoped to score an overwhelming victory.

Less than a year later House again traveled to Europe, visiting London, Paris, and Berlin. He found that neither the German nor the French government was yet ready to enter into meaningful negotiations. However, Britain's Edward Grey convinced House, and Wilson as well, that Allied war aims were moderate and reasonable.[10] As a result of this, Wilson approved of what came to be called the House-Grey Memorandum calling for a conference to discuss peace. As it turned out, the British were less enthusiastic about a peace without victory than the American leaders had thought, and no conference resulted.

Wilson made one final attempt at mediation after the 1916 election. In spite of opposition by Secretary of State Robert Lansing and Edward House, who thought that attempts to mediate at that time would only embarrass the Allies, the president would not be stopped in his efforts to bring the war to an end.[11] Thus, on December 18, 1916, he appealed to both sides, requesting that each state its war aims. Both sides demonstrated reluctance to state openly and fully what they hoped to achieve. The Allies were somewhat piqued when Wilson implied that their moral position was no better than that of the Central Powers.

On January 12, 1917, the Allies responded specifically to Wilson's inquiry. In summarizing the expectations of the Allies, Harley Notter comments, "The intention was plain: no peace before victory."[12]

Although the Central Powers had not stated what those nations hoped to achieve through the war and the Allied demands appeared to be discouraging, Wilson, in an address to the Senate on January 22, 1917, called for a "peace without victory." "Victory," said Wilson prophetically, "would mean peace forced upon the loser, a victor's terms imposed upon the vanquished. It would be accepted in humiliation, under duress, at an intolerable sacrifice, and would leave a sting, a resentment, a bitter memory upon which terms of peace would rest, not permanently, but only as upon quicksand."

All hope that peace could be achieved at this time was dashed a few days later when Germany announced that thereafter it would wage unrestricted submarine warfare. In a gamble that Germany was destined to lose, it had decided to score an all-out victory before an expected American entry into the war would make a difference.

Wilson's attempts to arbitrate the conflict indicate that he felt an obligation to bring the killing to an end. At least in part, this action sprang from a conviction that God would have it so. As he put it shortly after the war began,

> Christ came into the world to save others, not to save himself, and no man is a true Christian who does not think constantly of how he can lift his brother, how he can assist his friend, how he can enlighten mankind, how he can make virtue the rule of conduct in the circle in which he lives.[13]

In order to play the role of the honest broker, President Wilson had to convince both sides that he truly was impartial. As the war began, Wilson had urged his countrymen to be neutral in thought and action. He sincerely sought neutrality in order to be an effective mediator and because, as a Christian moralist, he eschewed hypocrisy as much as he could. On one occasion he said, "We must believe the things we tell the children."[14] Although Wilson seemed at times to waver, he sought mightily to maintain a neutral stance; he sought to practice his own words, to believe the words that he had told his "children."

On February 4, 1915, Germany announced that she planned to unleash her submarines against Allied merchant ships plying the English Channel and a wide zone of the seas around the British Isles. The Germans added that neutral ships might be endangered, because Allied vessels sometimes flew the flags of neutrals. Wilson responded to this announcement by stating that he would hold the German government to "strict accountability" if German submarines attacked American shipping.

The Wilson administration was tested on May 7, 1915, when the Germans sank the *Lusitania*, a British Cunard passenger liner. Some 128 Americans perished when the ship went down. Wilson, had he been less intent on keeping America out of the fray or had he been swayed by emotion, might have geared his nation for war. He did protest so strongly that Secretary of State William J. Bryan resigned. However, he would not be pushed over the brink. In a speech at Philadelphia's Convention Hall three days later he urged America to be a "special example." Said Wilson, "The example of America must be the example not merely of peace because it will not fight, but of peace because peace is the healing and elevating influence of the world and strife is not."

Earlier, on March 28, the Germans had sunk the British merchantman *Falaba*, which had resulted in the death of one American. The American press condemned the act as "barbarism run mad," a "triumph of horror," "an atrocity against which the civilized world should protest with one voice."[15] Robert Lansing urged Wilson to instruct the American ambassador to Germany, James W. Gerard, to protest vigorously this sinking and to demand that Germany disavow "the wanton act" and punish those responsible for it. On the other hand, Secretary of State Bryan urged moderation. He believed that the American who had boarded the *Falaba* was not "differently situated from those who by remaining in a belligerent country assume the risk of injury." Although in this case, Wilson felt the American killed had a legal right to be aboard the *Falaba*, he demonstrated some realism and a reluctance to be pushed into some untoward action by wondering whether the German commander who sank the *Falaba* might not be justified because the British government had advised merchantmen to arm themselves against submarines and ram them whenever possible.[16]

Wilson displayed similar restraint later in the same year when the British White Star passenger liner, the *Arabic*, was sunk with heavy loss of life including two Americans. Both House and Lansing urged a severance of diplomatic relations with Germany.[17] Daniel Smith says that Wilson rejected this advice, however, "primarily because of his love of peace and abhorrence of war."[18] Instead Wilson again sought to negotiate with Germany. For a time, Wilson's way seemed to be the right one, for Germany disavowed the act and pledged "Liners will not be sunk . . . without warning and without safety of the noncombatants."

When on March 24, 1916, an unarmed French channel steamer, the *Sussex*, was torpedoed, it appeared that the Germans had violated the *Arabic* pledge. This time, the president decided to go along with his chief advisors' recommendation that the United States explicitly threaten to break diplomatic relations unless Germany cease its wanton attacks against passenger ships. This came after much soul-searching. As Daniel Smith points out, "His instincts for peace and his continued desires to mediate the war seemed to make him vacillating and incapable of reaching a decision."[19]

Some have argued that from the start Wilson sided with the Allies and that an unfair double standard was set. The Germans were to be held strictly accountable, whereas the Allied violations of American neutrality were too easily overlooked. This was not Wilson's intent. The evidence suggests that Wilson genuinely sought to be evenhanded until the Americans themselves became involved. To some, American protests directed to Germany may seem more strident than those sent to the Allies. However, this did not stem from Wilson's partiality but from a firm conviction that Germany's infractions were more serious in that they resulted in the loss of human life.[20] As the *Boston Globe* put it, "One was a gang of thieves; the other was a gang of murderers."[21] Wilson believed murder a more serious crime than theft.

There is substantial evidence that President Wilson was genuinely upset over British violations of American neutrality. Early in the war when a number of American ships bound for neutral ports had been stopped by the British, President Wilson informed the State Department that he wanted a "vigorous protest," "one with teeth in it," prepared. It seems as though Wilson was concerned, at least at the outset, that war with Britain was possible if the United States absolutely refused to budge. Said he, "Madison and I are the only two Princeton men that have become president. The circumstances of the War of 1812 and now run parallel. I sincerely hope they will not go further."[22] In discussing America's controversies with Britain, Ray S. Baker states,

> Deep within him, deeper perhaps than any other aspiration, was the desire not only to keep America out of the war, but to be the instrument for making peace in the conflict then in progress, and beyond that, as he told Dr. Axson, he had a vision of a "new world order," wherein war should be abolished.[23]

In late 1914 and early 1915 the Englishmen became convinced that the Americans were siding against them. The *London Spectator* suggested the possibility of war with the United States. The government, in an effort to assuage the British, instructed Walter Page, the American ambassador to Britain, to "assure Sir Edward [Grey] that this government will adhere conscientiously to its course of neutrality" and that "it will not intentionally deviate a hair's breadth from the line, but it is powerless to prevent the increasing criticism which has been aroused by acts which have, from the American standpoint, seemed unnecessarily severe for the enforcement of belligerent rights."[24]

During most of 1915 the United States appeared to be more involved in controversy with Germany, but after the Germans pledged to live by the law in the *Arabic* and *Sussex* pledges, the conflicts with Britain again became more pronounced, so that by

1916 relations between Britain and the United States reached their nadir.

In July 1916 Wilson wrote Colonel House what Ray S. Baker describes as "one of the angriest letters of his career":[25] "I am, I must admit, about at the end of my patience with Great Britain and the Allies. This black list business is the last straw." (Wilson was referring to Britain's blacklisting of several American firms doing business with the Central Powers.) Wilson stated that he was considering "asking the Congress to authorize me to prohibit loans and restrict exportation to the Allies." He told House that he felt "obliged" to formulate a note to Britain "as sharp and final as the one to Germany on the submarines."[26]

The blacklist was a last straw, it seemed. The British had interfered with American trade for two years, never promptly responding to American protests, had captured U.S. ships and taken them into British ports, had been guilty of seizing American mail, and "for two years discouraged all his [Wilson's] plans for peace mediation."[27] To some Americans, the ruthless manner in which the English had handled the recalcitrant Irish seemed little different from Germany's treatment of the Belgians. Wilson told Ambassador Page that the war partly came down to a matter of "England's having the earth and of Germany wanting it."[28] Attempting to mediate for the last time in 1916, Wilson asserted that "the objects which the statesmen of the belligerents on both sides have in mind in this war are virtually the same, as stated in general terms to their own people and to the world."[29]

From the outset, then, Wilson had sought neutrality and noninvolvement in the war. He followed this path because he believed that he could serve as a mediator. He hoped that each side would compromise and that with the United States providing leadership and impetus the war would soon end. He felt that the international community would be better served with the United States remaining out of the war and that his nation, too, would benefit, for he knew that war would sear the American soul.

When in 1917 it became apparent to Wilson that the United States might have to fight, he agonized. In this regard, Arthur Link speaks of Wilson's Gethsemane. Frank Cobb of the *New York World* reported that the night before the president asked for a declaration of war he had "never seen him so worn down." "He looked as if he hadn't slept, and he said he hadn't."[30] He spoke of war as a cancer or infection. "Once lead this people into war," said Wilson, "and they'll forget there was such as thing as tolerance. To fight you must be brutal and ruthless, and the spirit of ruthless brutality will enter into the very fibre of our national life, infecting Congress, the courts, the policeman on the beat, the man in the street." According to Cobb, Wilson cried out, "If there is any alternative, for God's sake, let's take it."[31]

Since the United States entered the war only five months after the November 1916 election, some question might be raised concerning the integrity of the Democratic party, which had campaigned with a "He kept us out of war" slogan. Ray S. Baker believed that Wilson himself was bothered by the slogan because it implied that he had the power to keep America out of war.[32] Said Wilson to Secretary of the Navy Josephus Daniels, "I can't keep the country out of war. They talk of me as though I were a god. Any little German lieutenant can put us into the war at any time with some calculated outrage."[33] This comment and Wilson's genuine anguish as war approached seem to undercut any notion that Wilson was plotting war while running as a peace candidate in 1916.

Even so, a morally sensitive person may wonder why the United States decided to join the slaughter in April 1917. After Wilson's final attempt to achieve peace without victory failed, the Germans announced that they would conduct unrestricted submarine warfare. Although this seemed immoral to Wilson and diplomatic relations were severed with Germany, he continued to hope that Germany would not actually pull the trigger when American ships were sighted. However, events were to prove to Wilson that war could not be avoided. Early in 1917 the Americans became aware of a telegram sent by German Foreign Secretary Alfred Zimmermann proposing an alliance between Germany and Mexico with "an understanding on our part that Mexico is to reconquer the lost territory in Texas, New Mexico, and Arizona." The revolution that brought down the Russian czar made Russia "a fit partner" in Wilson's opinion, and thus he could with more conviction say that this nation was fighting to make the world safe for democracy. When American ships began to sink, Wilson felt he had no choice.

If a just war is one waged by a state for the purpose of restoring peace and achieving justice, the president was careful to define that such criteria existed before engaging the United States in the conflict. The United States entered the war because Wilson saw that the Germans no longer wanted him to act as a mediator. Whereas earlier Wilson believed that it was this nation's duty to end the war quickly by being the peacemaker, by 1917 he became convinced that the war would be shortened with the United States as a participant against a government that now seemed more evil than its opponent.

In asking Congress for a declaration of war, Wilson avowed, "Our object now, as then, is to vindicate the principles of peace and justice in the life of the world as against selfish and autocratic power and to set up amongst the really free and self-governed peoples of the world such a concert of purpose and of actions as will henceforth insure the observance of those principles." That this was more than mere rhetoric seems apparent from the frequent attempts made by the Wilson government to mediate the conflict. Also, when in the autumn of 1918 the German government approached Wilson concerning an armistice, Wilson proved to be receptive and opposed those who would prolong the war by refusing to quit until Allied troops had marched into Berlin.[34] Wilson's proposed League of Nations suggests that he not only wanted peace restored but also preserved.

Wilson's Fourteen Points, the disavowal by the president of material gains as the United States entered the war, Wilson's statement of September 27, 1918, in which he insisted that "impartial justice meted out must involve no discrimination between those to whom we wish to be just and those to whom we do not wish to be just," and his efforts to moderate peace terms for Germany give evidence of Wilson's concern for justice. A Christian can applaud these motives and aims, while being at the same time uneasy with a certain lack of humility in President Wilson when he asked for a declaration of war on April 2, 1917. As late as December 1916 Wilson had been critical of both sides, implying that neither adversary fought for noble ends. Curiously, therefore, a pious philosophy seems to pervade his war speech. Said Wilson, "We have no selfish ends to serve. We desire no conquest, no dominion. We seek no indemnities for ourselves, no material compensation for the sacrifices we shall freely make. We are but one of the champions of the rights of mankind." Whereas other warring nations may have hated each other, "we have no feelings towards them [the German people] but one of sympathy and friendship." This nation is made to seem morally superior to all the rest. There is a trace of condescension, too, when Wilson insists that his nation is not "allied" but only "associated" with America's cobelligerents. Those fighting the Central Powers were thus the Allied and Associated Powers.[35]

One also senses something ironic about Wilson's intent to fight in order to make the world "safe for democracy." George Kennan has pointed out that there has been a "failure to appreciate the limitations of war in general—any war—as a vehicle for the achievement of the objectives of the democratic state." Although Kennan admits that at times war may be necessary, he correctly asserts that "the democratic purpose does not prosper when a man dies or a building collapses or any enemy force retreats." It only prospers "when something happens in a man's mind that increases his enlightenment and the consciousness of his real relation to other people—something that makes them aware that, whenever the dignity of another man is offended, his own dignity, as a man among men, is thereby reduced."[36] War has a similar negative effect upon the Christian purpose. It seems apparent, therefore, that the very instrument employed to safeguard democracy can destroy the thing it is trying to preserve.

President Wilson had voiced concern about the high cost of hatred. He had good reason to be apprehensive, for not only did Americans learn to hate the enemy, but each other as well. In Cleveland, Ohio, a man was observed pulling a Liberty Bond poster from the rack above him and tearing it up. Immediately he was set upon by "patriots" who thought that he was opposed to Liberty Bonds. Finally, the victim, who was an alien not yet able to read and understand English, made it apparent that he objected not to the Liberty Bonds but to a picture of the Kaiser, which the artist had included "as a stimulus to patriotic generosity."[37]

Persons of German birth or with German names became suspect. Employers were requested to furnish information about employees having German names. Mark Sullivan writes that a street conversation in German or in any language other than English could generate suspicion. In many communities citizens were enjoined to conduct worship services in English. Because of his ethnic origin, Fritz Kreisler, a violinist of some renown, was prohibited from performing in East Orange, New Jersey. Robert

LaFollette, a respected senator from Wisconsin, was burned in effigy because of his opposition to the hysteria generated by the war.[38]

One can appreciate Wilson's anxieties over war's poisonous effects. However, the government that he headed must bear some of the blame for the venom that had such deleterious effects. The Committee on Public Information headed by George Creel manufactured hate as the United States was prepared for all-out war. The Congress passed the Alien Act in 1917 and the Sedition Act in 1918. The Espionage Act of June 15, 1917, called for penalties up to a $10,000 fine and a twenty-year incarceration for those who willfully caused or attempted to cause insubordination in the armed services or who obstructed recruiting. Persons were subjected to punishment who willfully made false reports and statements with intent to interfere with the operation or success of the military and naval forces. The postmaster general was authorized to bar from the mail any letter, pamphlet, book, or newspaper that violated any provision of the act or that advocated treason, insurrection, or forcible resistance to any law of the United States. The Sedition Act in sweeping language forbade disloyal, profane, scurrilous remarks about the form of government, flag, or uniform of the United States, or any language intended to obstruct the war effort in any way. Arthur Link and William B. Catton report that under these acts 2,168 persons were prosecuted and 1,055 were convicted. Of the number convicted only ten were found guilty of actual sabotage. Link and Catton add, however:

> But this reckoning gives little indication of the extent to which suppression of dissent was carried out by organized groups who lynched, whipped, tarred and feathered, or otherwise wreaked vengeance on labor radicals, German Americans, or any persons suspected of disloyalty. As Wilson had predicted in April 1917, many Americans forgot mercy and tolerance and compassion. In retrospect, the war hysteria seems the most fearful price that the American people paid for participation in the First World War.[39]

Unfortunately, this malevolent spirit is not easily suppressed when the fighting ends. Robert Murray notes this when he states that "wars produce a broader malaise than mere disillusionment or the release of passions." He says that they "breed a willingness of the human spirit to condone whatever brutality is necessary to resolve violently what men had hoped to resolve rationally by pacific means." Murray believes that "every scrap of the Christian code . . . is violated by war." The effects of this continue to be felt after the fighting ends: "As a reaction to this traumatic wartime exposure, men are likely in an immediate postwar period to continue to act in an aberrant way."[40]

This seems to be borne out after the First World War with the revitalization of the Ku Klux Klan. Membership in this organization mushroomed in the 1920s. The Palmer raids directed by Wilson's attorney general and the Red Scare generated hysteria and hatred toward those thought to be less than one hundred percent American. The immigration laws of the 1920s made a mockery of Emma Lazarus's "Give me your tired, your poor, your huddled masses yearning to breathe free" inscribed on the base of the Statue of Liberty.

Although one can surely assert that not all Christians were overcome by war's emotion and that not all forgot that a Christian owes prime allegiance to Christ,[41] still a thinking Christian is concerned over the manner in which many Christians and churches of the day met the challenge of the First World War. One might suppose that Christians would be less likely to be overcome by war's hysteria, that biblical injunctions to walk humbly, to seek mercy and justice, to love all men, and to give God allegiance even before the state would not be entirely forgotten by Christ's followers even in wartime. However, that often was not the case; Christians and the church no less than non-Christians and secular organizations spewed forth gall, manufactured hate, seemed smug and condescending toward other warring nations, and gave the state prime allegiance rather than God.

Henry Van Dyke, a prominent Presbyterian leader, called the Kaiser the "Potsdam Werewolf."[42] Dr. Van Dyke advocated hanging "everyone who lifts his voice against America's entering the war."[43] Dr. S. Parkes Cadman, pastor of the Central Congregational Church in Brooklyn, declared that the Lutheran church in Germany "is not the bride of Christ, but the paramour of Kaiserism."[44] Evangelist Billy Sunday prayed in the House of Representatives, "Thou knowest, O Lord, that no nation so infamous, vile, greedy, sensuous, bloodthirsty ever disgraced the pages of history."[45]

Dr. Newell Dwight Hillis, pastor of the Plymouth Congregational Church of Brooklyn and one of the most popular lecturers of the day, did much to stir up hatred against Germans by relating numerous tales of German atrocities. According to Dr. Hillis, German soldiers drank human blood out of their enemies' skulls; they murdered and raped as pastimes, specializing in crimes against women.[46] Ray Abrams asserts that Allied atrocity stories "became unusually valuable in working up the moral indignation and righteous wrath of church congregations." Abrams claims that many churchmen were so thoroughly indoctrinated that even today, though most of the stories have been proved to be absolutely false, they still believe what they read in the newspapers fifteen years later." Abrams concludes:

> The evidence on the war-time hysteria as it affected the ecclesiastical hierarchy leads to the conclusion that the church leaders, in spite of their priestly claim to depth of spiritual insight and knowledge of ethical values, displayed no such superior quality of moral judgment as has been assumed.[47]

Christians of that day demonstrated the same kind of smugness or condescension displayed by President Wilson in his war message to Congress. Whereas before our entry into the war many churchmen advocated neutrality because they believed neither side fought for the right reasons and were convinced that God was punishing the nations of the world for past sins, little of this was heard when the United States became a participant. The war seemingly had become a crusade, a holy war, because the United States was now involved. Prior to the American entry some American Christians believed God was using the war to deliver the Russians from "the curse of strong drink," and thus he was bringing good out of evil.[48] Others believed that the war was God's way of effecting a revival of religious faith and a return to him.

When America became involved, God's motive no longer appeared to be one of punishing or purging—the United States, at least, was not brought into the war because of past sins. This nation became the avenging angel. One clergyman from his pulpit in Washington stated that God had summoned America to the war: "It is his war we are fighting." He called the war a "crusade" that was the "greatest" and "holiest" in history: "Yes, it is Christ the King of Righteousness who calls us to grapple in deadly strife with this unholy and blasphemous power."[49] Frank Mason North, president of the Federal Council of the Church of Christ in America, asserted, "The war for righteousness will be won! Let the Church do her part."[50] The *Lutheran Quarterly* maintained that "we fight for the right and might of righteousness as over against a selfish and cruel creed of a pagan faith in force." Continued this periodical in the July 1918 issue:

> It is a contest in the world of spiritual ideas, a clash between the spirit of the German god Odin and the Christian God as revealed in the character and program of Jesus Christ. The two ideals cannot live on forever. One or the other must perish. We know, as Disraeli said, that "we are on the side of the angels."

Christians have always avowed that their master, Jesus Christ, is entitled to their foremost allegiance no matter what the circumstances. During this wartime, many Christians in America appeared to lose sight of this as they came to be servants of the state and as the Christian faith and patriotism were equated. George F. Pentecost, pastor of the Bethany Presbyterian Church of Philadelphia, maintained that he could not "draw any line between Christianity and patriotism," for "the two go together."[51] Worth M. Tippy, a secretary of the Federal Council of Churches, stated that requests from the government were "in a class by themselves" and that they "constitute a privilege and an opportunity for service which cannot be denied."[52] And James L. Vance, pastor of the First Presbyterian Church of Nashville, Tennessee, wrote in the *Christian Century* of September 1917, "We must keep the flag and the Cross together, for they are both working for the same ends."[53]

The Christian Reformed Church's periodical the *Banner*, in a display of superpatriotism, printed the following bit of doggerel, entitled "A Toast to the Flag," on a February 28, 1918, flag-bedecked cover:

> Here's to the Red of it—
> There's not a thread of it,
> No, nor a shred of it
> In all the spread of it
> From foot to head,

But heroes bled for it,
Faced steel and lead for it,
Precious blood shed for it,
Bathing it Red.

Here's to the White of it—
Thrilled by the sight of it,
Who knows the right of it
But feels the might of it
Through day and night?
Womanhood's care for it
Made manhood dare for it,
Purity's prayer for it
Keeps it so White.

Here's to the Blue of it—
Beauteous view of it,
Heavenly hue of it,
Star-spangled hue of it,
Constant and true,
States stand supreme for it,
Diadems gleam for it,
Liberty's beam for it
Brightens the Blue.

Here's to the Whole of it
Stars, stripes and pole of it,
Body and soul of it,
On to the goal of it
Carry it through.
Home or abroad for it,
Unsheath the sword for it,
Fight in accord for it,
Red, White and Blue.

Churchmen became recruiters for the armed forces and vigorous promoters of Liberty Bonds. Said Billy Sunday in urging enlistment, "The man who breaks all the rules but at last dies fighting in the trenches is better than you Godforsaken mutts who won't enlist."[54] Lyman Abbot, editor of *The Outlook* and a well-known Congregational clergyman, recommended that "in this house every Christian Church should be a recruiting office for the Kingdom of God."[55] In promoting the sale of Liberty Bonds, John Henry Jowett of the Fifth Avenue Presbyterian Church in New

York maintained that the Liberty Loan was a "consecration of our money to a sacred cause," while John M. MacInnis of the South Presbyterian Church of Syracuse, New York, called "every dollar and every service given to Uncle Sam for his army" "a gift to missions."[56] V.G.A. Tressler, a leader in the Lutheran Church in the U.S.A., said, "In this Liberty Loan we are in no small measure achieving the aspirations of this government and the commands of the gospel."[57]

President Wilson had insisted always that justice and fairness should prevail, even though in wartime that goal might be difficult to achieve. Thus, it was not surprising that the German government appealed to Wilson for terms as the war was ending in 1918. Wishing to avoid any unnecessary recriminations on the part of the Germans, Wilson resisted those who wished to march into Berlin.[58] He insisted that the Fourteen Points be the basis for the armistice, and when France and Britain balked, he threatened to sign a separate peace.[59]

From a Christian perspective, much of what Wilson did and hoped to achieve in the postwar period can be applauded. Wilson had long dreamed that a concert or league of nations would be essential in establishing an enduring peace. Thus, he went to Europe as one of the peacemakers, not as one who sought material gain for the United States, but as one determined to lay the groundwork for a lasting peace. He thus insisted that the League of Nations covenant or constitution be an integral part of what came to be called the Treaty of Versailles. He respected the rights and sensitivities of those who in previous times had been trampled upon when he called for self-determination and League of Nations' supervision of colonies taken from Germany. He had insisted that the former enemy be treated fairly and thus resisted the French demand that the west bank of the Rhine be separated permanently from the rest of Germany.[60] When reparations were discussed, he argued that Germany should not be saddled with more than it could realistically pay, although Wilson lost on this issue when the Allies presented Germany with a figure not based on Germany's capacity to pay. In the end, not only was Wilson's attitude more charitable, but Wilson the idealist in this case proved to be more realistic, for while Germany paid only a fraction of the total, an ocean of resentment was generated by the bill handed the Germans.

Wilson argued that the victorious powers should disarm just as they were insisting that Germany be disarmed. Thus, the American president proposed the abolishment of conscription, the prohibition of the manufacturing of implements of war by private parties, and the maintenance of armies large enough to preserve order and fulfill international obligations but no larger.[61] The French again opposed these strictures, and Wilson essentially lost when the final settlement made only a vague promise to undertake general disarmament in the future.

Just as Wilson felt obliged to end the awful war first by mediation and then by the participation of his country, so at the peace conference one senses Wilson's conviction that it must not happen again. Just as he felt compelled to act to end the war, so he felt some responsibility to do what he could to prevent a future holocaust.

At the Paris conference Wilson had shown some willingness to compromise, but he demonstrated more rigidity when he sought ratification of his work by the United States Senate. Wilson retorted that the Senate would have to take its medicine when amendments or revisions to the treaty were suggested. Some of Wilson's opponents were equally unyielding. The story of the Senate's failure to approve the treaty is familiar. Historians have long debated the reasons why the necessary two-thirds majority could not be procured. As it happened, neither side was entirely "pure of heart"; such sins as arrogance, jealousy, and selfishness in both the president and the Senate played some part in the result.

The League of Nations was established after the First World War with the intent of ennabling men to live at peace with one another, the condition that God requires. The United States should have been part of that effort. President Wilson sounded like a prophet when he said, "For I tell you, my fellow citizens, I can predict with absolute certainty that within another generation there will be another world war if the nations of the world do not concert the method by which to prevent it." No one can assert with certainty that the Second World War could have been avoided had the United States joined the League of Nations. As David F. Trask has said, "No one can argue that had the United States ratified the treaty, the future might have been devoid of warfare, but the decision of 1919 greatly inhibited the country's ability to act in behalf of just and lasting peace."[62]

In September 1939, a little more than two decades after the First World War ended, war came again. In reflecting on this, one realizes that not enough was done to avoid the conflict, and a Christian weeps for a world engaged in a war that again seemed to violate many of the basic tenets of the Christian religion and that fulfilled Wilson's fear of a greater holocaust than the world had ever experienced.

7 RICHARD V. PIERARD

WORLD WAR II

"WORLD WAR II WAS THE LAST WAR AMERICANS COULD BE PROUD OF" is a phrase often heard today. It was a conflict behind which the public enthusiastically rallied with war bond sales, waste paper drives, victory gardens, patriotic sloganeering, and the ubiquitous stars placed in the front windows of homes indicating that a son, husband, or brother was serving in the armed forces. Even the hardships of the war were borne cheerfully—rationing, blackouts, wage and price controls, shortages, transportation snarls, and the dislocation of families. Of course, enemy bombs and shells (with negligible exceptions) did not fall on the soil of the forty-eight states, and the combat casualties were minimal compared to the losses suffered by the other warring countries. After the first dark months of 1942 the radio, newspapers, and weekly newsreels heralded triumph after triumph as the Allies relentlessly ground away at the German, Italian, and Japanese empires in three continents, demanding and eventually forcing their "unconditional surrender."

The conflict is heralded as the purest example of a "just war" in which the United States has engaged.[1] It was fought under the auspices of the state, one whose rulers were accountable to the people they governed. The accepted codes of good faith and humanity, technically at least, were observed. These included the various Geneva Conventions, which dealt with the protection and humane treatment of prisoners and the wounded in war, the 1925 Geneva accord prohibiting the use of biological and gas warfare, and the recognition of the rights of neutral states. The Axis powers were guilty of aggression (Japan in Manchuria, 1931, and China, 1937; Germany in Czechoslovakia and Poland, 1939, Western Europe, 1940, and Russia, 1941; and Italy in Ethiopia, 1935, Albania, 1939, and France, 1940); they violated international agreements like the Kellogg-Briand Pact of 1928, whose signatories (eventually all but five countries in the world) renounced war as an instrument of national policy; they violated as well the various bilateral nonaggression pacts (the German-Polish treaty of 1934 and the German-Soviet treaty of 1939). In addition, the Pacific possessions of the United States in particular were the victims of an unprovoked attack by the Japanese in December 1941. In view of all the evidence, the American war effort clearly aimed at the restoration of peace.

Moreover, it was established at the Nuremberg (1945–46) and Tokyo (1946–48) trials that the Axis leaders, along with these "crimes against peace," were guilty of "war crimes"—violations of the various universally accepted laws of war—and of "crimes against humanity"—mass murder, deportations, torture, systematic persecution of entire racial groups like the Jews and Gypsies, and use of slave labor. Therefore, justice was "vindicated" by crushing the Axis tyranny. Finally, in accordance with just war theory the amount of violence used was restricted to that necessary to obtain satisfaction from the enemy. The entire populations of the defeated countries were not put to the sword, and sincere efforts were made to "rehabilitate" the German and Japanese people. The postwar occupations of these two lands were designed to eliminate the defects in their political and social structures that had enabled them to embark upon aggression, to rebuild their shattered economies, and to restore them to the family of nations where they would function in a peaceful, law-abiding fashion.

A Christian evaluation of America's involvement in World War II must look beneath the surface of what must be regarded as an "official" justification. Hard questions should be asked as to whether attitudes in this country contributed in some measure to the coming of the war. And, even if one is convinced that the war was thrust upon America, the problem of whether the country acted in accordance with the just war ideal still looms in the foreground. The current nostalgia about World War II, as reflected in the vast quantity of books, movies, games, toys, and models, unfortunately obscures some real difficulties about the conflict, difficulties that a sensitive Christian can ill afford to overlook.

REJECTION OF INTERNATIONALISM

The high moral aspirations of President Woodrow Wilson were not carried over into the peace settlement after World War I.[2] Under pressure from his political opponents at home and the Allies in Europe, he agreed to numerous compromises in the Paris treaties. These included the payment of reparations by Germany, winking at the freedom of seas, permitting France to occupy the Rhineland temporarily, Japanese and Italian violations of the principle of national self-determination, glossing over imperialistic actions through the mandate system, and signing a security agreement with Britain and France that sidestepped the League of Nations. The covenant of the League incorporated in the treaties contained concessions to placate Wilson's domestic critics, such as safeguarding the Monroe Doctrine, exempting tariff and immigration policy from League consideration, and recognizing the right of members to withdraw.

Nevertheless, after several months of public debate, the Senate rebuffed Wilson by rejecting both the Treaty of Versailles and American participation in the League of Nations. The Senate also turned down membership in the Permanent Court of International Justice (the "World Court"), which was formed in 1921. Gradually it became clear to perceptive observers that the unsatisfied aspirations of the participants in the Great War, the harsh peace imposed upon Germany, and the failure to create genuinely effective machinery to conciliate international differences made a second and even greater conflict virtually inevitable.

The central problem of the interwar years is summed up in the popular phrase "international anarchy."[3] This was compounded by the American withdrawal into hemispheric isolation, although it is incorrect to say that the United States ignored all international concerns. The Washington naval arms limitation conference of 1921–22 was convened on American initiative, as was the Geneva disarmament conference in 1927. The American secretary of state negotiated the 1928 Kellogg-Briand agreement (Paris Pact) outlawing war, and the country took part in subsequent disarmament conferences at London (1930), Geneva (1933), and London (1935–36). More attention was devoted to improving relations in Latin America, with the result that troops were withdrawn from the Dominican Republic, Nicaragua, and Haiti, the Roosevelt corollary to the Monroe Doctrine (the United States had a right to keep order in other countries so external powers would not have a pretext for intervention) was formally renounced at a meeting at Montevideo in 1933, and the "good neighbor policy" came to characterize the new attitude in Washington. In East Asia the United States endeavored through diplomatic and economic pressure to check Japanese expansion and encroachment upon China.

But all attempts to construct a harmonious international order foundered on the rock of nationalism. The political and economic policies of the various countries were dictated mainly by selfish considerations of national power and prestige. No land was prepared to surrender any of its precious sovereignty to enable the League of Nations to relieve political tensions or reduce armaments. No effective mechanism existed to permit those nations nursing grievances to obtain redress without having eventually to resort to armed force. The representatives at Geneva were committed to preserving the status quo, and those who wished change simply bypassed the League. As a result, the important international accords of the interwar years were arrived at in the traditional fashion of either bilateral treaties or conferences that involved several countries.

The anarchic effect of nationalism was particularly evident in economic policy.[4] The Unites States had loaned the Allies $10.3 billion during and immediately after the war and was demanding repayment. The Europeans regarded this as the American contribution to the war and felt the debts should be cancelled. In addition, the United States agreed to grant reconstruction assistance to Germany that resulted in a temporary recovery, but now Germany was also in debt to the Americans. Meanwhile, in spite of Wilsonian ideas about free trade, the American people as well as politicians were extremely fearful of the impact of foreign competition on industry and agriculture. Congress responded with a protective tariff bill in 1922 that raised duties to their highest levels in history, and the European debtor nations, unable to sell in the American market, found it more difficult than ever to repay their wartime obligations. This did not significantly benefit American exports, since European countries raised their own tariff barriers in retaliation. The ensuing tariff wars adversely affected international trade and fostered still more nationalism.

By the late 1920s the international economic order had begun to totter, and then it collapsed, ushering in the worst depression in modern history.[5] The United States responded in a shortsighted fashion by increasing duties through the Hawley-Smoot Tariff (1930) to even higher levels. By 1932 many nations had abandoned the gold standard and were in default on their debts, and the United States eased up on its demands for the time being. But President Franklin D. Roosevelt undermined the London Economic Conference in 1933 by refusing either to discuss the interrelated questions of tariffs, debts, and reparations or to go along with a program of currency stabilization based on gold. As more and more countries suspended payments, Congress acted vindictively by passing the Johnson Debt Default Act of 1934, which forbade loans to any nation in arrears on its obligations and barred the sale of that country's securities in the United States. This move blocked the possibility of international cooperation to ameliorate the depression, although the United States did loosen its tariff policies somewhat in the later 1930s through the use of reciprocal trade agreements.

Walter M. Van Kirk, a noted Christian leader, indicted his countrymen in forceful terms for their shortsightedness in an essay written in 1941:

> Along with other nations the United States must accept its full share of responsibility for Hitler. . . . We separated ourselves from the rest of the world. We closed our eyes. We closed our ears. We closed our minds. We closed our hearts. We did everything but close our mouths. And from that day [the Armistice] until the outbreak of the Second World War we preached international morality for others and practiced international anarchy for ourselves.[6]

It is true that churchmen in the United States, Britain, and elsewhere criticized these actions. Throughout the period ecumenical and denominational gatherings and individual clerics fervently supported disarmament measures. Well-known Christian lay people were directly involved in the aforementioned conferences, and churchmen were in the forefront of the various peace movements. They preached from their pulpits and lobbied in

Washington for the cause of international harmony and against the arms race.[7]

However, it is not clear that the liberal clergy really spoke for the mass of the American people, and because of their ambivalence on the question of pacifism they were not able to direct their followers away from the path of storm cellar neutrality. The isolationist sentiment in the mid-1930s was so strong that liberal internationalists (including President Roosevelt) were not able to obtain legislation committing the United States to a modest program of collective security.[8] Many congressmen rejected this approach, fearing it would mean some loss of America's highly prized freedom to act independently and might lead to involvement in war. The American policy as developed in the Neutrality Acts during 1935–37 was to embargo arms to both sides in any struggle. This was modified only after Hitler's assault on Poland, and even then there was considerable opposition by isolationists to any form of assistance to the beleaguered "democracies" of Europe and Asia. But the internationalists finally won the day when Hitler overran western Europe in spring 1940, and both presidential candidates that fall advocated doing everything possible short of sending American troops overseas to forestall a British defeat.[9] By then it was too late—the flames of war had engulfed the world.

THE PACIFIST DILEMMA

Pacifism was a strong element in American Protestant thinking after World War I. It drew its strength from several factors—the general disillusionment with the war and with the peace settlement, a reaffirmation of the New Testament emphasis on love, the traditional nonresistance doctrines of the historic peace churches, the liberal idea of human goodness, and the Marxist teaching about the nexus between capitalism and war. Pacifists were firmly internationalists in their outlook, opposed to "militarism" in all its forms, and for the most part critical of capitalism and its accompanying materialism. Their stance was eloquently summed up in a statement by Episcopal bishop George Oldham:

> A strident patriotism of the 100 percent American variety, scorning other races, looking condescendingly on other nations,

touchy about its own rights, and prating about "absolute sovereignty," is the greatest single danger to the peace of the world today.[10]

The rise of National Socialism, however, put them in a difficult position, particularly when Hitler's war machine rolled over one country after another. One pacifist, Reinhold Niebuhr of Union Theological Seminary, frankly acknowledged the problem when he pointed out that the imperial ambitions of Nazi Germany "represent a peril to every established value of a civilization which all Western nations share and of which we are all the custodians."[11] Theologian John C. Bennett admitted candidly "that the alternative to successful resistance to Germany is the extension of the darkest political tyranny imaginable over the whole of Europe with the prospect that . . . the whole world will be threatened by the Axis powers."[12] Nazism had dealt a severe blow to liberal humanistic pacifism, one from which it would never fully recover.

Nonpacifists such as Loraine Boettner, a conservative Presbyterian whose viewpoint on war accurately mirrored that of most evangelicals at the time, ridiculed the liberal pacifists for their short-sightedness and faulty theology, maintaining that their position could not cope with unprovoked aggression. In his opinion they failed to recognize that human nature is fallen, man is essentially selfish, and without forcible restraint there is no limit to the injustice he will commit. Pacifism is irresponsible, and "peace at any price" means certain tyranny. In these circumstances "combat is not only sanctioned by God but [also] it is our duty to perform it with all available resources."[13]

A radical shift took place in the months between the Munich agreement and the fall of France in the thinking of "mainline" theologians, many of whom had been pacifists and even socialists during the 1930s. The most important "revisionism" came from the pen of Reinhold Niebuhr. In numerous essays he struck at the theological foundations of pacifism, arguing that it is impossible "perfectionism."[14] Man is a sinner and lives in a world shot through with sin. Christians who live in and benefit from a society in which coercive relationships are taken for granted have no right to introduce the uncompromising ethics of the gospel into an issue like war. The kingdom of God is not a human possibility. The cross as a pure act of sacrifice can occur only outside of history and to make it normative for human behavior in a sinful world is illusory. The cross reveals what history ought to be, not what history is or can be. Within history people must settle for conflict and balance of power, because justice can only be achieved by protecting each life and interest against all others. However,

> most of our liberal Protestantism has neatly disavowed all the profounder elements of the gospel which reveal the tragic character of history and has made the gospel identical with the truism that all men ought to be good and with the falsehood that goodness pays. The end of pure goodness, of perfect love, is the cross.[15]

Further, pacifism has an element of impractical idealism. It springs from "an unholy compound of gospel perfectionism and bourgeois utopianism," the latter flowing from eighteenth-century rationalism. This kind of pacifism is not content with martyrdom and the rejection of political responsibility. It tries to fashion "political alternatives to the tragic business of resisting tyranny and establishing justice by coercion."[16] Nonviolent resistance is an example of this, but inevitably the result will be the acceptance of or connivance with tyranny. If one refuses to meet evil with evil, that is, tyranny with violent resistance, he becomes a party to the enslavement of nations and the suppression of freedom of thought and life.

John Bennett further exposed the inadequacy of peace at any price pacifism by examining some of their current arguments. He said nazism is not "the wave of the future," as many were contending, but rather a throwback to the remote past that has undone the results of previous revolutions. Moreover, there is no reason to believe that Germany will moderate its rule as its position in Europe becomes more secure. The opposite is more likely the case—tyranny will become even greater. Also inadequate is the view of many European Christians that nazism is a judgment on the sins of their churches and secularist democracy, and that it may lead to a cleansing of Europe and the development of a more Christian culture. As Bennett put it, the alternative to secularist democracy is not necessarily some kind of Christian authoritarian society but a blatantly secularist tyranny. Furthermore, a church driven underground loses touch with its society and is unable to shape the mind of the community in a Christian fashion.[17]

It is unfair to lay the responsibility for the spread of totalitarian dictatorships at the feet of liberal Protestants and secular pacifists in the Western democracies, and it is simply wrong to accuse them of cowardice in the face of mounting tyranny. But pacifists operated in a different world, and their ideas, although noble and admirable, were unworkable in the realities of the 1930s. They were unprepared to assume political responsibility and to support efforts in their countries to resist Axis aggression. They were undoubtedly convinced that righteousness was on their side, but they did not and would not involve themselves in the struggle against tyranny.

Therefore, doctrinaire pacifists constituted a source of weakness rather than strength in the Western democracies. Only when it was almost too late did many adherents realize its flaws and act accordingly to defend democracy, even if this required taking up arms. As Niebuhr wrote in the first issue of a new journal, *Christianity and Crisis*, the organ of those theologians who understood the failing of pacifism:

> Nazi tyranny intends to annihilate the Jewish race, to subject the nations of Europe to the dominion of a "master" race, to extirpate the Christian religion, to annul the liberties and legal standards which are the priceless heritage of ages of Christian and humanistic culture, to make truth the prostitute of political power, to seek world dominion through its satraps and allies, and generally to destroy the very fabric of western civilization. . . . We do know what a Nazi victory would mean; and our first task must therefore be to prevent it.[18]

FASCIST TENDENCIES

Another significant factor was the attraction that fascism had for many Americans during the depression years.[19] Several disturbing elements were evident in this native variety of the ideology that had carried Mussolini and Hitler to power. Anti-Semitism pervaded the outlook of most far-rightists, and even a respectable person, automobile manufacturer Henry Ford, carried on a campaign against the Jews in the 1920s. Although he later repented of these excesses, Ford did accept a medal from Hitler on his seventy-fifth birthday in 1938.[20] Populist demagogues such as Dr. Francis E. Townsend with his old age pension scheme and Senator

Huey Long with his "share the wealth" program had extensive followings among the discontented. A Roman Catholic radio preacher in Michigan, Father Charles E. Coughlin, stirred millions of listeners by attacking plutocracy, communism, and the New Deal. He openly referred to nazism and Italian fascism as a "defense mechanism" against communism and labeled Hitler, Mussolini, and Franco "as patriots rising to a challenge." Fascism "was and is Europe's answer to Russian Communism's threat of world revolution, and it is the bulwark against long active agencies of destruction." He subtly linked anti-Semitism with anticommunism by suggesting that Jews were persecuted because of their association with communism and their lack of patriotism.[21]

The new order in Europe found many admirers in the United States, and Christians were numbered among their ranks. Gerald Winrod, a popular fundamentalist preacher from Kansas and candidate for the U.S. Senate in 1936, wrote in his paper *The Defender*:

> Nazism and Fascism are patriotic and nationalistic; communism is not. . . . Of the three forms of government, Nazism and Fascism are as far in advance of Bolshevism as the twentieth century is from the Dark Ages. One stands for life, happiness and prosperity; the other, death, misery and starvation.[22]

Another prominent religious figure, Frank Buchman, the founder of Moral Rearmament, returned from the Olympic Games in Berlin and told a New York reporter that he "thanked heaven" for Adolf Hitler, who built "a front line of defense against the Anti-Christ of Communism."[23] William Randolph Hearst, although not known for his deep spiritual insights, yet being a newspaperman who should have been perceptive when dealing with political figures, was taken in just as effectively by Hitler. After meeting with the Führer in 1934, Hearst reported that he "is certainly an extraordinary man. . . . We estimate him too lightly in America." Hitler's "great policy, great achievement" was to have saved Germany from communism.[24]

There was no lack of fascist-style groups on American soil. The Ku Klux Klan, the most famous of all the hate organizations, whose program in the 1920s had primarily been anti-Catholicism, declined somewhat in importance during the 1930s, but many new ones appeared to supplement its work in spreading bigotry. Among the most notorious was the German-American Bund, headed by Fritz Kuhn, a German war veteran who emigrated to the United States in 1926. It was virulently anti-Semitic, maintained a private army of stormtroopers, and supported the policies of the Hitler regime. Another was the Silver Shirts, a group founded by William Dudley Pelley, which was a motley, ragtag vigilante organization. There were also literary fascists such as Seward Collins, editor of the *American Review*, the poet Ezra Pound who eventually settled in Italy, and Lawrence Dennis, a Harvard graduate who was the nearest thing to a "philosopher" of American fascism. Gerald L. K. Smith, a fundamentalist preacher who joined the Silver Shirts and then worked as an organizer for Huey Long, formed an isolationist and anti–New Deal group called the Committee of One Million, which boasted of being a "nationalist front against Communism."[25]

When war broke out in Europe, the influence of the fascist spokesmen rapidly waned. Many of them, however, were active in the isolationist America First Committee, a reasonably respectable group formed in 1940 and led by such dignitaries as Robert E. Wood, board chairman of Sears, Roebuck and Company, and aviator Charles A. Lindbergh. The committee definitely met with Nazi approval, for in a shortwave broadcast on January 2, 1941, the German propaganda ministry praised it as being "truly American and truly patriotic."[26] The committee eventually repudiated the support of the German-American Bund, but not that of Pelley's Silver Shirts, Father Coughlin's Christian Front, the Ku Klux Klan, or Gerald Smith. American fascism, aided and abetted by at least some conservative Christians, had contributed its part to the country's reluctance to resist German aggression and assist the embattled democracies.

ANTI-JAPANESE RACISM

The belief that the United States was a country where nonwhites had "no rights which the white man was bound to respect"[27] is undeniably one of the most pernicious influences in the nation's history. Negro slavery and ongoing discrimination against blacks is one manifestation of it, while the bloody record of violated treaties and unprovoked wars with the native American (Indian) population is another. Orientals have been a third minority victimized by white American racism, and unlike the other examples, their case seems to have had a direct bearing on the coming of World War II.

Immigration from East Asia began in the late 1840s when thousands of Chinese came to work in the gold mines and later on railroad construction. They were most numerous in California where they functioned as cheap labor and were perceived as a threat by white working people. Because of this economic consideration and their cultural differences, western whites viewed the Chinese as subhumans and subjected them to legal discrimination and mob violence. Finally the federal government responded to western demands to halt the Chinese influx by passing an exclusion bill in 1882. For the next seventy years immigration from China was not permitted.[28]

This formed a backdrop for the Japanese problem. Because Japan only legalized emigration in 1885, significant numbers of people from there did not arrive in the United States until the 1890s. And, compared to the total immigration between 1865 and 1924, the Japanese influx of 300,000 was minuscule, only 1 percent of the total to be precise. It was hardly the "yellow flood" that its detractors saw it to be.[29] They were an energetic, ambitious, upwardly mobile folk whose values of zeal, frugality, industry, honesty, and regularity, would, if practiced by white people, have surely been portrayed as the "Protestant ethic" in action. Their achievements in the field of agriculture were spectacular and contributed significantly to making California the leading farming state in the nation.[30]

Although the Japanese-Americans generally were not in direct economic competition with their white neighbors, like the Chinese they too became the target of racism. They experienced various forms of discrimination, the most egregious being the San Francisco school board's decision in 1906 to segregate Japanese students and the California Alien Land Law of 1913, which prohibited Japanese nationals from purchasing farmland. Various patriotic and economic organizations in California came together in 1919 to form the Oriental Exclusion League, a blatantly bigoted group that endeavored to bar Japanese immigration and to deprive Americans of East Asian extraction of their citizenship. Their efforts bore fruit in 1924 with the passage of the National Origins Act, whose frankly racist quota system not only severely limited immigration from southern and eastern Europe but also totally excluded the Japanese from coming to America. Nevertheless, in spite of white hostility and continuing discrimination, the second generation Japanese (the Nisei) were to some extent assimilated. They were citizens, and many even became hypernationalistic Americans.

The problem had international ramifications, because Japan with its industrial and military might was anything but a weak, minor Oriental power. The racist attitudes in the region where most of the Japanese lived had a profound impact on national policies.[31] President Theodore Roosevelt's Gentleman's Agreement of 1907–08 was one example of the efforts that had to be made from time to time to mollify Japanese feelings.

Moreover, many Americans suffered from an irrational fear of Oriental expansion and conquest, and from the 1890s on, jingoes talked about the "yellow peril" and the inevitable conflict with Japan for mastery of the Pacific. After Japan defeated Russia in 1905 the Hearst newspapers took a consistently anti-Japanese stance, while a minor military figure named General Homer Lea gained national acclaim with a sensationalist book published in 1909 which detailed how the Japanese would conquer the Philippines and then the West Coast states.[32] During the war the United States worked to block Japanese encroachment on China (the Twenty-one Demands, 1915), while public opinion was highly inflamed by the revelation in early 1917 (the Zimmermann Telegram) that the Germans had proposed an alliance with Mexico that would include Japan. The Japanese were rebuffed in their attempt to have a statement repudiating racism included in the Versailles treaty, while the Naval Conference of 1921–22 was designed as much to check their ambitions in the Pacific as it was to obtain disarmament.

Anti-Oriental racism linked with American fantasies about the yellow peril undoubtedly poisoned relations between the two countries. Added to this was the United States desire for Pacific hegemony, which went counter to Japanese intentions. As the military increasingly gained the ascendancy in Japan, they were less willing to accept an inferior status for their country and looked upon the United States as their chief antagonist. American moves to block Japanese expansion in Manchuria and China came to naught, while no attempt was made to conciliate Japan by relinquishing traditional aims in the western Pacific. The gulf between the two powers steadily widened as the United States sent aid to China and finally in 1941 cut off supplies of vital industrial and war materials. The Pearl Harbor attack was the Japanese response to the American "containment" policy in East Asia, but seen in perspective it was the last link in a long chain of events that reached back to the initial racism of the 1890s.[33]

Looking at American actions in the interwar years, one may conclude that the country fell short of the mark in several ways. Its leaders faithfully reflected the public attitude that the United States, although now the predominant industrial power in the world, should not accept responsibility for leading the global community. Too few Christians actively worked on behalf of this, and the majority preferred rather to retreat into isolationism or pacifism, both of which meant noninvolvement. The nation's moral position was further weakened by the way people went along with or at least winked at fascism and racism. Given the record of Axis aggression at the time, America's decision to go to war was justifiable, but viewing the situation from a Christian standpoint it was hardly an open-and-shut case of right versus wrong.

MORALITY AND THE WAR EFFORT

In spite of the best intentions of isolationists the United States was gradually drawn into the maelstrom of World War II. The neutrality legislation was laid aside, defenses in the Western hemisphere beefed up, conscription introduced, and America declared to be "the arsenal of democracy." The passage of the Lend-Lease bill in March 1941 made American neutrality a fiction, although Italy and Germany did not finally declare war until December 11. Once America was officially at war with the Axis powers, it quickly geared up for the most gigantic conflict in world history.

Although the people were solidly behind the war effort and viewed it as a righteous cause, the crusading spirit was not nearly as evident as in 1917 in spite of the title General Dwight D. Eisenhower gave to his memoirs, *Crusade in Europe*.[34] Roosevelt did, however, set a high moral tone when he proclaimed in his Pearl Harbor speech that "the American people in their righteous might will win through to absolute victory," and he held up the vision of a new order in the world "founded upon four essential human freedoms": freedom of speech and expression, freedom of worship, freedom from want, and freedom from fear.[35]

From the beginning American participation in the war was part of a larger coalition. In the Atlantic Charter of August 1941 the British and American leaders affirmed that the postwar goal would be that of peace and collective security for all countries, and in 1942 the United States assented to the Declaration of the United Nations, an alliance that committed its signatories to prosecute the war until victory was achieved. Throughout the conflict Roosevelt was in constant contact with Churchill and other Allied leaders, including the Russian dictator Joseph Stalin, and diligent efforts were made to coordinate strategy. In 1945 a world peacekeeping body known as the United Nations was created, and the United States committed itself to making the organization work. The mistakes of the previous world war would not, it was hoped, be repeated.

The level of domestic propaganda and censorship was milder and more sophisticated than in World War I and the treatment of conscientious objectors by the Civilian Public Service program was appreciably more responsible and humane.[36] There were, nevertheless, areas where American performance fell short of its moral ideals, and these cast a distinct pall over the "justness" of the struggle.

BOMBING OF CIVILIAN POPULATIONS

A moral question of vast significance was the deliberate bombing of civilian populations.[37] This first took place in 1937 when German planes supporting Franco attacked the Spanish town of Guernica and the Japanese bombed Nanking, the Chinese capital. The United States government strongly protested the latter: "Any general bombing of an extensive area wherein there resides a large populace engaged in peaceful pursuits is unwarranted and contrary to the principles of law and humanity."[38] At the outbreak of war in Europe Roosevelt urgently appealed to the parties involved to affirm they would not engage in air bombardment of civilian populations or unfortified cities. A year later he declared that the bombing of helpless and unprotected civilians was a tragedy that aroused the horror of all mankind: "I recall with pride that the

United States consistently has taken the lead in urging that this inhuman practice be prohibited."[39]

Hitler's aerial assaults on Warsaw, Rotterdam, and London were widely condemned as typical of his treachery and ruthlessness. The Allies felt the bombing of civilians was a form of attack used only by totalitarian dictators, and maintained that bombing should be directed at specific military targets. But confidence in the efficacy of precision bombing rapidly eroded in 1941 when the British Royal Air Force found that losses in daylight raids were becoming too great and that it was impossible to locate and hit important targets at night. As improved German air defenses forced the British to fly higher, thus causing a further decline in accuracy, they resorted increasingly to "area" or "saturation" bombing.

When Air Marshall Sir Arthur Harris took charge of the RAF Bomber Command in March 1942, all pretense of precision bombing was discarded. Because strategic bombing failed to cripple the industrial base of Germany's war economy, he opted for a direct assault on its urban population aimed at breaking the nation's morale and will to resist. The policy became that of "obliteration bombing," and 60 percent of the RAF's total tonnage in 1942–43 was dumped on German cities.

By 1943 the United States Eighth Air Force joined the RAF in massive operations over Germany, although at first the Americans concentrated on strategic actions. Roosevelt assured Congress that they were "not bombing tenements for the sadistic pleasure of killing, as the Nazis did. We are striking devastating blows at carefully selected, clearly identified strategic objectives—factories, shipyards, munitions dumps, transportation facilities, which make it possible for the Nazis to wage war."[40] Before long, however, the two air forces engaged in coordinated obliteration attacks using a combination of explosive and incendiary bombs. These often created raging firestorms that took huge tolls of lives in such cities as Hamburg, Cassel, Darmstadt, and above all Dresden, which in terms of total deaths (135,000) was the most costly bombing of the war.[41]

The United States began heavy B-29 air raids on Japan in the fall of 1944, at first using high-altitude daylight precision bombing. This proved ineffective, and General Curtis LeMay, head of the B-29 Bomber command, launched an obliteration campaign. On March 9–10, 1945, more than 300 planes unloaded

2,000 tons of incendiary bombs on Tokyo. A huge conflagration resulted that burned over fifteen square miles of the city and snuffed out the lives of nearly 100,000 people. Within three months LeMay's forces leveled the enemy's six largest industrial centers and then turned to the smaller cities. Their vulnerability was such that by summer Japan was on the verge of economic collapse. To accomplish the same in Germany had required three years of bombing. In fact, the progressive Allied advances on the eastern and western fronts did as much to force the Germans to their knees as the incessant air attacks had.[42]

Robert Batchelder notes that the shift from precision to saturation bombing in Japan had gone unnoticed just as it had in Europe. There was no outcry in the American press and churchmen did not protest: "The obliteration bombing of cities was accepted as a logical, normal, and routine part of accomplishing the defeat of Japan."[43] Thus, it logically followed that the United States would use its newly developed secret weapon, the atomic bomb. Further, the precedent of saturation bombing insured that it would be used on an urban target. It was too powerful a weapon to be reserved just for a single factory, dam, or railroad. Besides, American leaders no longer distinguished between purely military targets and urban areas. As far as they were concerned, the two were synonymous, because a city automatically was a war production center.

The decision to develop an atomic weapon was made early in the war. In the 1930s a number of prominent physicists who emigrated from Europe worked closely with their American colleagues on nuclear fission research. They persuaded Albert Einstein to inform Roosevelt and warn him that Germany was also engaged in the same research. The president reluctantly made a modest commitment of funds, but as the international situation deteriorated he decided just prior to Pearl Harbor to throw the whole weight of government behind the project. He feared what might happen to the civilized world if the Nazis were to develop an atomic weapon first.

What followed was a crash program, the top secret Manhattan Project, to produce fissionable material and transform it into a weapon of destruction.[44] Rumors of German progress added an awesome sense of urgency, although later it was learned that they had fallen far behind the Americans. Even though many

German scientists had fled the terrors of nazism, thus depriving Hitler of considerable topflight talent, those who remained did possess the know-how to build a bomb. But wartime conditions were such that the large-scale industrial plants needed to make fissionable material could not be built, while some scientists doubted whether it was actually possible to put together a bomb and believed that the Americans were far from accomplishing this goal. Also, the Führer was interested only in the development of new weapons that could become operational within a few months and was unwilling to divert funds to nuclear research.[45]

After feverishly constructing the huge plants to manufacture uranium 235 and plutonium, the Americans assembled an atomic weapon and tested in on July 16, 1945, over two months after the German surrender. Looking at the timing, some people have suggested that the United States would never have used the bomb on white people in Europe, but only on Asiatics; this, however, is sheer nonsense.[46] The very logic of obliteration bombing determined that it would be used to end the war as quickly as possible, and thus the decision was made to drop it on Hiroshima on August 6 and Nagasaki three days later.[47] As Winston Churchill accurately records in his memoir history of World War II:

> The historic fact remains, and must be judged in the aftertime, that the decision whether or not to use the atomic bomb to compel the surrender of Japan was never even an issue. There was unanimous, automatic, unquestioned agreement around our table [at the 1945 Potsdam conference]; nor did I ever hear the slightest suggestion that we should do otherwise.[48]

The evidence is convincing that the atomic bomb did shorten the war. It provided the peace party in Japan with sufficient clout to overcome the military clique and created a situation in which the emperor could use his authority to decide on surrender. It also saved hundreds of thousands of American lives that would have been lost in the projected invasion of Japan as well as millions of Japanese who would have died in defending their homeland, in the further air raids, and in military action on the Asiatic mainland.[49] The larger question of mass destruction of civilians by bombing, whether conventional or nuclear, remains unanswered. In a "just war" should such a draconian policy ever have been implemented in the first place? A Christian would be hard pressed to answer this affirmatively.

RACISM AND CIVIL LIBERTIES

The principal victims of racism in the United States were Negroes, who in 1940 made up 9.8 percent of the nation's population, but their status improved somewhat during the war years. Although of course they fell far short of achieving the goal of full civil rights, a noteworthy action was the creation of the Fair Employment Practices Committee by President Roosevelt in June 1941. The desperate need for labor by defense industries and the governmental pressure exerted through the FEPC made possible job opportunities for blacks in many fields that hitherto had been closed to them, and the work by black laborers across the country matched the best efforts of their white counterparts.[50]

Unfortunately, the armed forces remained segregated, and the World War II "crusade in Europe" for democracy and freedom was fought with a Jim Crow army and the "separate but equal doctrine" still intact as the law of the land. However, some progress was made in the integration of base facilities, the appointment of black officers, and the elimination of segregation in public transportation used by servicemen. The thousands of blacks who now were in the armed forces or who worked in northern defense factories had no desire to see a return to the old regimen of strict segregation, and World War II was an important stage in the drive for Negro civil rights.[51]

People of German extraction (and Italians as well) suffered little discrimination, quite unlike the first war. A few domestic Nazis and fascists were tried and convicted under the espionage laws, but the government's most ambitious venture—a mass sedition trial of twenty-eight pro-Nazis—ended in a mistrial after several weary weeks of court proceedings.[52] A more serious violation of civil liberties, however, was the treatment meted out to Japanese-Americans.

After Pearl Harbor, whites on the West Coast demanded that all people of Japanese lineage, regardless of whether they were American citizens, be evacuated to the interior.[53] Attorney General Francis Biddle, a firm civil libertarian, opposed the idea, but Assistant Secretary of War John J. McCloy told him bluntly: "If it is a question of the safety of the country [and] the Constitution, . . . why the Constitution is just a scrap of paper to me."[54] This mentality pervaded the thinking of those who engineered the relocation. Even the distinguished political pundit Walter Lippmann referred to the Japanese-Americans as a "Fifth Column on the Coast" and said there was "plenty of room elsewhere" for them to exercise their rights,[55] while Earl Warren, the California attorney general and later chief justice of the U.S. Supreme Court, added his voice to those demanding an evacuation. Finally, on February 19, 1942, President Roosevelt signed an executive order authorizing officials of the armed forces to designate "military areas" from which "any or all persons may be excluded" and to provide for them "transportation, food, shelter, and other accommodations as may be necessary . . . until other arrangements are made."[56]

Since military necessity really did not require such an evacuation (none took place in Hawaii where the percentage of the population of Japanese ancestry was much higher—one-third as opposed to merely 2 percent in California), this must be seen as a manifestation of anti-Oriental racism. The decision was greeted with enthusiasm not only in California and the West, but throughout the nation. Roosevelt realized that cracking down on the Japanese-Americans would enhance his popularity both in Congress and across the country generally. Moreover, he personally regarded them as a danger to national security and actually favored internment of the Hawaiian Japanese as well, but the military leaders stubbornly resisted such a rash move.[57]

What followed was a national scandal. In the spring, the War Relocation Authority, headed by Milton S. Eisenhower, brother of the general and a Washington bureaucrat, began the roundup of 120,000 Japanese-Americans. He had genuine misgivings about his position as the first director of concentration camps in American history, but he did try to make the program work. Although Eisenhower preferred simply to resettle the people in the interior, he backed down when the white residents of the intermountain states objected and instead established ten internment camps in isolated areas of the country.

After being forced to sell their property at a tremendous loss, the Japanese were herded into the camps. They were generally not brutal places and family units were allowed to remain together. They were more like that ancient American institution the Indian reservation than European concentration camps, but they were ringed with barbed wire and armed sentries. Most of the inhabitants submitted to the oppressive order of the camps and some even volunteered for military service (the Nisei regimental combat team which served in Italy and France was allegedly the "most decorated" unit in the American army),[58] but there were instances of passive resistance and civil disobedience. Appeals to the courts to halt such a blatant denial of civil liberties were unsuccessful, and the Supreme Court upheld the action in decisions handed down in June 1943 and December 1944.[59]

In early 1945 the relocation policy was terminated and the Nisei gradually returned to their homes. In many places they were rejected by their old neighbors and subjected to harassment, but responsible public officials, such as repentant Earl Warren, now governor of California, helped to ease tensions. Eventually they were reintegrated into their communities, awarded some damages, and recovered their legal and social status. Finally in 1952 a new immigration law restored a Chinese and Japanese quota and removed racial bars against naturalization, thus ending the last vestige of legal discrimination against Japanese-Americans.

TREATMENT OF DEFENSELESS GROUPS

Another stain on the American record in World War II was the treatment accorded to two defenseless groups, the Jewish victims of Nazi persecution and Russians who served in the German army. Hitler's anti-Jewish program was without equal in a modern industrialized nation, and other countries did little more than whimper about it, if even that, because after all it was a matter of "internal policy." In six short years the Nazis stripped the half million German Jews of citizenship, expelled them from the professions, deprived them of most of their wealth and property, and subjected them to innumerable types of discrimination. In November 1938 Hitler's henchmen unleased the *Kristallnacht* (Night of Breaking Glass) terror, which resulted in the burning and looting of countless Jewish homes, businesses, and synagogues. As more and more territories fell under German rule, the anti-Jewish measures became increasingly more horrifying with mass deportations, crowding people into ghettos, indiscriminate killings, and the ultimate act of barbarism, the so-called "final solution," namely, the systematic extermination of the entire Jewish population of Nazi-occupied Europe.[60]

Although the press kept Americans well informed during the 1930s about German misdeeds, little was done to combat them.[61] Acts of persecution such as *Kristallnacht* were publicly condemned, and liberal politicians and clergy tried to mount an aid program, but these protests amounted to little. There was strong resistance to permitting the entry of German Jews, and of course the drastic measure of humiliating Hitler by boycotting or cancelling the Berlin Olympics was not even given serious consideration. Fascist and right-wing groups kept up a steady drumbeat of anti-Semitic propaganda, organized labor opposed lowering the immigration barriers because of the possible effect upon the already high unemployment rate, and nativist and patriotic organizations looked upon a general influx of "foreigners" with a jaundiced eye.

In 1938 President Roosevelt took the initiative to call an international conference to deal with the refugee problem. It met at Evian, France in July but could accomplish nothing, since no nation really wanted to rescue the Jews. The United States certainly did not welcome Jewish immigrants from Nazi-held territories, and Roosevelt did not push the matter because he feared it would further harm his already low popularity.[62] In 1939 the Wagner Bill, which provided for the admittance of 20,000 German refugee children, was torpedoed by administration reluctance, and entry was refused to the shipload of Jews aboard the S.S. *St. Louis* who already had been turned away from Cuba. Breckinridge Long, the assistant secretary of state responsible for refugee matters, had little sympathy for their plight and openly expressed the fear that open admission would result in more "fifth columnists" sneaking into the country in refugee guise.[63]

By summer 1942 the State Department had learned of Nazi plans to exterminate the Jews, but officials in Washington chose not to publicize the fact widely. There were various reasons for this, such as skepticism about atrocity stories because of the experience with propaganda in the previous war, public indifference to the mass murder that had happened so frequently in recent times—the Armenian massacres, the extermination of Russian kulaks, the bombing of Spanish Republicans, and the Chinese victims of Japanese aggression—and the utter implausibility that the Nazis would try to eliminate ten million people in a calculated plan of slaughter. Also, the Nazis did everything possible to suppress disclosure about the truth of the "resettlement" program in the East. Even prominent Jews in the United States and Britain were incredulous about the stories leaking out of Europe, and deeply divided as to how they should respond to the situation.[64]

All efforts to help the beleaguered Jews came to naught. A conference at Bermuda in April 1943 could not secure changes in American immigration laws to accommodate refugees, the British approval of Palestine as a Jewish haven, or a public denunciation of the treatment of European Jews. Top American leaders, including Roosevelt and Secretary of State Cordell Hull, were fearful of the political repercussions that might result from a flood of aliens, since public opinion surveys now revealed Jews to be even more unpopular than Germans or Japanese.[65] Moreover, the American government refused to transport refugees to the United States in the ships that had carried troops and war material to Europe even though this easily could have been done, while the military authorities ruled out North Africa as a refuge for Jews. U.S. officials opposed all moves to provide direct assistance in feeding and clothing people in the ghettos and death camps or to ransom Jews. Once the Allies had gained air superiority in 1944, they declined to raid the camps or bomb the railway lines leading to them. Even after the war ended, American efforts to feed and house the surviving Jews were ineffective, and thousands more died.[66]

Historian Henry Feingold observes that it was relatively easy to intern the Nisei, an event that had some parallels with the early stages of the German treatment of the Jews, whereas the Roosevelt administration was unable to move on the rescue front even when it wanted to.[67] Since the European Jews were a "foreign" minority and their counterparts at home were unpopular, to engage in a wholehearted campaign of rescue involved too great a political risk for Roosevelt. In other words, the American energy, resources, and will committed to saving Jews did not even begin to match the Nazi determination to liquidate them. Therefore the United States was guilty of moral complicity in the Holocaust, a charge that was made as early as 1943 by a respected magazine, the *Nation*:

> In this country, you and I and the President and the Congress and the State Department are accessories to the crime and share Hitler's guilt. If we had behaved like humane and generous people instead of complacent, cowardly ones, the two million

> lying today in the earth of Poland and Hitler's other crowded graveyards would be alive and safe. And other millions yet to die would have found sanctuary. We had it in our power to rescue this doomed people and we did not lift a hand to do it—or perhaps it would be fairer to say that we lifted just one cautious hand, encased in a tight-fitting glove of quotas and visas and affidavits, and a thick layer of prejudice.[68]

As the end of the war approached, the Western forces in Europe took captive thousands of Russians wearing German uniforms. The Germans had compelled some of these to serve, while others were anti-Soviets who fought in General A. A. Vlasov's "Russian Liberation Army" or similar collaborationist units. Also, there were thousands of Cossack émigrés who had fled to the West after the Bolshevik revolution and who two decades later had joined Hitler's armies in the vain hope of winning freedom for their homeland. Because of a desire to hold the fragile alliance together, the British and American authorities acceded to the Soviet request to repatriate Russians taken by their forces. The Soviets agreed to do likewise when they liberated American and British prisoners on their front. Most of the Russians captured during the great offensives of 1941–42 had suffered under the Nazi yoke and wished to go home, but many did not want to return to Stalin's tyranny, especially those who had chosen to fight against him.[69]

At the Yalta Conference in February 1945 a secret agreement was concluded that formalized the decision to return all Soviet citizens held by the British and Americans. This was intended to paper over the cracks of discord developing in the alliance, ensure a favorable settlement (from the Western standpoint) of the Polish situation, and facilitate the return of the Western prisoners. Some were aware that Stalin regarded as traitors all Russians who had surrendered to the Germans without fighting to the death, and they did not want to see British and American war prisoners treated the same by the Soviets.[70] After V-E Day the British and Americans held to their word and began transferring to Soviet control the two million Russian prisoners and displaced persons that were in western Germany and Austria.

What followed were incredibly shocking scenes, as Russians who expected to receive political asylum resisted the efforts of their Western captors to send them back. The riots, mass suicides, and repeated incidents where doomed men were clubbed and forced into railroad cars at gunpoint constituted a melancholy final chapter in the Allied war effort, one that was faintly reminiscent of the Holocaust. The full extent of the operation was covered up, the victims were lied to and deceived regarding their fate, and the military personnel involved in the operation excused themselves by pleading they were just "following orders."

Aleksandr Solzhenitsyn later exposed and excoriated the repatriation in *The Gulag Archipelago*. He pointed out that "very few of the war prisoners returned across the Soviet border as free men," even those who had not collaborated in any way whatsoever with their captors. In this as well as many of their other political actions Roosevelt's and Churchill's "consistent shortsightedness and stupidity stood out as astonishingly obvious."[71] As the Soviet writer put it: "What was the military or political sense in their surrendering to destruction at Stalin's hands hundreds of thousands of armed Soviet citizens determined not to surrender?" Solzhenitsyn adds that turning over the 90,000-man Cossack corps to the Soviets was an "act of double-dealing consistent with the spirit of traditional English diplomacy."[72] Undoubtedly he goes too far, but his accusations do reflect the underlying reality that the Western leaders were prepared to trade off these Russian lives in the chimerical hope they could secure Stalin's acceptance of a lasting political settlement.

That of course did not happen, but one lesson was learned from this deplorable episode. In May 1952 during the peace talks in the stalemated Korean War, the communist side pressed the United Nations for a return of all Chinese and North Korean prisoners without regard to their individual wishes and by force if necessary. The American negotiators flatly rejected the demand because it was repugnant to the values for which they were fighting. As a result, the final settlement was considerably delayed but an important principle was upheld.[73]

JUSTICE AND VIOLENCE

In a penetrating analysis French social critic Jacques Ellul brings to light the real tragedy of World War II, namely, that Christians simply did not function as Christians should. Ellul observes that they "conform to the trend of the moment without introducing into it *anything* specifically Christian. Their convictions are determined by their social milieu, not by faith in the revelation; they lack the uniqueness which ought to be the expression of that faith."[74] Thus, they just went along with the passions and prejudices of the day. They did nothing creative to counter the vindictive peace after World War I or the swelling tides of nationalism, materialism, and racism. To the contrary, as has been shown throughout this essay, far too many Christians conformed to the prevailing thinking and even gave it the blessing of the church.

In fact, Ellul sees Hitler as the real victor in the war. His movement loosed the reign of violence in the world, and his methods—concentration camps, racism (both black and white), torture of enemies, extermination of entire populations—"are used by all regimes today, whether of the right or left, whether capitalist or socialist." Ellul goes on to say: "That violence is so generally condoned today shows that Hitler won his war after all: his enemies imitate him."[75] The argument has considerable merit, and one may point to examples like the Soviet Gulag Archipelago, the French war in Algeria, the United States involvement in Vietnam, and the innumerable Third World revolutionaries and dictators, all of which made violence a way of life.

There is no doubt that the war had an unhealthy effect on American values. People screamed "kill Japs," rejoiced in the destruction of large cities and their inhabitants, and became hardened to the misery of suffering populations, whether they be Jews or the masses of "displaced persons" milling about Europe in 1945. It is worth mentioning that food rationing was lifted immediately at the war's end, and within a few months the level of American consumption soared to new heights, even though vast numbers were starving in war-torn Europe and Asia. Also, the United States entered the conflict ostensibly to secure liberty and justice for all, but at the same time it denied these rights to its nonwhite citizens.

Theologian Roger Shinn, who served as an enlisted man in the army, excellently captured the ironical nature of the war in a personal anecdote. His unit was in combat on the western front and had suffered several casualties when a group of Germans pretended to surrender and then opened fire. After this the order was given to take no prisoners. The company was understrength and could neither afford any more casualties nor spare any men to escort prisoners to the rear. Just then a German surrendered and the sergeant who commanded the platoon involved faced a dilemma. Although he had his orders, he did not want to kill the prisoner in cold blood, and so he went to the unit's chaplain for help.

This was the "spiritual counsel" the sergeant received: Whatever he did in the situation, he would be no more guilty than the millions back home who manufactured his weapons. They were all tools in the impersonal medium of war. The acceptance of war meant the endorsement of the ruthless practices that were inevitably part of it. The chaplain then told him he could not evade his orders, even though the act could never be considered "right." Here was the guilt that was part of war, but God stood for a different way of life than the cruelty of battle. So the soldier had to go do his job, regardless of how unpleasant it was to him personally.[76]

There were some Christians like Niebuhr who supported their country's involvement in terms of "agonized participation." Their thinking went like this: War itself cannot be an act of justice, but it may sometimes be necessary to forestall an even greater evil that might result from permitting a morally perverse power to gain political dominance. In such a case war must be conducted with contrition, recognizing one's own guilt, and kept free of vindictive hatred for the enemy. Military victory is not the end but only the means for clearing the way for political and social programs that will establish reasonable order and justice. Also, the rights of Christians who are conscientious objectors must be guaranteed, as they too bear witness to a truth in the gospel and help those who are engaged in the war to keep their actions in Christian perspective.[77]

Did the United States measure up to this exacting standard? It was able to eliminate the aggressive, evil Axis regimes, but the equally wicked system of Stalinist Russia came out of the war stronger than ever. Adequate preparations were not made for a just postwar order, and tension and violence have continued to dominate the international scene since 1945. However, America did well in its attitude toward the defeated enemies and magnanimously helped them back onto their feet. It worked with the United Nations and sided with the cause of colonial liberation, until the developing Cold War sapped enthusiasm for that. Contrition over the wartime neglect of the Jewish plight resulted in the firm support given the state of Israel, and the right of conscientious objection became firmly enshrined in law. The effort to secure international justice encouraged the racial groups denied it at home to press harder their demands for full civil rights.

On balance, it may be said that the violence of World War II has brought a measure of justice that did not exist before, but it is still short of that which the righteous creator and judge requires. The hope of perfect peace with justice for all lies yet in the future.

8 ROBERT G. CLOUSE

THE KOREAN AND VIETNAM WARS

> An informed Christian recognizes that Communism and Christianity are completely incompatible and that there is no "half-truth" or "passion for social justice" in Communism. . . . It is an international conspiracy of gangsters. The Communist system exists for the very purpose of enforcing an evil, consciously atheistic code of behavior. . . . Communist rulers are the Devil's representatives who are engaged in total war to spread their Red Hell throughout the globe.[1]

> To counteract Communism, we need *courageous action*. Firmness is the only thing which Communists understand. Firmness must be backed up by military strength and force. . . . We should remind the Communists of their treaties and our rights, and declare that we will maintain access to Berlin whatever comes, even if this means using atomic weapons.[2]

THUS DID TWO EVANGELICAL SPOKESMEN EXPRESS THE ATTITUDE towards communism that led to the Korean and Vietnamese conflicts. The policy of containing communist expansion, which these wars and the Cold War represent, has been heartily supported by most American Christians. The United States and her allies have been identified with a righteous purpose, while communism has been regarded as a horrible, almost demonic, evil.

Events since World War II might have unfolded in a different fashion. During the war, Russia and the United States worked together to defeat the Axis powers. When the war ended, the Soviet Union wanted to secure her own borders and weaken Germany, a land that had attacked Russia twice in the twentieth century. The United States, however, remembering the depression and chaos that had resulted from the treatment of Germany after World War I, sought to rebuild Europe. By the spring of 1946 it was clear that wartime cooperation had given way to confrontation between the two superpowers, the United States and the Soviet Union.

Not only did Russian aims for Germany conflict with those of America but also the establishment of communist dictatorships in Poland, Rumania, Bulgaria, Hungary, and Czechoslovakia upset the West. A new policy to check the Soviet menace known as "containment" was spelled out by George Kennan in 1947. He maintained that Soviet ideology portrays capitalism as the major enemy. Although the fall of capitalism is inevitable in the communist view, it is most important that Soviet socialist power be promoted and supported. The Kremlin is under no timetable to complete its conquest of the world, because it deals in ideological concepts that are valid over a long period of time. Thus the Russians will make tactical withdrawals when firm barriers are set up in the path of communist advance, since ultimate victory is certain.

Kennan believed that "the main element of any United States policy toward the Soviet Union must be that of a long-term, patient but firm and vigilant containment of Russian expansionist tendencies."[3] This did not mean threats and tough talk, but rather the "application of counterforce at a series of constantly shifting geographical and political points" where the Russians try to encroach upon other territories.[4] Such action would place the Soviet regime under a strain that eventually would lead to either internal breakup or the gradual mellowing of Soviet power.

The first move in the new policy of containment came in Greece. A revolt supported by the neighboring communist countries broke out in 1946. Because of the postwar economic crisis, the British were unable to furnish help to the area. Consequently, the United States responded with an offer of aid to Greece and Turkey. In a speech to Congress on March 12, 1947, the American president laid down the "Truman Doctrine." He noted that there would be no lasting peace "unless we are willing to help free people to maintain their free institutions and their national integrity against aggressive movements that seek to impose upon them totalitarian regimes." Arguing that it must be American policy to "support free peoples who are resisting attempted subjugation by armed minorities or by outside pressures," he asked Congress to vote economic aid to Greece and Turkey.[5] Not only was such help given but also the United States began to rebuild its own armed strength, which had dwindled after World War II. The defense of the Western world fell upon the shoulders of the United States, and the nation assumed global leadership without an adequate public discussion of the burdens and risks involved.

The Truman Doctrine was followed in 1948 by the economic side of containment, the Marshall Plan. The scheme provided over $13 billion in American aid to sixteen noncommunist European nations. A political alliance to thwart the growth of communism was also established in 1949 after a Soviet blockade of Berlin and the fall of Czechoslovakia. This collective security pact, known as the North Atlantic Treaty Organization, provided that an armed attack on one of the members was an attack on all regardless of whether the aggression came in Europe or North America. When the United States joined the Western European states in NATO it was the first "entangling alliance" ratified by Congress since George Washington's famous warning. The containment policy tended to draw hard and fast ideological lines not only in Europe but in other parts of the world as well. No effort was made to distinguish between various types of socialist beliefs or to ascertain the level of communist involvement in legitimate anticolonial activity. To President Truman and his secretary of state Dean Acheson, the USSR was the evil force responsible for turmoil and revolution everywhere. The belief that communism was a monolithic threat with sinister military strength was also the view accepted by President Eisenhower and John Foster Dulles.

World events tended to reinforce the Cold War outlook when the forces of Mao Tse-tung seized power in China in 1949. This event prompted a storm of criticism against the Truman administration. Republicans took the lead in asserting that failure in Asia was due to weakness and subversion in Washington. They felt that many communists or communist sympathizers were working for the Truman administration. To some extent, the president's decision to send troops to Korea was due to such attacks on his administration by political opponents. He also believed that Korea could be the "Greece of the Far East" where the communist advance could be stopped.

The situation that developed in Korea originated at the Cairo Conference of 1943, where it was decided that eventually the country would receive its independence. Two generations of Japanese rule, however, had left the Koreans without the necessary experience in self-government. Consequently, for five years the land was to be under the trusteeship of the United States, the Soviet Union, Britain, and China. When the Japanese surrendered in 1945, American and Soviet troops occupied the peninsula. For the sake of convenience, the two powers divided the country at the 38th parallel. The Cold War froze this temporary boundary, and two competing regimes developed, each supported in its claim over the entire country by one of the superpowers. In the south was the Republic of Korea under Syngman Rhee, while in the north was the Democratic Peoples' Republic of Korea led by Kim Il-Sung.

American and Soviet troops were withdrawn in 1949 and the United Nations tried unsuccessfully to mediate between the two Korean governments. Meanwhile the Soviets equipped the North Korean army, and in the summer of 1950 eight divisions crossed the 38th parallel in order to "liberate" the south.[6] The United Nations branded the move as a breach of the peace and called on its members to aid the Republic of Korea to repel the attack. Although fifteen nations sent troops to fight under UN leadership, most of the forces were composed of Americans and South Koreans. The UN commander, General Douglas MacArthur, reported only to President Truman and later stated that he had no "direct" connection with the international body. For America, the method of involvement in the conflict, by means of a UN request rather than a conventional declaration of war, set an ominous precedent. The president acted unwisely when he did not consult with Congress before making key decisions and when he failed to obtain a declaration of support from that body. The Republican leader, Robert A. Taft, was one of the few who realized that the future could well hold more "presidential wars."

At the outset, the North Korean forces were victorious but MacArthur's brilliant Inchon landings behind the enemy lines soon took the war north of the 38th parallel. What started as a policy of containment now turned into a war of "liberation" as the UN forces occupied the northern half of the peninsula. MacArthur's forces reached the Yalu River on the border of Manchuria. At this point the Chinese intervened and sent hundreds of thousands of "volunteers" to stop the offensives. Within eight weeks the communists had pushed south once again. Later the UN forces recovered, and by January 1951 the fighting had stabilized near the 38th parallel. After two years of negotiations an armistice was signed on June 27, 1953, with the line of partition about where it had been in 1950.

Meanwhile, a bitter controversy over Cold War strategy broke out in the United States. In December 1950 President Truman, in consultation with Great Britain, had decided to abandon the objective of uniting Korea and to defend only the land south of the 38th parallel. The policy would be that of "limited war" in order to avoid accidentally precipitating a third world war. MacArthur, however, insisted that the conflict should be carried into Manchuria. He publicly protested against the political limitation on his freedom of military action. On April 11, 1951, Truman dismissed the general for insubordination, an action that caused a widespread protest among the American public. MacArthur returned home to a hero's welcome. In a speech to Congress he called for an economic and naval blockade of China as a prelude to further military action against her. Despite an outpouring of emotional support for the general, subsequent hearings by congressional committees supported the president's actions. Important military spokesmen such as George Marshall and Omar Bradley also defended the concept of limited war.

Perhaps from the point of view of the containment policy the Korean War could be seen as a victory. Communist aggression had been repelled while total war was averted. The conflict also stimulated the growth of collective security to hold back communism. The United States and its allies pushed ahead with rearmament and either created new defense pacts or strengthened existing systems. However, from another point of view the division of Korea was unnatural and remained a seedbed for later quarrels. The repressive regime in the north was matched by an authoritarian state in the south. American troops were forced to remain on duty there and constituted a continuing drain on national resources.

Although attention was focused on the Korean War, during the same period, in a more quiet fashion, the United States became involved in Vietnam. Americans had never been very interested in Southeast Asia. President Franklin D. Roosevelt had opposed French colonialism in the area; he felt that the French should not be allowed to reoccupy Indochina after the defeat of Japan. Roosevelt understood the situation correctly, because the Vietnamese had been trying to throw off the colonialist yoke ever since World War I.[7] Over one hundred thousand Vietnamese soldiers and laborers were sent to Europe during that war, and on their return they brought a knowledge of the West and a desire to improve conditions in their homeland. The French tried to satisfy some of their demands by authorizing elected assemblies, but these were chosen by such a small electorate that they did little to quiet the unrest. In 1925 a young revolutionary named Nguyen Ai Quoc (Ho Chi Minh) founded the Revolutionary Youth League, which became the nucleus for the future Indochinese Communist Party.[8] Ho was educated in France, where he became a Marxist, and only later did he travel to Moscow. For the rest of his life he was to show a single-minded dedication to the cause of revolution in Vietnam. In 1927 Ho joined with a number of other Vietnamese revolutionaries to form the Vietnam Quoc Dan Dang, or VNQDD, with the advice and assistance of the Kuomintang Party of China. The VNQDD fomented a series of uprisings in 1930, which the French ruthlessly suppressed. Villages were strafed and bombed, prisoners tortured, hostages executed, and finally almost the entire leadership of the VNQDD was caught and liquidated.

In 1933 a new emperor, Bao Dai, returned from his schooling in France. (The French continued to keep a puppet emperor on the throne during the years they occupied the land.) The imperial court was for a short time a center of attempts to loosen French control. Ngo Dien Diem, a reform-minded nationalist, was appointed minister of the interior and also made secretary of a commission on reform. When he realized the insincerity of the French, he resigned in disgust and went into exile. World War II brought Japanese control to Vietnam, but they ruled through the French and little change occurred. In fact, it should be noted that the French were the only Western power to retain control in Asia during World War II. When defeat in the conflict appeared imminent, the Japanese promoted the establishment of an independent Vietnamese government at Hue in 1945.

The independent Vietnamese state that the Japanese encouraged Bao Dai to form had a serious rival in the north. In late 1944, Ho Chi Minh, who had been directing guerrilla activity in northern Vietnam during the war, formed a provisional government and was chosen president of the Vietnamese Republic. The Chinese refused to let French troops go north of the 16th parallel after the fall of Japan, and this helped Ho to consolidate his regime. In March 1946 the French recognized the northern republic and promised to hold a referendum in the south to see if the country could be unified. They hoped to make the Indochinese Federation part of a worldwide French Union on the order of the British Commonwealth of Nations. This scheme did not gain much support in Vietnam, so France organized a separate state in Cochinchina and declined to hold the election. The Vietnamese reply to this was to attack the French garrisons in 1946. The leadership in the fight for independence was taken by the Vietminh organization of Ho Chi Minh, which aligned with more moderate resistance groups.

The French persuaded Bao Dai to head an opposition government. However, Dai's dependence upon foreigners and the fact that he continued to live the life of a playboy in France cost him a great deal of support. Still, there was considerable anticommunist sentiment behind his government, especially among the Catholics of Tongking and the different religious sects in the area of Saigon. The Tongking Roman Catholics numbered two and one-half million out of a population of nine million. The bishops held political as well as religious power in the rural villages, and they organized militia units to fight the communists. Bao Dai and his representatives distrusted these forces and refused to cooperate with them. The religious sects in the south were another potentially powerful force that Bao Dai and his troops did not care to encourage. These exotic sects included some like the Caodaists, who had their own hierarchy, including a pope and cardinals, and a theology that combined Buddhist and Christian elements and featured such patron saints as Victor Hugo. Only one sect found favor with Bao Dai, namely, the Xuan, which operated a Mafialike organization in the Saigon area that controlled such activities as prostitution and gambling. Another obstacle was the French demand that the Vietnamese army should not be allowed to organize into its own large forces, but its soldiers must rather serve in small companies with the Europeans.

Thus the Bao Dai government was handicapped by internal dissension and French caution, while Ho Chi Minh received considerable help from his communist allies. Many feel that Ho was forced to rely on the Chinese and the Russians because of the pro-French stance of the United States. By 1947 the Truman administration had dropped the American anticolonialist position toward Indochina, because it concluded that the Vietnamese revolutionaries were not to be trusted. Despite Ho's penchant for quoting Jefferson and his indication that Vietnam would be a "fertile field for American capital and enterprise," the United States supported the French in Southeast Asia. Frightened by the domino theory and eager for French cooperation in Europe, the United States began its support of a colonial war in Asia.

The major American concern in the postwar world was to rebuild Western Europe. Early in 1950 Washington agreed to fund the major part of the Indochinese conflict in return for French support for the economic revival of Germany as an anchor of anticommunism in Europe. With the beginning of hostilities in Korea, France's war in Vietnam was perceived by the American government as part of the worldwide confrontation between communism and the free world. The loss of Vietnam, it was believed, would lead to the collapse of the other nations of Southeast Asia. First employed to justify aid to Greece in 1947, this "domino theory" once applied to Southeast Asia quickly became an article of faith. The easy acceptance of this theory reflects the experience of World War II, when Hitler's forces overran Western Europe in three months and the Japanese conquered Southeast Asia in even less time.

It now seems that the assumptions upon which American policy was based during the French phrase of the Vietnam War were wrong. The Southeast Asian revolution was not inspired by Moscow but by nationalism. Although both the Russians and the Chinese tried to control the Vietnamese, they were not able to accomplish this. The psychology of the Cold War, with its virulent anticommunism, helped to transform the French attempt to reestablish their colonial power in Asia into a crusade against communism. As Alexander Kendrick states:

> The Sino-Soviet treaty and Peking's support of Hanoi, taken in conjunction with developments in Europe—Soviet consolidation of a Communist bloc, the 1948 Communist coup in Czechoslovakia, the Berlin blockade and the Allied airlift, the formation of the rival NATO and Warsaw Treaty organizations—helped transform the French colonial war in Indochina,

a war of guilt and shame to many in France, into a salient of the worldwide anti-Communist deployment of the United States. It became not only justified, for the sake of "Western civilization," but even moral.[9]

When the French military effort in Vietnam began in 1946, the French had every assurance of a quick victory. However, Ho understood the conflict better when he predicted, "If ever the tiger [Vietminh] pauses the elephant [France] will impale him on his mighty tusks. But the tiger will not pause and the elephant will die of exhaustion and loss of blood."[10] The Vietminh evaded major engagements and launched surprise attacks in places where they were assured of victory. Ho's forces came to dominate the countryside while the French held the major towns and cities. By 1950 Mao Tse-tung had recognized the revolutionary government in Vietnam. Communist recognition brought more than moral support and before long there were camps in South China where Vietminh forces were taught to use modern weapons. These newly trained troops enabled Ho to change his tactics from guerilla warfare to open battles with large concentrations of manpower. To prevent the movement of Ho's forces out of Hanoi to the west and south, the French had placed a garrison at Dien Bien Phu. In the spring of 1954 this fortress was besieged and captured. Not only did the Vietminh win a decisive military victory when this center was overrun but also they scored a decisive psychological success against the French. This enabled the Vietnamese to obtain a settlement at a conference in Geneva (May to July 1954) that ended the sixty-year domination of France over the area. There were representatives at this meeting from Britain, the Soviet Union, France, the United States, China, Cambodia, and Laos as well as the French-backed South Vietnamese government and the North Vietnamese Democratic Republic.

The decisions reached at this conference included the following: (1) Vietnam was to be divided temporarily along the 17th parallel until general elections could be held in July 1956 to reunify the country; (2) French troops were to be withdrawn from the north; (3) the Vietnamese people were to have three hundred days to move to either the north or south zone as they chose; (4) military personnel and supplies were not to be increased in either zone; (5) an International Control Commission consisting of India, Canada, and Poland was to see that these agreements were followed; and (6) Laos and Cambodia were to be established as independent nations. Although the United States did not sign these agreements, it did promise to refrain from the use of force to disturb the Geneva settlement.

As a result of these accords, there was a dramatic move of approximately one million mostly Catholic refugees from North Vietnam to the south. These people had enjoyed a privileged status under the French, and since they had fought against the Vietminh, they feared reprisals. The United States sent a team to aid the refugees, and one of the young naval officers assigned to this duty was Thomas A. Dooley. He came not only on a naval assignment but also as a Roman Catholic Christian who sympathized with his fellow Catholics. Tom Dooley's experiences led him to become a writer, and he came to exert considerable influence on American public opinion. According to the Gallup poll of 1960, he was one of the ten most admired Americans. Kendrick observes:

> To Dooley, with his penchant for vivid prose, the mainly Catholic resettlers were making "the epic Passage to Freedom" from "terror-ridden North Vietnam." The American presence in Vietnam as he saw it was based on "gentleness." "We had come late to Vietnam but we had come," he wrote, "and we brought not bombs and guns but help and love." In contrast to American generosity and friendship were "the godless cruelties of Communism."[11]

Tragically mistaken about the realities of Southeast Asia, this young man believed that America had not really been involved in Vietnam. Actually, during the years 1950 to 1954 the United States had given the French $2.6 billion to restore European control in the area. Depending too much on ill-informed opinions like Dooley's, America increased her commitment and gave large amounts of aid directly to the government of South Vietnam. Many believed that this area could be developed into an Asian counterpart to West Germany.

However, South Vietnam continued to be racked with problems. In addition to the difficulties of the refugees from the north, there were still communists in the south and sects such as the Caodaists who considered themselves autonomous. The need for effective leadership caused Bao Dai to ask Ngo Dinh Diem to become prime minister in 1954. Diem acted in a vigorous manner to secure the withdrawal of French troops, to put down the rebellious sects, and to stall the election for reunification of the country. By 1955 he had become head of state in place of Bao Dai and replaced the empire with a republic. From this date the United States assumed the role of the French in supporting the government of South Vietnam. With the establishment of the republic the people of the south had expected economic development and social reform. This was slow to come, and aside from an improvement in the legal status of women, which was passed at the insistence of his sister-in-law, Madame Nhu, Diem made few improvements. To an ever increasing degree his goal became simply the abolition of opposition so that orderly reform could be carried out in his own way. Diem also halted exports to the north, and since the rice production of South Vietnam was necessary to feed the industrial population of the north, this was a serious blow. Finally, his refusal to allow elections in 1956 sparked the resumption of intensive guerilla warfare in the country. It should be remembered that the Geneva agreements did not provide for two Vietnams but rather for a truce in order that something other than a military solution could be found for the nation. Now it looked as though the only hope for those noncommunist opponents of the southern regime lay in the use of violence. Thus the insurgents at first were not primarily communists, but rather members of religious sects, Buddhists, and former Vietminh fighters who would have been annihilated by Diem's policy of crushing the opposition. The North Vietnamese entered the conflict in the south only after the factions in the south itself had started fighting.

While the southern part of the country continued to suffer the agonies of civil war, North Vietnam rebuilt her economy with Soviet and Chinese aid. Land was consolidated into collective farms, and while the industrial output increased, food production did not. The Lao Dang, or Workers Party, tightened its hold on North Vietnamese life, especially with the establishment of a new school system. Morale was high enough and prosperity sufficiently adequate that Ho was able to aid the guerrillas in the south.[12]

Although Diem's government was never very popular in South Vietnam, it certainly was well received in the United States. Senator John Kennedy called it "the cornerstone of the Free World in Southeast Asia, the keystone in the arch, the finger in the dike," and predicted that if the "red tide of Communism" should pour into it, the rest of Asia would be threatened. Not only was its economy essential to all Southeast Asia, but its "political liberty" was an "inspiration to those seeking to obtain or maintain their liberty in all parts of Asia—and indeed of the world."[13] The building of a strong, prosperous nation-state in South Vietnam became one of the major goals of American foreign policy. Upset over the Geneva accords, the United States was to look on Vietnam and the SEATO alliance as a possible basis for military action in the area if it should prove necessary.

To ensure the survival of the Diem government, the United States poured over $1 billion in economic and military assistance into South Vietnam between 1955 and 1961. By the late 1950s there were over 1,500 American advisors in the country. Most of the aid program focused on building an effective army to deal with both internal subversion and a possible invasion from the north. Other significant results of the American help included the rebuilding of highways, railways, and canals as well as improvements in agriculture and education. However, much of the aid money was wasted on consumer goods. An observer concluded in 1963 that the progam had turned into a large-scale relief project. The assistance made Vietnam dependent upon the United States, but it did not build a foundation for a genuinely independent state. While attention was focused on economic and military matters, the Americans tended to ignore politics, perhaps the most important aspect of nation building. Despite the acceptance of a constitution that made provisions for a president and a legislature elected by popular vote, Diem was determined to rule with an iron hand. He believed that the people should be controlled by those who knew what was best for them.

By the time John F. Kennedy became president, Diem's regime was in a great deal of trouble. Kennedy had previously taken a personal interest in Vietnam and came to feel that it was a test case of America's resolve to honor its commitments and to meet the new threat of communist subversion of third world nations. Other events such as the Bay of Pigs debacle, the United States's recognition of a neutralist regime in Laos, and his acceptance of the Berlin Wall seemed to make a strong stand in Vietnam necessary. In May 1961, Kennedy sent 400 Special Forces and 100 military advisors to Saigon. Urged on by close associates such as Walt Rostow and by Vice President Lyndon Johnson, he applied the domino theory to Vietnam and increased the United States's commitment to 15,000 troops in 1963. Much of this was done secretly, because it violated the Geneva accords.

The introduction of American men and weapons into the war on a larger scale gave a boost to South Vietnamese morale. The government forces (ARVN) conducted extensive operations against the guerrillas (Vietcong) in 1962. This new spirit on the part of Diem's forces proved to be short lived, and by 1963 the Vietcong regained the military initiative. Many Americans were increasingly disturbed by the techniques used in the military operations in Vietnam. It was difficult to tell the difference between innocent civilians and guerrillas, and ARVN soldiers did not exert much effort to make such distinctions. Civilians were killed, villages were bombed and strafed, and napalm and defoliants were widely used. Later, when the fighting was taken over by American forces, the Americans adopted these same techniques.

Diem proved incapable of handling the revolution in his land, and finally even the United States deserted him. In November 1963, three weeks before the assassination of President Kennedy, Diem and close members of his family were killed by a coup led by his own anticommunist generals. The death of Diem led to a period of political chaos in Saigon, but a series of military governments finally were able to keep the land under control.

Some have expressed the view that John Kennedy would have revised his policy in Southeast Asia and reduced American involvement if he had lived. Whatever his ultimate intentions might have been, he left to his successor, Lyndon Johnson, a more difficult situation than he himself had inherited from Eisenhower. Johnson assured the Vietnamese of American support and, while running as a "peace" candidate against Barry Goldwater in 1964, approved secret operations in Vietnam that included air reconnaissance and destroyer patrols. An enemy attack upon American naval units operating in North Vietnamese waters in August led to the speedy and nearly unanimous congressional approval of the Gulf of Tonkin resolution. This vague statement granted the president the power "to take all necessary measures to repel any armed attack against the forces of the United States and to prevent further aggression."[14] President Johnson used this resolution to justify a major buildup of American forces in Southeast Asia. During 1964 American troop strength in Vietnam increased from 16,000 to 23,300. In February 1965, a Vietcong attack that killed 8 Americans and wounded 109 led to Operation Rolling Thunder, a campaign of extensive bombing of North Vietnam. Instead of ending the war as the administration had promised, the bombing led Ho's government to send more men into the south. In response, the American presence grew to 35,000 men in May 1965, 120,000 in September, and 184,000 by the end of the year. During 1965–68 United States generals in Southeast Asia continued to argue that more men and planes would enable them to win the war. Lyndon Johnson usually gave them what they wanted, without bothering to tell the American people. Finally, General William C. Westmoreland, the supreme field commander for Vietnam, requested 542,000 men in June 1966 and promised complete victory within eighteen months. The increase in troop strength enabled the United States to take over most combat operations in the war during 1966–67, while ARVN forces were assigned to "pacification" of the countryside.

In the meantime a new military government headed by Nguyen Van Thieu and Nguyen Cao Ky had taken over in South Vietnam. By this time the traditional bases of Vietnamese society, the village and the family, were largely eroded. Much of the population of the country was living in slums near army installations or near cities like Saigon. American military and social involvement created a new kind of colonialism in Southeast Asia. As Francis Fitzgerald noted:

> So when Americans often—I mean, I'm talking about, I don't know, colonels or aid representatives—would say with all goodness of heart that they were trying to help the Vietnamese, trying to build wells, trying to start chicken production or so on, they didn't see this very fundamental principle, that the people they were dealing with were being pulled farther and farther away from their own society. In the end what happened was that we recruited almost everybody into the army or the bureaucracy. There was something like a million men in the South Vietnamese army and in a population of eighteen million that means about all of the ablebodied men; and so what we'd done was simply as it were hired them. It went no further than that.[15]

Another development as the war escalated under the Johnson administration was the use of heavy planes for bombing missions against Vietnam. Individuals such as Bernard Fall felt that the huge aircraft, originally intended for dropping nuclear bombs on the Soviet Union, changed the moral and the military character of the war. He believed that unlimited aerial warfare by B-52s denied all the high-sounding claims for American involvement in exchange for a military victory by destruction. Flown from places as far away as Guam, these planes released their bombs from thirty thousand feet on South as well as North Vietnam, hitting unseen targets that included industrial installations, infantry units, and jungle hideouts as well as houses, roads, bicycles, trucks, and civilians. Despite the expense, which reached $6 billion in lost aircraft alone by 1968, Washington retained its faith in the efficiency of aerial bombardment. By the end of the war the Americans had dropped 7.4 million tons of bombs on Vietnam. Alexander Kendrick describes the mechanized, impersonal nature of these attacks in the following manner:

> The B-52s, chauffeured by skilled young technicians, went out in waves over both North and South Vietnam, blowing huge craters in the terrain below. From heights of 30,000 to 50,000 feet the air strikes came without warning. The big machines fixed their targets by radar and dropped their bombs without seeing where they fell. In the long slow flight from Guam the crews ate TV dinners and blueberry pies from the commissary, warmed up in galley ovens. The six men of a B-52 crew, remote from the reality of the war, acted as an extension of the computer which governed their plane. They constituted the most detached and impersonal operation in the history of warfare. The triumph of technology was complete.[16]

The large-scale bombing of Vietnam created other problems as well. Captured American airmen gave the communists hostages, who became ever more important in the stalemated war. Also, the continued bombing of a small, backward nation by the world's strongest military power furnished North Vietnam with an excellent propaganda theme. In addition, opposition to the war within the United States was galvanized by the aerial warfare. In October 1965, 70,000 people marched and attended rallies in sixty cities, and the following month another 30,000 participated in a march on Washington to demonstrate for peace in Vietnam. President Johnson responded by sending representatives to various foreign capitals to secure support and to try to contact the North Vietnamese so that talks leading to a negotiated peace could begin.

As frustration and stalemate increased, many Americans in key places joined members of the press in opposition to the conflict. Several liberal congressmen condemned the tragic, undeclared war. By 1967, Secretary of Defense Robert McNamara had become disenchanted and left the Pentagon to become head of the World Bank. His successor, Clark Clifford, was supposed to be committed to the conflict, but he soon became a leading spokesman for disengagement.

The tragic story of Vietnam reached a climax for most Americans during the period from January through March 1968. The turning point of the war, the Tet offensive, began on January 30, when the Vietcong launched a series of attacks on the major cities of South Vietnam. In Saigon they struck the U.S. embassy, Tan Son Nhut airport, the headquarters of the ARVN general staff, and the presidential palace. The town of Hue was occupied by the Vietcong, and it took three weeks of heavy fighting to recapture it. During the Tet offensive an estimated 32,000 insurgents were killed, while American losses reached 4,114 dead, 19,275 wounded, and 604 missing. In addition the South Vietnamese forces lost 2,300 dead and 23,000 captured. Whatever optimism had been created by official reports that the war was going well was wiped out by the Tet campaign. The American command claimed that enemy losses in the offensive were so heavy that it represented a victory for the United States and its ally. However, the added social dislocation and the need to withdraw ARVN forces from the countryside to secure the cities raised grave doubts about this interpretation. As one writer has concluded: "As with much of the war, there was a great deal of destruction and suffering, but no clearcut winner or loser."[17]

The administration had given the American public unduly optimistic reports about the war, and consequently the Tet battles were a great shock that widened an already large credibility gap. In March, Senator Eugene McCarthy, a strong opponent of the war, won 42 percent of the New Hampshire Democratic primary vote compared to Johnson's 49 percent. On March 31, the president announced over national television that the bombing would cease, negotiations would begin, and that he had withdrawn from the presidential race. By this time, the true cost of the war in both lives and national treasure was becoming apparent to everyone. The president's approval rating had been below 50 percent for two years, and the Great Society that he had proclaimed was in shambles. He had promised Americans guns and butter, but domestic programs were continually sacrificed to pay for rising military expenses. These cuts led to increased resentment and bitterness among those whose hopes had been stirred by the president's speeches. Johnson also opposed efforts to raise taxes so that the costs of war could be met. As a result the national debt increased to over $300 billion during the 1960s and prices soared because of the inflation caused by the deficit.

While the period after Tet brought pressure against the war at home, in Southeast Asia there was a heightening of Vietnamese-American tension. The South Vietnamese felt that the Americans were planning to desert them, and the U.S. servicemen, frustrated by a war they could not win, began to show hatred toward all Vietnamese. The murder of over three hundred men, women, and children in the village of My Lai by an American company under the command of Lieutenant William Calley in March 1968 demonstrated the depth of this hostility. By the spring of the same year peace talks began in Paris between North Vietnam and the United States. Despite this activity Lyndon Johnson's preferred candidate, Hubert Humphrey, was defeated in his bid for the presidency by Richard Nixon. The Republican was able to benefit from the Vietnam issue without revealing how he proposed to end the war. Once in office, his peace plan turned out to be a vague attempt to have the Russians put pressure on the North Vietnamese to negotiate with the Americans. Although he promised "peace with honor," Nixon pursued the same goal as his predecessor, namely the establishment of an independent, noncommunist state in South Vietnam. This was to be achieved by a massive military buildup of the Saigon government and by applying the same kinds of pressure on the North that had failed so often before. The result was four more years of war in Southeast Asia and a period of domestic strife in the United States.

To disarm his critics, Nixon began to withdraw U.S. forces from Vietnam in early 1969. At the same time he used sporadic violence to try to win concessions from the enemy. Meanwhile, negotiations continued in Paris in an effort to stop the fighting. Total American troop strength in Vietnam declined from a peak of 543,400 in January 1969 to 415,000 at the end of 1970, to 239,000 a year later, and to only 48,000 at the close of 1972.

Despite the reduction in troops, Nixon enlarged the geographical extent of the war by offensives into Cambodia and Laos. The purpose of these campaigns was to deny sanctuary to enemy forces and to cut off supply routes.

The periodic use of force to try to secure what he considered a just negotiated peace was Nixon's method of operation during his first presidential term. The main task of working out a settlement was not accomplished at the Paris peace talks; rather, it was achieved through secret negotiations between the North Vietnamese representative, Le Duc Tho, and Nixon's national security advisor, Henry Kissinger. A settlement was almost reached in June 1971, but Hanoi's continued desire to discuss political as well as military matters made agreement impossible. To secure a stronger position for the United States, Nixon negotiated detente with China and the Soviet Union. These steps tended to isolate the North Vietnamese and to limit the support they could expect from other communist lands. Early in 1972 the president's visit to China led to agreements that ended two decades of hostility between that land and the United States. Because Moscow and Peking did not trust each other, it was obvious to most observers that the old Cold War view of a world divided between a monolithic communism and the "free world" no longer had any validity.

The Nixon-Kissinger diplomacy seemed to accomplish its goals. When the United States bombed Hanoi and Haiphong and mined the North Vietnamese harbors, neither communist nation interfered. The war dragged on into the fall of 1972 when Nixon promised that it would not be an election issue. Despite such assurances Kissinger announced on October 26 that peace was at hand. The Democratic candidate, George McGovern, denounced this as a trick, and nothing came of the peace talks. After the election, in December 1972, the United States resumed the heavy bombing of Hanoi-Haiphong for twelve days. By late January 1973, American and North Vietnamese representatives in Paris signed an armistice. The agreement had the effect of allowing the North to take over the South either through elections or military action. Kissinger was later to remark that if one group of Vietnamese proved superior "that is no American concern." Despite years of angry words, blood, and death the domino theory was forgotten and the United States simply gave up in Southeast Asia. Following a "decent interval," in the spring of 1975 North Vietnamese troops overran the south and unified the land under communist control.

Looking back over the conflict, one may well ask how a Christian should react to Vietnam. At the time most believers supported the war, but a vocal minority spoke against it. It was in fact a rather easy conflict to criticize. There was no issue such as slavery or a Pearl Harbor attack to draw America into a costly Asian war. The conflict had a vague beginning, unclear objectives, and an inconclusive ending. When American troops withdrew, the political situation was about what it had been twenty years before. Little had been accomplished to justify the expenditure of so much treasure and so many lives. Driven on by the rhetoric of a moral crusade against communism, America had allowed a minor colonial struggle to reach grotesque proportions. Several examples of this miscalculation stand out: the cost of the war in 1968 and again in 1969 had risen to at least nine times the value of North Vietnam's gross national product; the largest American overseas airbase was built at Long Binh, Vietnam, where it covered 17,000 acres, an area larger than the entire city of Saigon; the cost of the Vietnam War has been estimated by the government at $140 billion, which is approximately 242 percent of the value of all American aid to underdeveloped countries in the world from 1945 to 1970. Robert Stevens concludes:

> In other words, the United States government spent almost 2½ times as much fighting for the status quo in one small underdeveloped country as it spent "promoting economic development" in all less developed countries in a quarter of a century.[18]

Not only did the war represent a gigantic waste of lives and resources but it also devastated the land America was ostensibly trying to save. Vietnam was blasted with a severity almost unparalleled in the history of warfare. Napalm, white phosphorus bombs, rockets, antipersonnel devices, chemical warfare—a whole science fiction arsenal was unleashed on Southeast Asia. The war moved steadily toward a systems analysis, body count, automated approach. As one writer described the mentality:

> One of the Westmoreland improvements to the science of war was the body count, described by another general as an attempt to overcome the Vietnamese birth rate. . . . The body count made its victims impersonal by turning them into statistics.

There were only "gooks," "slopes," or at most "oriental human beings."[19]

Because the Vietcong lived like "fish" in the "sea of people" it was necessary to destroy villages and relocate their inhabitants. Correspondents noticed the revulsion felt by American soldiers who were ordered to burn villages and shoot chickens, ducks, water buffalo, and pets. One observer remarked:

> I simply cannot help worrying that, in the process of waging this war, we are corrupting ourselves. I wonder, when I look at the bombed-out peasant hamlets, the orphans begging and stealing on the street of Saigon, and the women and children with napalm burns lying on the hospital cots, whether the United States or any nation has the right to inflict this suffering and degradation on other people for its own ends.[20]

When the Vietnam War veterans returned to the United States they brought the physical and psychological burdens of the conflict home to Americans. Individuals twisted by brutality and violence had a difficult time adjusting to a peaceful society.

Another obvious casualty of the war was the failure of Lyndon Johnson's Great Society. The conflict in Southeast Asia won out over the war on poverty in two ways. First, it distracted the attention of the president and his top aides away from domestic issues to Vietnam, and consequently it deprived the antipoverty program of the leadership that it needed to survive. Second, after 1965 Great Society programs were hurt because of funding cuts to provide money for the war in Vietnam. The war proved to be much more expensive than President Johnson thought it would be. The compromise he tried to strike between "guns and butter" could not be maintained. As an economist points out:

> At first he tried to protect the war against poverty . . . from being overbalanced by the war in Vietnam. But his failure to accomplish this impossible balancing act brought on the worst of both worlds: inflation for the economy and disappointment for those who had believed him when he promised to fight the war against poverty.[21]

The year 1966 saw the abandonment of President Johnson's domestic reform. In January 1965 the administration had urged Congress to double appropriations for the war on poverty, but a year later the president's economic message scarcely mentioned the antipoverty crusade. The domestic situation was overshadowed by the struggle in Vietnam. The Office of Economic Opportunity received about $1.5 billion during the 1965–66 fiscal year but $1.6 billion in 1966–67. Because the agency was new and its activities were expanding at a rapid pace, the slight increase in budget forced a cutback in its program. This was a drastic blow to an agency in its third year of life. The war that mattered to the administration was the one against a small Asian land rather than the one against poverty in America. Because of continuing reductions, a malaise of despair and disappointment swept through the Office of Economic Opportunity. James Reston expressed the mood in 1967 when he wrote that the problem of poverty in the United States "is defined; the programs all have vivid names; the machinery, still new and imperfect, is nevertheless in place; but the funds are lamentably inadequate to the gigantic scope of the problem."[22] As John C. Donovan explained:

> The conclusion is inescapable. Lyndon Baines Johnson became so involved in a war in Vietnam which he did not start and which he did not want that he soon lost sight of the war on poverty which he initiated and which only he could lead if it were to be fought with courage and skill. A controversial social welfare program . . . became particularly vulnerable to Congressional and bureaucratic controls—and to local political resistance—once presidential leadership was deflected.[23]

If one considers what might have happened had America's resources been used to deal with domestic problems rather than being squandered in a foreign war, then the tragedy of Vietnam takes on an enormous significance. Based upon statistics provided by Arthur Okun, a former chairman of the Council of Economic Advisors, the conclusion is obvious that the government would have had $11 billion more a year by 1969 to spend on civilian projects if the nation had not been engaged in the Vietnam War.[24] This amount could have eliminated poverty in the United States. Whether the funds would have been used in this manner cannot be known, but such expenditures would have been possible. The entire quality of life in the United States might have been transformed. The poor could have entered the mainstream of the land rather than remaining in a subculture of hopelessness, drugs, violence, and crime. Martin Luther King, Jr., called the war

"America's tragic distraction" as he explained:

> There is at the outset a very obvious and almost facile connection between the war in Vietnam and the struggle I and others have been waging in America. A few years ago there was a shining moment in that struggle. It seemed as if there was a real promise of hope for the poor, both black and white, through the poverty program. There were experiments, hopes, new beginnings. Then came the buildup in Vietnam, and I watched the program broken and eviscerated as if it were some idle political plaything of a society gone mad on war, and I knew that America would never invest the necessary funds or energies in rehabilitation of its poor so long as adventures like Vietnam continued to draw men and skills and money like some demonical destructive suction tube. And so I was increasingly compelled to see the war not only as a moral outrage but also as an enemy of the poor, and to attack it as such.[25]

It was also during the Vietnam War that Washington developed the habit of governing by dishonesty. Senator Taft had pointed out at the time of the Korean War that there was a grave danger of further "presidential wars," future conflicts when the executive branch would involve the nation in military action without the considered judgment of the Congress. The Vietnamese conflict certainly developed in such a fashion. The irony of the situation is that congressional support could have been secured, because in the early 1960s the government's policies were supported by the majority of the population. At that time there was a national Cold War consensus developed by the three leading recent secretaries of state: Dean Acheson, John Foster Dulles, and Dean Rusk. It should not be forgotten that the only two men to challenge the anticommunist approach by voting against the Gulf of Tonkin Resolution, Senators Gruening and Morse, were both defeated in the next election.

Despite the initial public support for the war, much of the buildup of troops and materials in Southeast Asia was done in secret by the Johnson administration. While official statements pointed to "the light at the end of the tunnel" and gave optimistic predictions about the time for the end of the conflict, the Indochina situation required a constantly growing commitment on the part of the United States. Gradually, as the war dragged on the cold war political consensus dissolved. It became necessary to conduct the conflict in a secret manner. It was almost as if the president had two constituencies: on the one hand the American people who elected him, and on the other a military–foreign-policy establishment that defined the national interest and suggested the strategy for conducting the Cold War. When the interests of these two groups clashed, it was almost a foregone conclusion that the civilian side would lose. Robert Warren Stevens describes the overwhelming influence of the military–foreign-policy group:

> [Their] claims are typically couched in terms of sweeping, simplistic slogans, and they are articulated by men who exude a strong sense of mission ("save the world from communism"). Moreover, they are advanced by men who have been rigorously trained to spare no effort in looking for threats and in devising strategies to preempt them. In such circumstances a President, perhaps without being aware of it, slips into the language of military strategy and into calculations of probability, adopting unconsciously a technology-oriented approach to the subtleties and nuances of international relations.[26]

In order to carry out the plans suggested by the foreign policy establishment it was necessary for the president to deceive the voters who placed him in the White House. During the Johnson era the difference between what the administration said and what it did was called "the credibility gap." Many Americans agreed with Senator Fulbright's statement that the Great Society had become the "sick society." The Tet offensive seemed to bring to a focus the feeling that the government was lying to the people. Televised scenes of the fighting in Saigon and Hue made the optimistic reports of Johnson and Westmoreland appear ridiculous.

The secrecy and misrepresentation involved in the conduct of the war during the Johnson administration continued under Richard Nixon. It was also during his presidency that the worst consequences of the policy appeared, when the practice of dishonesty was transferred from the realm of foreign affairs into the domestic scene through the Watergate situation. This affair, which eventually forced Nixon from the White House, involved a burglary in June 1972 at the national headquarters of the Democratic party in a Washington office complex. The dramatic events that followed as a special Senate committee investigated Watergate in 1973 led to impeachment proceedings against Nixon and his resignation on August 9, 1974. The anticommunist concern with national security that caused the Cold War, the Korean War, and the Indochina conflict had now resulted in illegal actions against the president's domestic opponents. Alexander Kendrick sums up the situation:

> Like Vietnam, Watergate was not an aberration but the logical extension of authority, indeed the political form of Vietnam. The unaccountable exercise of power in the war was meshed with the power being exerted at home to give the White House control of the cabinet departments, to place the President's men in federal agencies, to dictate the budget by veto or impoundment of funds. . . . The Gestapo mentality that the chairman of the Senate committee investigating Watergate discerned behind this domestic counter-insurgency plan was possessed by men who almost stole America, in the words of another committee senator. . . . The blurring of American values always present to some degree in the realm of Making It, had apparently been widened as never before. The decade that began with John F. Kennedy's ringing inaugural speech closed with a measurable loss of national confidence and hope. Ask not what your country can do for you, the new young President had declared in 1961. In May 1972 his only surviving brother wrote the era's epitaph. How often, asked Senator Edward Kennedy, has the average American been failed by his country?[27]

By and large, evangelicals supported the Cold War mentality. There were, however, some outstanding, articulate exceptions to this rule. Perhaps the range of opinions can be seen most clearly in a brief comparison of the statements and attitudes of two well-known evangelical spokesmen, Billy Graham and Mark Hatfield. Although Graham has moderated his views today, at the time he supported the outlook that led to the Vietnam War. Indeed, in his first major crusade in 1949 he described the world as divided into two camps: a Christian West and a vast, godless communist realm under the sway of Satan. During the Korean War he looked on that conflict as a life and death struggle against the false faith of communism. This anticommunist theme continued in his sermons and writings throughout the 1950s and well into the 1960s. In 1964 he wrote in the forward to *The Challenge of World Communism in Asia*, "Today no single movement gives more concern than does communism," because it poses "a threat to the peace of the whole world."[28] With this outlook it was natural that Graham should support the Vietnam War. Although he later tried to hedge on some of his comments, essentially he backed the Johnson and Nixon administrations as they conducted the conflict. In his sermons, advice, and visits to Vietnam he did his best to support the war interests. A 1965 statement lays down his attitude:

> I have no sympathy for those clergymen who have signed ads recently, urging the U.S. to get out of Vietnam. The world is involved in a battle with communism. The President and most members of Congress are well united in their determination to stay in Vietnam. People who become personally acquainted with the facts and the situation in that part of Asia agree with the President. . . .
>
> We are dealing with naked aggression, with infiltration. If we pull out we will lose face with the people of many small countries in that part of the world and they won't ever trust our word again. Communism had to be stopped somewhere, whether it is in Hawaii or on the West Coast. The President believes it should be stopped in Vietnam.[29]

In the following year he again affirmed his support for the war in a sermon preached at the National Prayer Breakfast in Washington on February 17. He commended President Johnson and pictured the struggle as necessary to defend freedom. Jesus, the evangelist assured his listeners, was not afraid to use force, and consequently his followers must also be willing to fight. Warming to the occasion he declared:

> Those who hate tyranny and love freedom will take sides when little nations suffer terror and aggression from those who seek to take their freedom from them. But Jesus warned, "When you take sides, you will be opposed by those who do not understand the deep problem of human nature and the true definition of love." To preserve some things, love must destroy others. Love is never, never, never neutral.[30]

During December 1966, Graham visited Vietnam, and when he returned he noted the high morale of the troops there as well as their dedicated work in a "tremendous pacification and peace program." He also assured his fellow countrymen that "the American people have every reason to be very proud of the American personnel we have in Vietnam today."[31]

During the years of the Johnson administration Graham often sent messages of support to the president. In April 1967, he criticized Martin Luther King, Jr., for opposing the war. He claimed that "there is no relationship between civil rights and the war policy," and he warned the black leader that "millions of negroes are going to rebel" against King's actions.[32] Graham also condemned other opponents of the Vietnam War because he believed their opposition was encouraging the enemy and prolonging the conflict. As the war escalated during the years 1965 to 1968 many more Christians spoke out against it. Graham doggedly continued to view Vietnam as a necessary and just war. Remembering World War II and the lessons of Hitler and Munich, he saw Johnson as another Churchill. Vietnam, he told a student audience at a North Carolina college, was essentially a repetition of the 1930s when "the war in Europe seemed far away, too."[33] He again toured the battle area in 1968 and returned to make optimistic statements about the prospects of building a strong, free nation in Southeast Asia. "I am certain," he assured the president, "that history is going to vindicate the American commitment if we don't lose the peace in Paris."[34]

When his personal friend Richard Nixon entered the White House, Graham continued to support the war. The brutality of the Nixon-Kissinger plan to use intermittent bombing to gain concessions in the peace talks strained his patience, but he would not condemn the actions. In fact he tried to minimize the importance of these savage attacks by stating:

> It's all over the world, this business of civilians being killed. There is tragedy everywhere. Violence is something worldwide. I deplore the suffering and the killing in the war, and I pray it can be ended as soon as possible, but we also have to realize that there are hundreds of thousands of deaths attributed to smoking. . . . A thousand people are killed every week on the American highways and half of those are attributed to alcohol. Where are the demonstrations against alcohol?[35]

In the end, after peace came to Indochina and Nixon resigned, Graham tried to explain his attitude by insisting that he was not a "hawk" on Vietnam. He claimed that he had never been a chaplain to the president and that God had called him to be a New Testament evangelist rather than an Old Testament prophet. His mission was to preach salvation and personal righteousness rather than social reform and political activism.

Perhaps the best known evangelical spokesman who dissented from the prowar, proadministration views of Graham was

Senator Mark Hatfield. The Senator's perception of Vietnam began in 1945 when he visited the area while serving in the navy. He had seen action in the Pacific theatre during World War II, and when hostilities ended, his ship was sent to Haiphong to pick up nationalist Chinese soldiers in order to transport them to northern China to fight the communists. In a letter sent to his parents at that time he noted:

> It was sickening to see the absolute poverty and the rags these people are in. We thought the Philippines were in a bad way, but they are wealthy compared to these exploited people. The Philippines were in better shape before the war, but people here have never known anything but squalor since the French heel has been on them. . . .
>
> I tell you, it is a crime the way we occidentals have enslaved these people in our mad desire for money. The French seem to be the worst and are followed pretty closely by the Dutch and the English. I can certainly see why these people don't want us to return and continue to spit upon them.[36]

Hatfield might have allowed Southeast Asia to slip into the dim recesses of old memories had it not been for American involvement in a war there. Once he finished his naval duty he returned home and earned a graduate degree in political science at Stanford University. After completing his master's degree he became a professor at Willamette University and entered Oregon Republican politics. He served as governor of the state for two terms before his election to the Senate in 1966. Deeply influenced by the evangelicalism in which he was reared, Hatfield tried to apply his faith to politics. In speeches, books and articles, and legislative activities he worked against the Vietnam War. He became convinced that the conflict had distorted the nation's priorities. Disturbed by phrases such as "kill ratio," "body count," and "kill a Commie for Christ," he declared "In God's eyes the life of a Viet Cong is as valuable as one of ours."[37]

Soon after his election to the Senate Hatfield put forward a plan to end the Indochina war. He believed Americans should reduce their presence in the conflict, organize an all Asian peace conference, and establish a Southeast Asian common market. He became popular as a speaker and explained his position on Vietnam to many audiences. On March 16, 1967, he spoke at Harvard

University, where he stressed a knowledge of Vietnamese history as basic for an understanding of the war. Not communism, he claimed, but nationalism was the driving force behind the efforts of Ho Chi Minh to unify the land. The Tet offensive intensified Hatfield's belief that the war was a dismal failure. That the United States might be fighting just to "save face," he stated, was "immoral and unconscionable." His moral outrage was even more incensed when he learned of the My Lai massacre in 1968. Americans could not blame such events just on the soldiers, he declared, because

> There is a collective guilt that all of us share, for we as a nation embarked upon a foreign civil war. We, as a people, have helped create and perpetuate this situation which is compounded by the fact that our involvement in Vietnam has been and continues to be [morally and legally] wrong.[38]

In 1968, Hatfield presented his ideas on Vietnam in a book, *Not Quite So Simple*. This work accused the Johnson administration of deliberately misrepresenting the nature of the struggle in Southeast Asia. In reality, the senator told his readers, the Vietnamese did not want to join some global communist conspiracy, but rather they wanted to be free of foreign domination. Ho Chi Minh represented the force of nationalism, while the government of South Vietnam was associated with foreigners. As Hatfield stated:

> It is absolutely vital that our policy-makers recognize the causes of the conflict and the basic nature of the war. David Schoenbrun . . . has summed it up very nicely: "From the very start there has been a civil war among the Vietnamese, not a Korean-like aggression by the North against the South. And if this fundamental truth cannot be accepted, then any kind of an honorable settlement is beyond hope. You can't settle a fight if you do not know what it is all about."[39]

The book continued with rebuttals of all the familiar arguments for the war. The domino theory was shown to be false, and the claim that the United States was fighting for the freedom of Southeast Asia was disproven. Hatfield demonstrated that the South Vietnamese did not have freedom of the press, freedom of speech, freedom of assembly, or the freedom to petition the government for redress of grievances. He accused the Saigon government of using gestapo tactics and of conducting dishonest elections. The senator also condemned the bombing of Vietnam as useless and brutal. He proceeded to defend the rights of those Americans who opposed the war. Dissenters, he claimed, should not be condemned for encouraging the enemy, because such charges were based upon the false belief that America was winning the war when this was not the case. Those who opposed the war wanted to save the lives of American soldiers by stopping the conflict. In his discussion of dissent he cautioned his fellow Christians against an uncritical patriotism:

> Those who question the loyalty of the dissenters often subscribe to a perverted patriotism, a patriotism based on a flag-waving, heart-pounding commitment to "my country right or wrong." I would counsel these people not to confuse patriotism with blind endorsement of bad policy. Responsible dissenters are sincerely convinced that our policies in Vietnam are wrong and that they must be corrected if the best interests of the United States are to be served. Just like the superpatriots, we want what is best for our country and the world, but we don't think that our present policies, or a red-white-and-blue obeisance to these policies for the sake of "national unity," serves the long-term interests of the United States. Believing this, we have a *duty* to speak out, to try and change bad policy.[40]

Not only did Hatfield speak and write against the war, he also took a major part in the congressional effort to halt the conflict. He joined Senator McGovern and others in sponsoring a series of amendments that would have ended the war in 1970–71. These actions set limits for the time that troops could remain in Southeast Asia and provided for a reduction in funding for the war. Although none of them passed, they served to focus antiwar feeling and put Hatfield's name on Richard Nixon's "enemy list."

It is well to point out in conclusion that the senator's attitude toward Vietnam grew out of his Christian faith. He expressed this most clearly in an interview published in *HIS* magazine in 1967:

> My views are naturally influenced by my beliefs, by my faith, because no man can isolate or divide himself into tight little compartments that do not relate to one another. We're an organism in which there are interdependencies, interrelationships. We are also related to our environment, and our environment tends to influence us. My concern about Vietnam

> is primarily a political concern because I feel that we are involved there in a situation which has been going on for twenty years . . . and in twenty years a policy that has brought neither victory or solutions, I think, needs careful review. . . . I just cannot accept the idea that ultimate victory will be achieved by killing more people, killing more people, and killing more people. I think we should take peace, prosperity, and food and love to these people. Paul teaches us that love is the most powerful instrument in the world. I think it is far more powerful than the atomic bomb, and we ought to use our genius and our ingenuity to find an honorable way to solve this problem.[41]

The same Christian faith that encouraged Billy Graham to support the war led Senator Hatfield to oppose it. The difference seems to be in the way these two men related their faith to communism. As was pointed out at the beginning of this essay, many evangelicals during the Cold War period gave an eschatological significance to communism. These individuals were so preoccupied with a paranoid fear of international Marxism that it was impossible for them to judge accurately different international situations. Engrossed by this view, preachers like Billy Graham could not understand that Vietnam began as an anticolonial conflict and then turned into a civil war with the United States backing one side. Graham thought of it as part of an international struggle against evil rather than as a local problem involving nationalism and socialism. Hatfield was able to make the necessary distinctions so that he could accurately assess the situation. Most evangelicals sided with Graham because of the simplistic, Manichaeanlike tendencies implicit in their world and life view. It is comforting for such people to have "evil" communists who oppose the "good" Western society. Another point that encouraged evangelical anticommunism was the ideological, almost religious, claims of Marxism. Countering such beliefs gives gospel preaching a currency and relevance that gains adherents. Nevertheless, despite the attention it draws, such preaching is dangerous and can lead to Christian support for new Vietnams wherever they may be found in the world.[42]

AFTERWORD—AND FUTURE WORD

THE AMERICAN WAY OF WAR reveals much about the American way of life. American attitudes about the nation's wars turn on the foundational beliefs that Americans have had and continue to have about the nature and destiny of their nation. While the historian ought to be appropriately cautious about reducing the thoughts and experiences of so diverse a nation into a prevailing ideology, some tentative general contours emerge when we take in the long view of American history,

If there is a prevailing American ideology, it is largely found in our confidence about the future. If there is a central American myth, it is what Russel B. Nye has called "the myth of anticipation," a myth "which has found its classic expression in the quest, the mission, the journey toward destiny."[1] Walt Whitman, perhaps the most notable "American" poet, brought the central myth to articulation:

> The promise of thousands of years, til now deferr'd
> Promis'd to be fulfilled, our common kind, the race.
> The new society at last, proportionate to Nature . . . ,
> Fresh come, to a new world indeed, yet long prepared,
> I see the genius of the modern, child of the real and ideal,
> Clearing the ground for broad humanity, the true America,
>   heir of a past so grand,
> To build a grander future.[2]

The histrionic nature of American life has given its central myth the quality of a moral drama in which Europeans, both potential emigrants and intellectuals who visited the New World, were as much interested as Americans themselves.[3]

The ideology of the moral drama was typically set in religious terms, although the explicitly Christian foundations of the ideology were later to be secularized.[4] America was, to many Americans, what Ernest L. Tuveson has called a "Redeemer Nation."[5] The two aspects of the biblical drama were believed to be present in America: it was "Eden," in that it was pure and undefiled by the worldly corruptions so prevalent in Europe; but it was also "Israel," in that the old world, indeed humanity, would be redeemed by the development of the new world and the new man in America. The refuge of the pure in heart would be the light to which the Gentiles would someday turn. Embedded in this vision of the secular millenium is the danger of the temptation into which Americans frequently fell: the belief "that what is good for America is good for the world, that saving the United States is saving mankind."[6]

The mission of American destiny, always latent, came to most authentic and articulate expression in times of crisis; hence the illumining qualities of war.[7] Given the prevailing ideology, Americans could not help but think that their wars were "just," precisely because their historic role in the world was "just." Thus Americans often fell into the temptation noted above and converted their "just wars" into "crusades," because no less than the fate of the world depended upon an American victory. As we have seen in the previous essays, America entered none of its wars as a crusade initially, but in the prosecution of the war, the high stakes involved became apparent, and the ideology came to clear and heightened expression.

One of the most important commentators on warfare in modern America is Paul Ramsey, whose work on the ethics of war has received wide acclaim.[8] He makes clear, in the title of an essay germane to this study, "What Americans Ordinarily Think About Justice in War."[9] Americans have typically viewed war in terms of "the aggressor-defender" doctrine, that is, aggressive wars are unjust while defensive wars are just. Americans believe that their wars have not only been just but justified because they have been wars of "defense," not merely of the national territory, but of greater importance, of democracy and self-determination. This is particularly important for American wars from 1898 onward, all of which were fought on foreign soil. Most Americans apparently have believed, and still believe, that the use of force to ensure that the "right thing" is done between nations is not only a legitimate act of the state but also an act that follows naturally from America's conception of itself, if not as "redeemer" nation, at least as God's avenging angel, seeing to it that the sin of international aggression is extirpated.

Even in the nuclear age, the potential use of the dramatically advanced technology of warfare has not changed the basic American conviction that the use of force to do right is not only morally acceptable but is a moral imperative. Ramsey poses for us the fundamental question of whether or not there is a substantial difference between nuclear weapons and the merest weapon when a nation has decided to use force—and to take life—in the pursuit of public policy. He cites a quotation from *Time* magazine that may well represent "typical" American thinking:

> [There is] no moral problem in the H-bomb that was not present in the A-bomb, none in the A-bomb that was not present in the mass bombing of cities, and none of these that is not present in war itself, and no grave problems in war that are not present in the basic question of the permissibility of force in any circumstances.[10]

Although the complicated questions involved in just war theories are not easily reducible to one, the resolution of those questions does depend on a prior decision regarding the legitimacy of the use of force as an instrument of governmental policy. Where do, or ought, Christians stand on the matter of the use of force?

The dialogue about these and other matters of the Christian attitude toward society has received much attention in recent years. A book receiving wide acclaim, yet the occasion of much controversy, is John Howard Yoder's *The Politics of Jesus*.[11] Yoder writes out of the Anabaptist tradition, and, predictably, his views accord with those of the traditional pacifist position. But lest Yoder's work be too easily categorized, the "nonpacifist" Christian must admit that too often the pacifist position has been more caricatured than analyzed. Not to listen to Yoder would be foolish, because he presents the pacifist argument with such power and yet with such subtlety that Christians of all persuasions should at least listen. Yoder's reasons for the rejection of force—hence war—is developed through his theory of "revolutionary subordination," the net result of which is a commitment *not* to try to "manage" society for God.[12] For historians, like those in this book, who are appreciative of Niebuhr's "ironic" perspective, Yoder speaks both to us and for us:

> . . . when men try to manage history, it almost always turns out to have taken another direction than that in which they thought they were guiding it. This may mean that man is not morally qualified to set the goals toward which he would move history; it at least means that he is not capable of discerning and managing its course when there are in the same theater of operation a host of other free agents, each of them in his own way also acting under the same assumptions as to his capacity to move history in his direction.[13]

The Christian dialogue about society was continued by Richard J. Mouw in *Politics and the Biblical Drama*, in which Yoder's views are carefully addressed.[14] If Mouw disagrees with Yoder at all, it is not over whether or not Christians should be participants in (what Yoder terms) "the War of the Lamb," but over *how* the warfare should be conducted. Specifically on the matter of force, Mouw partially accepts Yoder's corrective that Christian (especially Calvinist) attempts to "manage" society have seldom had the results hoped for. Yet, while admitting that such management in the past has often gone awry, Mouw maintains that a case must nevertheless be made for limited attempts to manage society—such management as accords with Christian demands for justice in God's creation.[15]

The case for limited attempts to accomplish justice by managing society must take Yoder's views into account, so Mouw asks several questions of the "subordinationist" position:

> How does it relate to the biblical mandate for human beings to "have dominion" in the created order? If human beings are created with the capacity for assessing situations, projecting into the future, planning strategies, and the like, would it not seem a judicious exercise of created abilities to put these gifts to use, even in the area of social and political planning? And if God does require us to do these things, some attempt to "run his world for Him" might be an important means of praising Him.[16]

Surely Mouw is correct in noting that we can do better than a simple antithesis in articulating Christian views on coercive activities; a meaningful distinction can be made between "engaging in actions that will have the effect of coercing other human beings and acting out of a desire to coerce and dominate others."[17] Yoder's defense of eschewing coercive action must mean "a rejection of significant political activity."[18] If Yoder is correct in stating that good actions can have unintended bad consequences, he must recognize that well-motivated inaction can also result in unintended and unacceptable results. In completely rejecting the use of force, one has not given a "final" answer to the problem of ethical activity. On the other hand, however, one who accepts the social use of force has the more difficult problem of distinguishing between justice and injustice.

The dialogue continues in the work of a British ethicist, Oliver O'Donovan.[19] He fears that if the pacifist argument about war is founded on a claim that government can do without coercive force—"institutionalized violence," if you will—then the argument must retreat to anarchism after all. "Force" is exercised by legitimate governments, "violence" by terrorists. It is not merely a cynical distinction to say that "the difference between force and violence is not what is done, but who does it,"[20] because it does matter that only governments may do what individuals and private groups may not do. However, lest O'Donovan's position be misrepresented, let it be noted that he writes in an irenic spirit, in hopes of building a bridge of communication between those who hold a just war view and those who are pacifists. He recognizes that no war is fully just and that many are grossly unjust (notwithstanding what participants in the war may claim). Even though notions of justice come to us ambiguously, he holds that Christians have a duty to do that which is more just. Even though the justice that war may bring is relative, Christian duty sometimes obtains in aiding the state in the only and extreme way in which that relative justice can be realized. Assuming an attitude of an almost sanctified exasperation, he concludes that God has given us government "as a severe blessing for our mediocre world. Government is good for people in a nasty sort of way. The government that exists must be recognized, damn it."[21]

To return to Paul Ramsey's question—on the permissibility of force in certain circumstances—recent Christian thought seems to indicate a "conditional necessity" for force if a society of love and justice is to emerge. The use of force to obtain or to maintain justice must always be tempered by the ethic of love that "does not seek its own way."

Most of the writers in this book accept the notion that our Christian commitment requires us to be active in society, and that we accept, however reluctantly, the notion that coercive force must be allowed. Philosophically, at least, we accept the notion of "just war." (This view is not accepted by one of the authors, Ralph Beebe, whose pacifist convictions remain unmoved.) While allowing for the philosophical plausibility of "just war," however, we are not generally convinced that America's wars have been just merely because Americans claimed they were.

In conclusion, there is no need to rehearse the arguments of the various essays, much less reduce to a single sentence the proportions of justice we have judged to be present in particular wars (although George Marsden's essay on America's first war as a nation frames many of the recurring questions). Since we are agreed, with E. H. Carr, that history is a dialogue between past and present, we may ask other than factual questions of the situations described in the particular wars. To ask how Christians might have acted in particular wars is to ask how Christians in our day might act in future wars.

How, for instance, might the situation have been different? Is it possible, we can ask, for Christians in a given situation to distinguish a just cause from an unjust one with relative assurance, and furthermore to avoid turning their support of just causes into unwarranted crusades? For this to happen, it seems, Christians would have to be both full participants in a nation's political activities and yet be sufficiently detached from the partisanship and prejudices of their day to assess causes with some true discrimination. From what we have seen of American wars, however, such a stance seems difficult to achieve. Christian participants, far from being more detached and somewhat immune to the dangers of partisanship, seem more often to be particularly prone to them—especially when they have Bible in hand. With supporting texts, not only are they likely to perceive their partisan self-interest as just, but they are likely to inflate their cause, seeing the conflict as a struggle between the absolute righteousness of God and Satanic aberration.

Yet surely Christians must presuppose that despite the feebleness of our visions, the blinding light of prejudices, and the distortions of preconceptions, we are able to tell right from wrong in real historical settings and to act as responsible agents. While we recognize these dangers and pitfalls, we must affirm also that God has made us in such a way that we can indeed recognize and stand on the principles of peace and justice in the service of Christ.

What it seems necessary to do more effectively is to mount a massive effort to develop some sense of real detachment as well as responsibility among Christians today. Religion has been too intimately and too long involved in supporting specific political options to provide a stance distinct from the prevailing political options of the day. Christianity has been co-opted, called into the service of partisan political concerns.

We live in an age that is highly politicized, where the pressures, especially in times of crisis, are great to enlist Christianity in the service of one form or another of partisan politics. If we are to avoid such a danger, we must prepare ourselves in advance of such crises by strenuously cultivating a sense of first allegiance that is given to a cause other than the nation-state or various reforming or revolutionary options. George Marsden rightly encourages in us a strong sense that our first allegiance is to the city of God and our subordinate loyalties and responsibilities are to the city of the World. We do recognize that we have responsibilities to both cities. Yet we must recognize that the civilizations of the world, despite the relative virtues that one or another may possess are in the last analysis built on principles of self-interest, power, and violence—principles opposed to Christian virtues. This means that though in the exercise of our political responsibilities we may have to make hard political choices and commitments, nevertheless we should seldom expect to identify Christianity fully with any one side of a political struggle. We must not allow even the good causes that we endorse to become idols as though *they* were the essence of the kingdom. To cultivate such a sense, we must develop habits in our own thought, and teach our children only those habits, that emphasize that our characteristic stance is that of a party of reconcilers.

We cannot wait until times of crisis and wartime to cultivate such a stance. If we do, we are very likely to end up as Christians for whom the world has turned the gospel upside down. If we do not anticipate the dangers, as the present volume hopes to help us do in its small way, we shall too often, like the Americans we have considered in this book, find ourselves beating our plowshares into swords in the name of Christ and for the sake of America.

NOTES

INTRODUCTION

1. Maldwyn A. Jones, "American Wars," in *The United States: A Companion to American Studies*, ed. Dennis Welland (London: Methuen, 1974), pp. 153–154.

2. Quoted in ibid., p. 154.

3. Quoted in Adrienne Koch, ed., *The Philosophy of Thomas Jefferson* (Chicago: Quadrangle, 1964), p. 187.

4. *The Rising Glory of America* (Philadelphia, 1772).

5. Frank Thistlethwaite, *The Great Experiment* (New York: Cambridge University Press, 1955), esp. pp. 319–321.

6. Michael Kammen, *People of Paradox* (New York: Vintage, 1972), p. 9.

7. Gordon Wood, "Rhetoric and Reality in the American Revolution," *William and Mary Quarterly*, 23 (1966), 3–32.

8. Thomas A. Bailey, "The Mythmakers of American History," *Journal of American History*, 55 (1968), 5–21.

9. Jones, "American Wars," p. 154.

10. The following discussion is drawn largely from Reinhold Niebuhr, *The Irony of American History* (New York: Charles Scribner's Sons, 1952), esp. pp. vii–viii and 151–174.

11. See the compelling account of Brown's life in Stephen B. Oates, *To Purge This Land With Blood: A Biography of John Brown* (New York, Harper, 1970).

12. Richard Hofstadter, *The American Political Tradition* (New York: Vintage, 1974), p. 3.

13. Niebuhr, *The Irony of American History*, p. 42.

14. Ibid., p. 147.

15. Ibid., p. 155.

16. Ibid., p. 156.

17. Herbert Butterfield, *Christianity, Diplomacy, and War* (New York: Abingdon, Cokesbury Press), p. 4.

18. Ibid., p. 5.

19. Much of the discussion to follow is based upon Roland H. Bainton, *Christian Attitudes Toward War and Peace* (New York: Abingdon Press, 1960), esp. pp. 230–268.

20. A lucid description of the just war theory can be found in Arthur F. Holmes, *War and Christian Ethics* (Grand Rapids: Baker, 1975), pp. 61–83.

21. Bainton, *Christian Attitudes Toward War and Peace*, p. 15.

1. THE AMERICAN REVOLUTION

1. Mark A. Noll, *Christians in the American Revolution* (Grand Rapids: Christian University Press, 1977), presents from an evangelical Christian perspective a valuable analysis of the variety of Christian responses. Noll also presents (pp. 177–190) a rather extensive bibliographical essay that would serve as a valuable supplement to the present essay.

2. Robert A. Gross, *The Minutemen and Their World* (New York: Hill and Wang, 1976), indicates that before the actual killing began at Concord in April 1775 both sides displayed some scruples in their treatment of each other and were concerned that they fight only defensively, rather than fire the first shot. For the citizens of Concord, at least, Christian considerations explicitly shaped these attitudes, even though they seemed to take for granted that warfare might be the natural outgrowth of their other resistance.

3. Garry Wills, *Inventing America: Jefferson's Declaration of Independence* (Garden City, N.Y.: Doubleday and Co., Inc., 1978), points out strong influences of Scottish philosophy on Jefferson, but does not, in my opinion, successfully demonstrate the lack of very strong influences of Locke in the Declaration.

4. The chief advocates of this view have been historians of the "imperial school," led in America by Charles M. Andrews (1863–1943). Such interpreters emphasize that British administration of the empire and taxation of the colonies was essentially legal and just.

5. Carl L. Becker, *The History of Political Parties in the Province of New York, 1760–1776* (Madison: University of Wisconsin, 1909).

6. Two other prominent interpretations of this era were those of the "imperial school," mentioned above, and of the "Namierist school," founded by the English historian Sir Lewis B. Namier, which presented a rather positive view of the internal politics surrounding George III.

7. Edmund S. Morgan, *The Birth of the Republic, 1763–1789* (Chicago: University of Chicago Press, 1956), p. 100.

8. Morgan's influential essays on the Revolution are collected in *The Challenge of the American Revolution* (New York: W. W. Norton & Co., 1976).

9. The differences between these two views are apparent in Edmund S. Morgan's reviews of seventeen bicentennial publications, *The New York Review of Books*, July 15, 1976, pp. 14–18; August 5, 1976, pp. 29–33.

10. Noll, *Christians in the American Revolution*, summarizes well recent scholarship on this question. Also notable is Alan Heimert's controversial *Religion and the American Mind From the Great Awakening to the Revolution* (Cambridge: Harvard University Press, 1966). Harry S. Stout, "Religion, Communications, and the Ideological Origins of the American Revolution," *William and Mary Quarterly*, 34 (1977), 519–541, sheds some new light on these issues.

11. Gordon S. Wood, "The Democratization of Mind in the American Revolution," *Leadership in the American Revolution*, Library of Congress Symposium, 1974, pp. 70–73, points out how eighteenth-century rhetoric differed from twentieth-century propaganda.

12. These views and their influence on the revolutionaries are very well summarized in Bernard Bailyn, *The Ideological Origins of the American Revolution* (Cambridge, Mass.: Harvard University Press, 1967); and Gordon S. Wood, *The Creation of the American Republic, 1776–1787* (New York: W. W. Norton & Co., 1969).

13. Wills, *Inventing America*, demonstrates the importance of this theme in Jefferson's thought.

14. These conclusions have emerged from the work of the "imperial" and "Namierist" schools, mentioned above (n.6). A good summary of such views is Lawrence Henry Gipson, *The Coming of the Revolution, 1763–1775* (New York: Harper & Row, 1954).

15. John Adams, a liberal Congregationalist, develops this theme in one of his early tracts, "A Dissertation on the Canon and the Feudal Law" (1765).

16. See Bailyn, *Ideological Origins*, and Wood, *The Creation*.

17. Essays by Edmund S. Morgan, "The Puritan Ethic and the Coming of the American Revolution," and Perry Miller, "From the Covenant to the Revival," develop these themes. Both these essays are reprinted in the excellent collection *The Reinterpretation of the American Revolution, 1763–1789*, ed. Jack P. Greene (New York: Harper & Row, 1968). Morgan's essay is also found in his *Challenge*.

18. Carl Bridenbaugh, *Mitre and Sceptre: Transatlantic Faiths, Ideas, Personalities, and Politics, 1689–1775* (New York: Oxford University Press, 1962).

19. Samuel West, *A Sermon Preached before the Honorable Council* . . . (Boston, 1776), pp. 58–63, quoted in Nathan O. Hatch, *The Sacred Cause of Liberty: Republican Thought and the Millennium in Revolutionary New England* (New Haven: Yale University Press, 1977), pp. 55 and 87. Hatch's is the best discussion of these millennial themes, although he suggests a more exclusively nonpolitical character to the millennialism of the Great Awakening than I would.

20. These themes are traced in many works. Two good examples are Hatch, *The Sacred Cause*, and Ernest Lee Tuveson, *Redeemer Nation: The Idea of America's Millennial Role* (Chicago: University of Chicago Press, 1968). John F. Berens, *Providence and Patriotism in Early America, 1640–1815* (Charlottesville: University Press of Virginia, 1978), is a recent review of such themes.

21. Of the many recent works on this subject, probably the best introduction is Russell E. Richey and Donald G. Jones, eds., *American Civil*

Religion (New York: Harper & Row, 1974). As Martin Marty's essay and others in the volume indicate, there are varieties of civil religion, and varieties of definitions, not all of which are negative. The definition in the present essay focuses on one aspect of most civil religion that presents the greatest difficulties in terms of Christian profession.

22. Noll, *Christians in the American Revolution*, pp. 79–102.

2. THE WAR OF 1812

1. James D. Richardson, *Messages and Papers of the Presidents, 1789–1907* (Washington, D.C.: Bureau of National Literature and Art, 1908), I, 505.

2. There is no universally accepted definition of "Christian pacifist." My own views can be supported by the following: John Howard Yoder, *Nevertheless* (Scottdale, Pa.: Herald Press, 1971), gives a variety of pacifist approaches. Roland H. Bainton, *Christian Attitudes Toward War and Peace* (New York: Abingdon, 1960), supplies a valuable historical perspective. Ronald J. Sider, *Christ and Violence* (Scottdale, Pa.: Herald Press, 1979), is an extremely valuable resourse. See also Peter Brock, *Pacifism in the United States* (Princeton, N.J.: Princeton University Press, 1968); Jean Lasserre, *War and the Gospel* (Scottdale, Pa.: Herald Press, 1962); Norval Hadley, ed., *A New Call to Peacemaking* (published by the Faith and Life Movement, Friends World Committee for Consultation, Section of the Americas, 1976); Edward Guinan, ed., *Peace and Non-Violence* (New York: Paulist Press, 1973); Jacob Enz, *The Christian and Warfare* (Scottdale, Pa.: Herald Press, 1972); William Keeney, *Lordship as Servanthood* (Scottdale, Pa.: Herald Press, 1975); John H. Yoder, *The Politics of Jesus* (Grand Rapids, Mich.: Eerdmans, 1972); Arthur F. Holmes, *War and Christian Ethics* (Grand Rapids, Mich.: Baker Book House, 1975); John Lamoreau and Ralph Beebe, *Waging Peace: A Study in Biblical Pacifism* (Newberg, Oregon: Barclay Press, 1981).

3. George Rogers Taylor, ed., *The War of 1812* (Boston: D.C. Heath and Company, 1963); Bradford Perkins, ed., *The Causes of the War of 1812* (New York: Holt, Rinehart and Winston, 1962); Morton Borden, *Parties and Politics in the Early Republic, 1789–1815* (New York: Thomas Y. Crowell Company, 1967), pp. 98–100.

4. John P. Foley, ed., *The Jeffersonian Cyclopedia* (New York: Funk and Wagnalls Company, 1900), p. 917.

5. Ibid., p. 918.

6. Ibid.

7. *Historical Statistics of the United States, Colonial Times to 1957* (Washington: Government Printing Office, 1960), p. 538.

8. Foley, *Jeffersonian Cyclopedia*, p. 916.

9. *Historical Statistics of the United States*, p. 538.

10. W. Alison Phillips and Arthur H. Reede, *Neutrality: Its History, Economics and Law* (New York: Columbia University Press, 1936), II, 20.

11. Augustus J. Foster, *Notes on the United States* (London, 1841), quoted in *the Quarterly Review* (London), 68 (1841), 50.

12. Samuel Flagg Bemis, *A Diplomatic History of the United States* (New York: Henry Holt, 1936), p. 145.

13. Jefferson to Gov. William H. Cabell of Virginia, November 1, 1807, quoted in Andrew A. Lipscomb, ed., *The Writings of Thomas Jefferson* (Washington, D.C.: The Thomas Jefferson Memorial Association of the United States, 1904), XI, 397.

14. Jefferson to General John Armstrong, July 17, 1807, quoted in ibid., pp. 283–284.

15. Foley, *Jeffersonian Cyclopedia*, p. 919.

16. Jefferson to William Duane, as quoted in Lipscomb, *Writings of Jefferson*, p. 291.

17. Proclamation by the King of England, October 16, 1807, quoted in *American State Papers, Foreign Relations* (Washington, D.C.: Gales and Seaton, 1832), III, 26.

18. Foley, *Jeffersonian Cyclopedia*, p. 916.

19. *Republican Spy*, March 9, 1808, quoted in Walter Wilson Jennings, *The American Embargo, 1807–1809*, University of Iowa Studies in the Social Sciences, no. 8 (Iowa City: University of Iowa Press, 1929), p. 42.

20. *Washington Monitor*, July 20, 1808, quoted in ibid., p. 43.

21. See, for example, Thomas A. Bailey, *A Diplomatic History of the United States* (New York: Appleton-Century-Crofts, 1950), pp. 119–120.

22. *The Massachusetts Spy or Worcester Gazette*, April 13, 1808.

23. Fletcher Pratt, *The Heroic Years: Fourteen Years of the Republic, 1801–1815* (New York: Harrison, Smith, McLeod, 1934), p. 138.

24. *Historical Satistics of the United States*, p. 538.

25. B. R. Mitchell, *Abstract of British Historical Statistics* (Cambridge: Cambridge University Press, 1962), pp. 289–290.

26. Louis Martin Sears, *Jefferson and the Embargo* (Durham, N.C.: Duke University Press, 1927), p. 287.

27. Bailey, *Diplomatic History*, p. 123.

28. Felix Grundy to Andrew Jackson, November 28, 1811, quoted in John Spencer Bassett, ed., *Correspondence of Andrew Jackson* (Washington, D.C.: Carnegie Institute of Washington), I, 208.

29. *Annals of Congress of the United States*, 12th Congress, 1st Session, Part I (Washington, D.C.: Gales and Seaton, 1853), p. 599.

30. Ibid., p. 519.

31. Ibid., pp. 686–687.

32. Ibid., pp. 600–601.

33. Ibid., pp. 467–468.

34. Ibid., pp. 414–415.

35. Ibid., p. 426.

36. J. Leitch Wright, Jr., *Britain and the American Frontier, 1783–1815* (Athens: University of Georgia Press, 1975), is a helpful recent source on the frontier problems.

37. *Nashville Clarion*, April 28, 1812, quoted in Julius W. Pratt, *Expansionists of 1812* (Gloucester, Mass.: Peter Smith, 1957), p. 14.

38. *Annals of Congress*, p. 657.

39. Ibid., pp. 518–519.

40. John Stevens, April 8, 1813, as quoted in William Gribbin, *The*

Churches Militant; The War of 1812 and American Religion (New Haven, Conn.: Yale University Press, 1973), p. 61.

41. Quoted in ibid., p. 74.
42. Ibid., p. 23.
43. Ibid., p. 55.
44. Ibid., p. 67.
45. Ibid., p. 88.
46. Ibid., p. 16.
47. Ibid., p. 41.
48. Ibid., p. 57.
49. Ibid.
50. Ibid., p. 27–28.
51. Ibid., p. 121.
52. Ibid., p. 126.
53. Samuel Eliot Morison and Henry Steele Commager, *The Growth of the American Republic* (New York: Oxford University Press, 1950), p. 424.
54. Samuel Eliot Morison, "Dissent in the War of 1812," in *Dissent in Three American Wars* (Cambridge, Mass.: Harvard University Press, 1970), pp. 3–4.
55. Gribbin, *The Churches Militant*, p. 134.
56. Roger H. Brown, *The Republic in Peril: 1812* (New York: Columbia University Press, 1964), pp. 190–191.
57. The *Niles Weekly Register*, February 18, 1815, p. 1.
58. Ibid.

3. THE WAR WITH MEXICO

1. Norman A. Graebner, review of *The Diplomacy of Annexation*, by David M. Pletcher, *Journal of American History*, 61 (1974), 190.
2. Alexander DeConde, *American Diplomatic History in Transformation* (Washington: American Historical Association, 1976), p. 19.
3. David M. Pletcher, *The Diplomacy of Annexation: Texas, Oregon and the Mexican War* (Columbia: University of Missouri Press, 1973), p. 4.
4. Robert L. DeVries, "Moral Principle and Foreign Policy-Making," *Christian Scholar's Review*, 6 (1977), 303–316.
5. "The Causes of the Mexican War: A Note on Changing Interpretations," *Arizona and the West*, 6 (1964), 289–302.
6. *North America Divided: The Mexican War, 1846–1848* (New York: Oxford University Press, 1971), esp. pp. 192–193.
7. *The Mexican War, 1846–1848* (New York: Macmillan, 1974), p. xx. Other historians also follow Smith quite closely, especially William H. Goetzman, *When the Eagle Screamed: The Romantic Horizon in American Diplomacy* (New York: Wiley, 1966).
8. Pletcher, *The Diplomacy of Annexation*, p. 3.
9. *North America Divided*, p. vi.

10. *The War with Mexico*, I, ix.

11. *North America Divided*, p. vi.

12. Richard W. Van Alstyne, *The Rising American Empire* (New York: Norton, 1974), pp. 1–28; Frederick Merk, *Manifest Destiny and Mission in American History* (New York: Vintage, 1963), pp. 3–23.

13. Albert K. Weinberg, *Manifest Destiny: A Study of Nationalist Expansionism in American History* (Chicago: Quadrangle, 1963), p. 2.

14. *Manifest Destiny and Mission*, pp. 25–26.

15. The remainder of the immediate discussion of "Manifest Destiny" is drawn freely from Merk, *Manifest Destiny and Mission*, pp. 27–60.

16. Quoted in ibid., pp. 31–32.

17. Quoted in ibid., p. 32.

18. Quoted in ibid., p. 50.

19. Charles G. Sellers, *James K. Polk, Continentalist* (Princeton, N.J.: Princeton University Press, 1966), esp. pp. 213–266.

20. Bauer, *The Mexican War*, p. 12.

21. Van Alstyne, *The Rising American Empire*, pp. 101–102.

22. Bauer, *The Mexican War*, p. 11; Frederick Merk, "Dissent in the Mexican War," in Samuel Eliot Morison, Frederick Merk, and Frank Freidel, *Dissent in Three American Wars* (Cambridge, Mass.: Harvard University Press, 1970), p. 35.

23. Smith, *The War with Mexico*, I 470–471.

24. Goetzmann, *When the Eagle Screamed*, pp. 58, 60–61.

25. The account of Whig opposition is drawn from Merk, "Dissent in the Mexican War," pp. 38–44.

26. Stephen B. Oates, *With Malice Toward None: The Life of Abraham Lincoln* (New York: New American Library, 1977), pp. 86–87.

27. Merk, "Dissent in the Mexican War," pp. 43–45.

28. Norman A. Graebner, *Empire on the Pacific: A Study in Continental Expansionism* (New York: The Ronald Press, 1955).

29. Merk, *Manifest Destiny and Mission*, p. 39.

30. A good account of Polk's policy toward California and a lucid treatment of the American conquest is Walton Bean, *California, An Interpretive History* (New York: McGraw-Hill, 1968), pp. 90–107.

31. Quoted in Sellers, *James K. Polk*, p. 334.

32. A revisionist account of hostilities in California, centering on Captain John Fremont, is Ronald A. Wells, "A Re-Examination of the American Conquest of California," *Christian Scholar's Review*, 4 (1974), 95–109.

33. Smith, *The War with Mexico*, I, 104.

34. Excellent discussions of the important issue of Mexican perception of the United States in the 1840s are: Frank A. Knapp "The Mexican Fear of Manifest Destiny in California," in Thomas E. Cotner and Carlos E. Casteneda, eds., *Essays in Mexican History* (Austin: University of Texas Press, 1938), pp. 192–208; Gene M. Brack, *Mexico Views Manifest Destiny* (Albuquerque: University of New Mexico Press, 1975).

35. Quoted in Knapp, "The Mexican Fear," p. 200.

36. Reprinted in the newspaper *El Amigo del Pueblo*, November 4, 1845, and quoted in Knapp, "The Mexican Fear," p. 201.
37. Brack, *Mexico Views Manifest Destiny*, p. 173.
38. Ibid., p. 170.
39. Smith, *The War with Mexico*, I, 115
40. Brack, *Mexico Views Manifest Destiny*, p. 173.
41. Ibid., p. 181.
42. Pletcher, *The Diplomacy of Annexation*, pp. 607–608.
43. Shomer S. Zwelling, *Expansion and Imperialism* (Chicago: Loyola University Press, 1970), pp. 86–88.
44. John D. P. Fuller, *The Movement for the Acquisition of All Mexico* (Baltimore: John Hopkins University Press, 1936). A good analysis of Fuller's work is Paul F. Lambert, "The Movement For the Acquisition of All Mexico," *Journal of the West*, 11 (1972), 317–327.
45. The cabinet discussion for June 30, 1946, can be found in Allan Nevins, ed., *Polk: The Diary of a President* (New York: Longmans, Green, 1952), pp. 117–118.
46. "Dissent in the Mexican War," p. 47.
47. Ibid., p. 62.
48. Clayton Sumner Ellsworth, "The American Churches and the Mexican War," *American Historical Review*, 45 (1940), 301–326.
49. "Dissent in the Mexican War," p. 63.
50. "Polk and Fremont," *Pacific Historical Review*, 7 (1938), 227.
51. Arthur M. Schlesinger, Sr., "Rating American Presidents," *New York Times Magazine*, July 29, 1962.
52. Pletcher, *The Diplomacy of Annexation*, p. 3.
53. An especially good review of "new left" historiography is Irwin Unger, "The 'New Left' and American History: Some Recent Trends in United States Historiography," *American Historical Review*, 72 (1967), 1237–1263.
54. Glenn W. Price, *Origins of the War with Mexico* (Austin: University of Texas Press, 1967).
55. A life of Josiah Royce can be found in Ronald A. Wells, "A Portrait of Josiah Royce" (unpublished Ph.D. diss., Boston University, 1967).
56. Josiah Royce, *California, A Study in American Character* (Boston: Houghton Mifflin, 1886), p. 151.
57. Ibid., pp. 500–501.
58. Odie B. Faulk, "The Mexican War: A Seminar Approach," *Journal of the West*, 11 (1972), 212.
59. Seymour V. Connor, "Attitudes and Opinions About the Mexican War, 1846–1970," *Journal of the West*, 11 (1972), 361.
60. Ibid., p. 366.

4. THE AMERICAN CIVIL WAR

1. Cf. Lincoln's Second Inaugural Address in Roy P. Basler, ed., Marion Dolores Pratt and Lloyd A. Dunlap, asst. eds., *Collected Works of Abraham Lincoln* (New Brunswick, N.J.: Rutgers University Press, 1953–1955), VIII, 332–333.

2. Alice Felt Tyler, *Freedom's Ferment: Phases of American Social History to 1860* (New York: Harper, 1962), p. 1; Winthrop S. Hudson, *Religion in America: An Historical Account of the Development of American Religious Life* (New York: Charles Scribner's Sons, 1973), pp. 210–211.

3. Kenneth M. Stampp, ed., *The Causes of the Civil War*, rev. ed. (Englewood Cliffs, N.J.: Prentice Hall, Inc., 1974), p. 1; Dennis Welland, ed., *The United States: A Companion to American Studies* (London: Methuen, 1974), p. 171.

4. Thomas J. Pressly, *Americans Interpret Their Civil War* (New York: Free Press, 1962), pp. 145f. See Howard K. Beale, "What Historians Have Said About the Cause of the Civil War," *Theory and Practice in Historical Study: A Report of the Committee on Historiography*, Social Science Research Council Bulletin, no. 54 (New York, 1946); D. W. Brogan, "Historical Revisions LIII—The Origins of the American Civil War," *History* (London), NS 15 (1938), 47–58; Harnott T. Kane, "The Cannon Are Silent, But the Bugles Still Blow," *The New York Times Book Review*, February 6, 1955, p. 5; Dexter Perkins, "American Wars and Critical Historians," *Yale Review*, 40 (1951), 682–695; Charles W. Ramsdell, "The Changing Interpretations of the Civil War," *Journal of Southern History*, 3 (1937), 3–37; Edwin C. Rozwenc, ed., *The Causes of the American Civil War* (Lexington, Mass.: D. C. Heath and Company, 1961), pp. 225–230; C. Vann Woodward, "The Irony of Southern History," *Journal of Southern History*, 19 (1953), 3–19.

5. David Donald, "American Historians and the Causes of the Civil War," *South Atlantic Quarterly*, 59 (1960), 351–355.

6. David Brion Davis, *The Problem of Slavery in Western Culture* (Ithaca, N.Y.: Cornell University Press, 1966), and Edmund S. Morgan, "Slavery and Freedom: The American Paradox," *Journal of American History*, 59 (1972), 5–29. Both stress the centrality of slavery to the American experience.

7. David Potter, *The South and the Sectional Conflict* (New York: Harper & Row, 1968), p. 146.

8. Eric Foner, "The Causes of the American Civil War: Recent Interpretations and New Directions," *Civil War History*, 20, No. 3 (1974), 198.

9. Ibid., p. 199.

10. The major works of "new political history" dealing with prewar politics are Lee Benson, *The Concept of Jacksonian Democracy: New York as a Test Case* (Princeton, N.J.: Princeton University Press, 1961); Ronald P. Formisano, *The Birth of Mass Political Parties: Michigan, 1827–1861* (Princeton, N.J.: Princeton University Press, 1971); Paul Kleppner, *The Cross of Culture* (New York: Free Press, 1970); Frederick C. Luebke, ed., *Ethnic Voters and the Election of Lincoln* (Lincoln: University of Nebraska Press, 1971); and Michael F. Holt, *Forging a Majority: The Formation of the Republican Party in Pittsburgh, 1848–1860* (New Haven, Conn.: Yale University Press, 1969).

11. Foner, p. 199. Foner discusses the methodological problems in his footnote no. 7.

12. Ibid., p. 200; cf. James E. Wright, "The Ethnocultural Model of Voting," *American Behavioral Scientist*, 16 (1973), 653–674; James R.

Green, "Behavioralism and Class Analysis: A Review Essay on Methodology and Ideology," *Labor History*, 13 (1973), 89–106.

13. Don E. Fehrenbacher, "The Republican Decision at Chicago," in *Politics and the Crisis of 1860*, ed. Norman A. Graebner (Urbana: University of Illinois Press, 1961), p. 36; Joel H. Silbey, "The Civil War Synthesis in American Political History," *Civil War History*, 10 (1964), 130–140.

14. B. F. Telft, "Progress of Society," *Ladies' Repository*, 8 (June 1848), 186, quoted in James H. Moorhead, *American Apocalypse: Yankee Protestants and the Civil War, 1860–1869* (New Haven, Conn.: Yale University Press, 1978), p. 5.

15. Joseph Brady, "The Magnetic Telegraph," *Ladies Repository*, 10 (February 1850), 61–62, quoted in Moorhead, *American Apocalypse*, p. 6.

16. Harry V. Jaffa, *Equality and Liberty* (New York: Oxford University Press, 1965), pp. 118–119.

17. "History of Opinions Respecting the Millennium," *American Theological Review*, 1 (1859), 655, quoted in Moorhead, *American Apocalypse*, p. 9.

18. George M. Marsden, *The Evangelical Mind and the New School Presbyterian Experience: A Case Study of Thought and Theology in Nineteenth Century America* (New Haven, Conn.: Yale University Press, 1970), p. 197.

19. Moorhead, *American Apocalypse*, pp. 6–7.

20. Ralph Henry Gabriel, "Evangelical Religion and Popular Romanticism in Early Nineteenth-Century America," *Church History*, 19 (1950), 46–47.

21. Timothy Dwight, *A Discourse on Some Events of the Last Century* (New Haven, Conn., 1801), p. 43.

22. Ernest Lee Tuveson, *Redeemer Nation: The Idea of America's Millennial Role* (Chicago: University of Chicago Press, 1968), p. 189.

23. Robert Baird, *Religion in America*, ed. by Henry Warner Bowden (New York: Harper & Row, 1970), p. 153.

24. Philip Schaff, *America: A Sketch of Its Political, Social, and Religious Character*, ed. Perry Miller (Cambridge, Mass.: The Belknap Press of Harvard University Press, 1961), p. 47.

25. *Chicago Western Citizen*, August 3, 1852.

26. Ibid.

27. *Joliet* (Illinois) *Signal*, December 31, 1850.

28. Gilbert Hobbs Barnes, *The Antislavery Impulse, 1830–1844* (New York: Appleton, 1933), pp. 196–197; Seymour Martin Lipset, "Religion and Politics in the American Past and Present," in *Religion and Social Conflict*, ed. Robert Lee and Martin E. Marty (New York: Oxford University Press, 1964), pp. 77–79; Don E. Fehrenbacher, *Prelude to Greatness: Lincoln in the 1850's* (Stanford, California: Stanford University Press, 1962), pp. 11–14; Ronald D. Rietveld, "Lincoln and the Politics of Morality," *Journal of the Illinois State Historical Society*, Abraham Lincoln Issue, 68 (1975), pp. 28–29.

29. Calvin Colton, ed., *Private Correspondence of Henry Clay* (New York: A. S. Barnes & Company, 1856), p. 525; Lincoln, *Collected Works*, II, 452; III, 310, 313.

30. *Congressional Globe*, 31st Congress, 1st sess., p. 453; Richard K. Cralle, ed., *The Works of John C. Calhoun* (New York, 1854), IV, 557–559.

31. Cralle, ed., *The Works of Calhoun*, IV, 559.

32. *Presbyterian Herald*, quoted in Chester Forrester Dunham, "The Attitude of the Northern Clergy Toward the South, 1860–1865" (unpublished Ph.D. diss., University of Chicago, 1939), p. 2.

33. Ronald D. Rietveld, "The Moral Issue of Slavery in American Politics, 1854–1860" (unpublished Ph.D. diss., University of Illinois, 1967), pp. 16–17.

34. Fehrenbacher, *Prelude to Greatness*, pp. 11–12.

35. Avery O. Craven, "The Fatal Predicament," in Graebner, ed., *Politics and the Crisis of 1860*, p. 131; *New York Herald*, June 7, 1860; *New York Independent*, June 14, August 2, 1860.

36. Clyde S. Griffin, *The Ferment of Reform, 1830–1860* (New York: Crowell, 1967), pp. 37, 88; *New York Independent*, November 5, 1860; Count Agenor de Gasparin, *Uprising of a Great People* (New York: Scribner's, 1861), p. 227.

37. Carl Schurz to Lincoln, November 7, 1860, Abraham Lincoln Papers, Library of Congress; *New York Independent*, November 15, 1860.

38. *New York Independent*, November 8, 22, 1860; de Gasparin, *The Uprising of a Great People*, pp. 21–22.

39. "Why We Resist and What We Resist," *De Bow's Review*, 30 (February 1861), 235.

40. *New York Independent*, November 5, 1860.

41. De Gasparin, *The Uprising of a Great People*, p. 227.

42. Ibid., p. 11; *New York Independent*, November 22, 1860; Charles Hodge, "The State of the Country," *Biblical Repertory and Princeton Review*, 33 (January 1861), 1–36; *New York Independent*, January 17, 1861, quoted in Moorhead, *American Apocalypse*, p. 34.

43. Quoted in Tuveson, *Redeemer Nation*, p. 196.

44. Quoted in Dunham, "The Attitude of the Northern Clergy Toward the South, 1860–1865," p. 112.

45. William N. Polk, *Leonidas Polk: Bishop and General*, 2 vols. (New York, 1893), I, 325; Sydney E. Ahlstrom, *A Religious History of the American People* (New Haven, Conn.: Yale University Press, 1972), pp. 670–671.

46. For representative proslavery statements, see Hibrie Shelton Smith, Robert T. Handy, and Lafferts A. Loetscher, *American Christianity: An Historical Interpretation with Representative Documents* (New York: Charles Scribner's Sons, 1960–1963), II, 177–178; 182–186; 201–210.

47. Moorhead, *American Apocalypse*, p. 43.

48. Henry E. Jacobs, *A History of the Evangelical Lutheran Church in the United States* (New York, 1893), p. 452; Ahlstrom, *A Religious History of the American People*, p. 674.

49. Quoted in Gross Alexander, *History of the Methodist Episcopal Church, South*, II (New York, 1894), 72; Ahlstrom, *A Religious History of the American People*, p. 675.

50. Ahlstrom, *A Religious History of the American People*, pp. 676–677.

51. Ibid., pp. 677–678.

52. Tuveson, *Redeemer Nation*, pp. 205–206; Robert N. Bellah, "Civil Religion in America," *Daedulus*, 95 (Winter 1967), 1–21.

53. Lincoln, Annual Message to Congress, December 1, 1862, in *Collected Works*, V, 518–537.

54. James Wilson in the *North American Review*, December 1896, p. 667.

55. Lincoln, "Meditation on the Divine Will" (September 2, 1862?) in *Collected Works*, V, 403–404.

56. Ibid., pp. 343, 346.

57. Lincoln, Second Inaugural Address, March 4, 1865, in ibid., VIII, 332–333.

58. Lincoln to Thurlow Weed, March 15, 1865, in ibid., p. 356.

59. William F. Fox, *Regimental Losses in the American Civil War* (Albany, 1889), pp. 46–47, 554; Thomas L. Livermore, *Numbers and Losses in the Civil War in America*, 1861–1865 (Boston and New York, 1901), pp. 3–7.

60. John S. Rosenberg, "Toward a New Civil War Revisionism," *The American Scholar*, 38 (1969), 250–272. The article was reprinted in Gerald N. Grob and George Athan Billias, *Interpretations of American History* (New York: Free Press, 1967), pp. 459–479.

61. Phillip S. Paludan, "The American Civil War: Triumph Through Tragedy," *Civil War History*, 20, No. 3, 239–250.

62. Ibid., pp. 246–247; Eugene Genovese, *The Political Economy of Slavery* (New York: Pantheon Books, 1965); Kenneth Stampp, *The Peculiar Institution* (New York: Knopf, 1956), pp. 383–418; Robert Starobin, *Industrial Slavery in the Old South* (New York: Oxford University Press, 1970); Alfred H. Conrad and John R. Meyer, "The Economics of Slavery in the Antebellum South," *Journal of Political Economy*, 65 (1958), 95–122.

63. Paludan, "The American Civil War," pp. 247–250; Ecclesiastes 3:1–8.

64. Paludan, "The American Civil War," p. 250; Lincoln to U. S. Grant, April 30, 1864, in *Collected Works*, VII, 324.

65. Paludan, "The American Civil War," pp. 535–536.

5. THE SPANISH-AMERICAN WAR

1. Frank Freidel, *The Splendid Little War* (Boston: Little, Brown and Company, 1958), p. 3; on the theme of irony, see Reinhold Niebuhr, *The Irony of American History* (New York: Charles Scribners' Sons, 1962); James D. Richardson, ed., *A Compilation of the Messages and Papers of the Presidents, 1789–1908* (Bureau of National Literature and Art, 1909), X, 16.

2. *The Search for Order, 1877–1920* (New York: Hill and Wang, 1967), p. 44.

3. Quoted in David Healy, *U.S. Expansionism: The Imperialist Urge in the 1890s* (Madison: The University of Wisconsin Press, 1970), p. 46.

4. Hofstadter develops the theme of "psychic anxieties" in "Cuba, The Philippines, and Manifest Destiny" in his *The Paranoid Style in American Politics and Other Essays* (New York: Vintage Books, 1967), pp. 145–151.

5. *American Imperialism: A Speculative Essay* (New York: Atheneum, 1968).

6. Milton Plesur, *America's Outward Thrust: Approaches to Foreign Affairs, 1865–1890* (DeKalb, Ill.: Northern Illinois University Press, 1971), pp. 82, 74–86; my general discussion of the background themes to American expansion is drawn from the following: Wiebe, *The Search for Order*, pp. 1–110; Sam Bass Warner, Jr., *The Urban Wilderness* (New York: Harper and Row, 1972), pp. 55–112, 153–179; Harold U. Faulkner, *Politics, Reform and Expansion* (New York: Harper Torchbook edition, 1963), pp. 1–93; Charles S. Campbell, *The Transformation of American Foreign Relations, 1865–1900* (New York: Harper and Row, 1976), pp. 140–160; Robert L. Beisner, *From the Old Diplomacy to the New, 1865–1900* (New York: Thomas Y. Crowell Company, 1975), pp. 66–77; Josiah Strong, *Our Country*, ed. Jurgen Herbst (Cambridge, Mass.: The Belknap Press of Harvard University Press, 1963), pp. 200–218; Walter LaFeber, "That 'Splendid Little War' in Historical Perspective," reprinted in *American Expansionism: The Critical Issues*, ed. Marilyn Blatt Young (Boston: Little, Brown and Company, 1973), pp. 42–49, and *The New Empire, An Interpretation of American Expansion, 1860–1898* (Ithaca, New York: Cornell University Press, 1963), pp. 150–196, 300–311; Marilyn Blatt Young, "American Expansion, 1870–1900: The Far East," in *Towards a New Past: Dissenting Essays in American History*, ed. Barton J. Bernstein (New York: Vintage Books edition, 1969), pp. 176–185; William A. Williams, *The Tragedy of American Diplomacy* (New York: Dell Publishing Company, rev. ed., 1962), pp. 21–50; Healy, *U.S. Expansionism*, 34–47, 159–177; Frederick Merk, *Manifest Destiny and Mission in American History, A Reinterpretation* (New York: Vintage Books, 1963), pp. 231–247; also see Thomas J. McCormick, *China Market: America's Quest for Informal Empire, 1893–1901* (Chicago: Quadrangle Books, 1967), pp. 17–107; and for a still masterly summary of "The Roots of Imperialism" consult Richard W. Leopold, *The Growth of American Foreign Policy* (New York: Alfred A. Knopf, 1962), pp. 119–129.

7. Williams, *Tragedy*, pp. 1–3; Young, ed., *American Expansionism*, xii.

8. John Higham, "Hanging Together: Divergent Unities in American History," *The Journal of American History*, 61 (1974), 10–16; Robert D. Linder and Richard V. Pierard, *Twilight of the Saints: Biblical Christianity and Civil Religion in America* (Downers Grove, Ill.: InterVarsity Press, 1978), pp. 65–69.

9. Plesur, *America's Outward Thrust*, pp. 82–84; Robert T. Handy, *A Christian America: Protestant Hopes and Historical Realities* (New York: Oxford University Press, 1971), pp. 117–123 (the quote by Gulick is on p. 123); Paul A. Varg, "Motives in Protestant Missions, 1890–1917," *Church History*, 23 (1954), 68–82; Sydney E. Ahlstrom, *A Religious History of the American People*, 2 vols. (Garden City, New York: Image Books edition, 1975), II, 343–345; LaFeber, *New Empire*, p. 307.

10. Three useful collections of articles on the background to the Spanish-American war and imperialism are Young, ed., *American Expansionism*; A. E. Campbell, ed., *Expansion and Imperialism* (New York: Harper and Row, 1970); and Thomas G. Paterson, ed., *American Imperialism and Anti-Imperialism* (New York: Thomas Y. Crowell Company, 1973).

11. Merk, *Manifest Destiny*, p. 210; Richard W. Van Alstyne, *The Rising American Empire* (Chicago: Quadrangle Paperback Books, 1965), pp. 87–88, 147–163; Campbell, *Transformation*, p. 3; Lester D. Langley, *The Cuban Policy of the United States: A Brief History* (New York: John Wiley and Sons, Inc., 1968), pp. 1–51.

12. Beisner, *Old Diplomacy to the New*, pp. 50–51; Langley, *Cuban Policy*, pp. 55–70.

13. Beisner, *Old Diplomacy to the New*, pp. 51–54; Langley, *Cuban Policy*, pp. 70–81; Campbell, *Transformation*, pp. 53–59; Leopold, *Growth of American Foreign Policy*, pp. 56, 78–79.

14. Langley, *Cuban Policy*, pp. 83–88; Philip S. Foner, Introduction to José Marti, *Our America*, ed. Philip S. Foner (New York and London: Monthly Review Press, 1977), pp. 11–53.

15. Jacques Ellul, *Violence: Reflections from a Christian Perspective*, trans. Cecelia Gaul Kings (New York: The Seabury Press, 1969), pp. 93–108.

16. Philip S. Foner, *The Spanish-Cuban-American War and the Birth of American Imperialism, 1895–1902*, 2 vols. (New York and London: Monthly Review Press, 1972), I, 15–34, 76–78, 98–118; Campbell, *Transformation*, pp. 239–243; Langley, *Cuban Policy*, p. 89; for a summary of how the American press described the atrocities, see Marcus M. Wilkerson, *Public Opinion and the Spanish-American War: A Study in War Propaganda* (New York: Russell and Russell, 1932), pp. 29–53.

17. John A. S. Grenville and George Berkeley Young, *Politics, Strategy, and American Diplomacy: Studies in Foreign Policy, 1873–1917* (New Haven, Conn.: Yale University Press, 1966), p. 180; Olney is quoted in Ruhl J. Bartlett, ed., *The Record of American Diplomacy: Documents and Readings in the History of American Foreign Relations* (New York: Alfred A. Knopf, 1956), p. 344.

18. On Cleveland and Cuba see Ernest R. May, *Imperial Democracy: The Emergence of America as a Great Power* (New York: Harper Torchbooks, 1961), pp. 69–93; Grenville and Young, *Politics*, pp. 181–200; LaFeber, *New Empire*, pp. 285–300; Beisner, *Old Diplomacy to the New*, pp. 104–106; Langley, *Cuban Policy*, pp. 90–95; Olney's note is reprinted in Bartlett, ed., *Record of American Diplomacy*, pp. 373–374; on the role and impact of the nation's press and correspondents both during the Cleveland and McKinley administrations, see Wilkerson, *Public Opinion and the Spanish-American War*; Joseph E. Wisan, *The Cuban Crisis as Reflected in the New York Press, 1895–1898* (New York: Octagon Books, Inc., 1965); Charles H. Brown, *The Correspondents' War: Journalists in the Spanish-American War* (New York: Charles Scribner's Sons, 1967).

19. Two helpful biographies of McKinley are Margaret Leech, *In the Days of McKinley* (New York: Harper and Brothers, 1959), and H. Wayne Morgan, *William McKinley and His America* (Syracuse, N.Y.: Syracuse University Press, 1963); also see Morgan's *America's Road to Empire:*

The War With Spain and Overseas Expansion (New York: John Wiley and Sons, Inc., 1965), pp. 17–21, and Grenville and Young, *Politics*, pp. 239–247.

20. Reinhold Niebuhr, *Moral Man and Immoral Society* (New York: Charles Scribner's Sons, 1932), p. 99.

21. LaFeber, *New Empire*, pp. 327–334; May, *Imperial Democracy*, pp. 114–130; Campbell, *Transformation*, pp. 244–249.

22. Richardson, (ed.), *Messages and Papers*, X, 31; Grenville and Young, *Politics*, pp. 248–251; Morgan, *Road to Empire*, pp. 23–28; LaFeber, *New Empire*, pp. 335–340.

23. Richardson, ed., *Messages and Papers*, X, 37, 38; Morgan, *Road to Empire*, pp. 30–35; Niebuhr, *Moral Man*, p. 97.

24. Quoted in Grenville and Young, *Politics*, p. 254.

25. Langley, *Cuban Policy*, p. 105.

26. LaFeber, *New Empire*, pp. 343–348; Campbell, *Transformation*, pp. 250–253; Morgan, *Road to Empire*, pp. 37–46; Grenville and Young, *Politics*, pp. 253–256.

27. Quoted in May, *Imperial Democracy*, p. 141.

28. Morgan, *Road to Empire*, pp. 48–52; May, *Imperial Democracy*, pp. 143–152; Campbell, *Transformation*, pp. 255–257; LaFeber, *New Empire*, pp. 349–351, 370–393, 403–406.

29. May, *Imperial Democracy*, p. 154.

30. Campbell, *Transformation*, pp. 260–267; Morgan, *Road to Empire*, pp. 54–59; Grenville and Young, *Politics*, pp. 256–262.

31. Richardson, ed., *Messages and Papers*, X, 56–67.

32. Paul S. Holbo, "Presidential Leadership in Foreign Affairs: William McKinley and the Turpie-Foraker Amendment," *American Historical Review*, 72 (1967), 1333, 1331–1338; Campbell, *Transformation*, pp. 274–278; David F. Healy, *The United States in Cuba, 1898–1902: Generals, Politicians, and the Search for Policy* (Madison: University of Wisconsin Press, 1963), pp. 21–29; Leopold, *Growth of American Foreign Policy*, pp. 147–179.

33. On the just war see Edward LeRoy Long, Jr., *War and Conscience in America* (Philadelphia: The Westminster Press, 1968), pp. 22–33; Ralph Luther Moellering, *Modern War and the Christian* (Minneapolis: Augsburg Publishing House, 1969), pp. 42–54; Arthur F. Holmes, "War and Christian Ethics," *Reformed Journal*, January and February 1974, pp. 12–15, 19–21; Michael Walzer, *Just and Unjust Wars* (New York: Basic Books, Inc., Publishers, 1977), pp. 86, 101; also see, Roland H. Bainton, *Christian Attitudes Toward War and Peace: A Historical Survey and Critical Evaluation* (New York: Abingdon Press, 1960) and Paul Ramsey, *The Just War: Force and Political Responsibility* (New York: Charles Scribner's Sons, 1968), esp. pp. 19–69, 141–167.

34. Although my interpretation may differ, I have drawn insights from Campbell, *Transformation*, pp. 273–278; Morgan, *Road to Empire*, pp. 59–63; Langley, *Cuban Policy*, pp. 110–113; Beisner, *Old Diplomacy to the New*, pp. 113–115; Grenville and Young, *Politics*, pp. 264–266; Leech, *McKinley*, pp. 180–191; Leopold, *Growth of Foreign Policy*, pp. 174–177; Walzer, *Just and Unjust Wars*, pp. 102–103.

35. Morgan, *Road to Empire*, pp. 65–75; Grenville and Young, *Politics*, pp. 267–282; Campbell, *Transformation*, pp. 279–295; William Reynolds Braisted, *The United States Navy in the Pacific, 1897–1909* (Austin: University of Texas Press, 1958), pp. 21–32.

36. Quoted in Healy, *United States in Cuba*, p. 179.

37. My summary of immediate postwar events in Cuba is drawn from Healy, *United States in Cuba*; Langley, *Cuban Policy*, pp. 115–139 (quotes from 126); Jules Robert Benjamin, *The United States and Cuba: Hegemony and Development, 1880–1934* (Pittsburgh: University of Pittsburgh Press, 1974), pp. 7–14.

38. Niebuhr, *Moral Man*, p. 99; Walzer, *Just and Unjust Wars*, p. 104.

39. Walzer, *Just and Unjust Wars*, pp. 104–105.

40. Richard E. Welch, Jr., *Response to Imperialism: The United States and the Philippine-American War, 1899–1902* (Chapel Hill: The University of North Carolina Press, 1979), pp. 3–6; Grenville and Young, *Politics*, pp. 285–296; Beisner, *Old Diplomacy to the New*, pp. 118–120.

41. McCormick, *China Market*, p. 117; LaFeber, *New Empire*, p. 416.

42. Both quotes were in John Edwin Smylie, "Protestant Clergymen and America's World Rule, 1865–1900: A Study of Christianity, Nationality, and International Relations" (unpublished Th.D. diss., Princeton Theological Seminary, 1959), pp. 490, 501; on the role of public opinion groups see also May, *Imperial Democracy*, pp. 243–259.

43. Quoted in Smylie, "Protestant Clergymen," p. 506; see also Leech, *McKinley*, pp. 343–346.

44. Welch, Jr., *Response to Imperialism*, pp. 7–8, 15.

45. On the anti-imperialist arguments see Robert L. Beisner, *Twelve Against Empire: The Anti-Imperialists, 1898–1900* (New York: McGraw-Hill Book Company, 1968), esp. pp. 215–239 for a summary; also Welch, Jr., *Response to Imperialism*, pp. 43–149; Leopold, *Growth of Foreign Policy*, pp. 188–194; on the connection between American imperialism and Indian policy see Walter L. Williams, "United States Indian Policy and the Debate over Philippine Annexation: Implications for the Origins of American Imperialism," *Journal of American History*, 66 (1980), 810–831.

46. Paolo E. Coletta, *William Jennings Bryan: Political Evangelist* (Lincoln: University of Nebraska Press, 1964), pp. 220–237, 263–284.

47. On the Philippine-American war and its aftermath, see Leon Wolff, *Little Brown Men* (London: Longmans, Green and Co., Ltd., 1961); Welch, Jr., *Response to Imperialism*, pp. xiii, 3–42, 150–159; Garel A. Grunder and William E. Livezey, *The Philippines and the United States* (Westport, Conn.: Greenwood Press reprint, 1973), pp. 3–103.

48. Quoted in Wolff, *Little Brown Men*, p. 201.

49. Welch, Jr., *Response to Imperialism*, p. 155.

50. Ellul, *Violence*, p. 88.

6. WORLD WAR I

1. George M. Trevelyan, *Grey of Fallodon* (Boston: Houghton Mifflin Co., 1937), p. 302.

2. Robert R. Palmer and Joel Colton, *A History of the Modern World*, 3rd ed. (New York: Alfred A. Knopf, Inc., 1965), pp. 660–661.

3. Thomas A. Bailey, *A Diplomatic History of the American People*, 6th ed. (New York: Appleton-Century-Crofts, Inc., 1958), p. 563.

4. Arthur S. Link, *Wilson: The New Freedom* (Princeton, N.J.: Princeton University Press, 1956), p. 64.

5. Arthur S. Link et al., eds., *The Papers of Woodrow Wilson*, 36 vols. (Princeton, N.J.: Princeton University Press, 1966–), XXIII, 377.

6. Arthur S. Link, *The Higher Realism of Woodrow Wilson* (Nashville: Vanderbilt University Press, 1971), p. 17.

7. Ibid.

8. Ibid.

9. Harley Notter, *The Origins of the Foreign Policy of Woodrow Wilson* (Baltimore: The Johns Hopkins Press, 1937), p. 653.

10. Link, *Higher Realism of Woodrow Wilson*, p. 101.

11. Daniel Smith, *The Great Departure* (New York: John Wiley and Sons, Inc., 1965), p. 73.

12. Notter, *Origins of the Foreign Policy of Woodrow Wilson*, p. 597.

13. Link, *Papers of Woodrow Wilson*, XXXI, 221.

14. Richard Hofstadter, *The American Political Tradition* (New York: Alfred A. Knopf, Inc., 1948), p. 245.

15. Arthur Walworth, *Woodrow Wilson*, 3rd ed., 2 vols. (New York: W. W. Norton and Co., 1978), II, 13.

16. Ibid.

17. Smith, *The Great Departure*, p. 61.

18. Ibid.

19. Ibid., p.64.

20. Ray S. Baker, *Woodrow Wilson: Life and Letters*, Potomac ed., 7 vols. (New York: Charles Scribner's Sons, 1946), V, 326.

21. Bailey, *Diplomatic History of the American People*, p. 594.

22. Charles Seymour, *The Intimate Papers of Colonel House*, 2 vols. (Boston: Houghton Mifflin Co., 1926), I, 304.

23. Baker, *Wilson*, IV, 211–212.

24. Ibid., p. 243.

25. Ibid., V, 312.

26. Ibid.

27. Ibid., p. 313.

28. Ibid., p. 324.

29. Ibid., p. 399.

30. Ibid., pp. 505–506.

31. Arthur S. Link, *Wilson: Campaigns for Progressivism and Peace* (Princeton, N.J.: Princeton University Press, 1965), p. 399.

32. Baker, *Wilson*, V, 257–258.

33. Ibid., p. 258.

34. Thomas A. Bailey, *Woodrow Wilson and the Lost Peace* (Chicago: Quadrangle Books, 1963), p. 40.

35. Ibid., p. 20.

36. George F. Kennan, *American Diplomacy, 1900–1950* (Chicago: University of Chicago Press, 1951), pp. 88–89.

37. Mark Sullivan, *Our Times: The United States, 1900–1925*, 6 vols. New York: Charles Scribner's Sons, 1926–1935), V, 473.

38. Ibid., pp. 473–474.

39. Arthur Link and William B. Catton, *American Epoch*, 3rd ed., 3 vols. (New York: Alfred A. Knopf, Inc., 1967), I, 212.

40. John A. Garraty, *Interpreting American History: Conversations With Historians*, 2 vols. (New York: Macmillan Co., 1970), II, 148.

41. See William R. Hutchison, *The Modernist Impulse in American Protestantism* (Cambridge, Mass.: Harvard University Press, 1976), pp. 232–243; also two chapters titled "Groups of Irreconcilables" and "The Non-Conformist Clergy" in Ray H. Abrams, *Preachers Present Arms* (Scottdale, Pa.: Herald Press, 1969), pp. 177–207. It should be understood that although almost all religious leaders in America supported the war effort, and, as William R. Hutchinson states in his *The Modernist Impulse in American Protestantism*, almost all mainline liberals were willing "to state a moral preference for the Allied cause," a large number opposed the frenzied chauvinism generated by a number of Americans, including some clergymen. Even though this is true, in retrospect a Christian experiences some uneasiness when one realizes that a sizable segment of Christian leaders became "infected" by war's hysteria.

42. Abrams, *Preachers Present Arms*, p. 105.

43. Mark Sullivan, *Our Times*, V, 467–468.

44. Ibid.

45. Ibid.

46. Abrams, *Preachers Present Arms*, pp. 99–100.

47. Ibid., p. 124.

48. Robert Bolt, *U.S. Involvement in World War I* (Grand Rapids; National Union of Christian Schools, 1974), p. 8.

49. Abrams, *Preachers Present Arms*, p. 55.

50. Ibid., p. 58.

51. Ibid., pp. 72–73.

52. Ibid., p. 82.

53. Ibid., p. 50.

54. Ibid., p. 83.

55. Ibid.

56. Ibid., p. 85.

57. Ibid., p. 86.

58. Link, *Higher Realism of Woodrow Wilson*, pp. 108–109.

59. Smith, *The Great Departure*, p. 108.

60. Arthur S. Link, *Wilson the Diplomatist*, 2nd ed. (Chicago: Quadrangel Books, 1963), p. 110.

61. Ibid., pp. 118–119.

62. David F. Trask, *Woodrow Wilson and World War I* (St. Charles, Mo.: Forum Press, 1975), p. 15.

7. WORLD WAR II

1. See the definition of just war contained in Roland H. Bainton, *Christian Attitudes Toward War and Peace* (Nashville: Abingdon, 1960), pp. 14, 33, 38, 95–99, and Edward LeRoy Long, Jr., *War and Conscience in America* (Philadelphia: Westminster, 1968), pp. 22–33.

2. N. Gordon Levin, *Woodrow Wilson and World Politics* (New York: Oxford University Press, 1968); Arno J. Mayer, *Politics and Diplomacy of Peacemaking* (New York: Knopf, 1967); Thomas A. Bailey, *Woodrow Wilson and the Lost Peace* (New York: Macmillan, 1944), and *Woodrow Wilson and the Great Betrayal* (New York: Macmillan, 1945); Ralph Stone, *The Irreconcilables: The Fight Against the League of Nations* (Lexington: University of Kentucky Press, 1970).

3. Roger Dingman, *Power in the Pacific: The Origins of Naval Arms Limitation, 1914–1922* (Chicago: University of Chicago Press, 1976); Robert H. Farrell, *Peace in Their Time: The Origins of the Kellogg-Briand Pact* (New Haven, Conn.: Yale University Press, 1952), and *American Diplomacy in the Great Depression: Hoover-Stimson Foreign Policy, 1929–1933* (New Haven, Conn.: Yale University Press, 1957); Melvyn P. Leffler, *The Elusive Quest: America's Pursuit of European Stability and French Security, 1919–1933* (Chapel Hill: University of North Carolina Press, 1979); Selig Adler, *The Isolationist Impulse: Its Twentieth Century Reaction* (New York: Abelard-Schuman, 1957), and *The Uncertain Giant, 1921–1941: American Foreign Policy Between the Wars* (New York: Macmillan, 1965).

4. Robert K. Murray, *The Politics of Normalcy: Governmental Theory and Practice in the Harding-Coolidge Era* (New York: Norton, 1973); Joan Hoff Wilson, *American Business and Foreign Policy, 1920–1933*(Lexington: University of Kentucky Press, 1971); Herbert Feis, *The Diplomacy of the Dollar, 1919–1932* (New York: Norton, 1966).

5. John Kenneth Galbraith, *The Great Crash, 1929* (Boston: Houghton Mifflin, 1955); Charles P. Kindleberger, *The World in Depression, 1929–1939* (Berkeley: University of California Press, 1973).

6. Walter W. Van Kirk, *Religion and the World of Tomorrow* (Chicago: Willett, Clark, 1941), pp. 116–117.

7. Ruth Rouse and Stephen Charles Neill, *A History of the Ecumenical Movement, 1517–1948* (Philadelphia: Westminster, 1967); Samuel McCrea Cavert, *The American Churches in the Ecumenical Movement, 1900–1968* (New York: Association Press, 1968); Charles Chatfield, *For Peace and Justice: Pacifism in America, 1914–1941* (Knoxville: University of Tennessee Press, 1971).

8. Wayne S. Cole, *Charles A. Lindbergh and the Battle against American Intervention in World War II* (New York: Harcourt, Brace, Jovanovich, 1974); R. A. Divine, *The Illusion of Neutrality* (Chicago: University of Chicago Press, 1962); William L. Langer and S. Everett Gleason, *The Challenge to Isolation: The World Crisis of 1937–1940 and American Foreign Policy* (New York: Harper, 1952).

9. Manfred Jonas, *Isolationism in America, 1935–1941* (Ithaca: Cornell University Press, 1966); Robert A. Divine, *The Reluctant Belligerent: American Entry into World War II* (New York: Wiley, 1965); John E. Wiltz, *From Isolationism to War, 1931–1941* (New York: Crowell, 1968).

10. George Ashton Oldham, *The Church's Responsibility for World Peace* (Washington: National Council for Prevention of War, 1928), p. 10. On American pacifism see Chatfield, *For Peace and Justice*.

11. *Christian Century*, Dec. 18, 1940, p. 1578.

12. Ibid., Dec. 4, 1940, p. 1506.

13. Loraine Boettner, *The Christian Attitude Toward War* (Grand Rapids, Mich.: Eerdmans, 1940), pp. 73–74. He also said: "True religion and true patriotism have always gone hand in hand, while unbelief, doubt, modernism, etc. have invariably been accompanied by socialism, communism, radicalism, and other enemies of free government" (pp. 83–84).

14. For evaluations of Niebuhr's political views see Ronald H. Stone, *Reinhold Niebuhr: Prophet to Politicians* (Nashville: Abingdon, 1972); John W. Coffey, *Political Realism in American Thought* (Lewisburg, Pa.: Bucknell University Press, 1977); and Donald E. Meyer, *The Protestant Search for Political Realism, 1919–1941* (Berkeley: University of California Press, 1960). Niebuhr's thinking can best be seen in two collections of his essays, *Christianity and Politics* (New York: Scribners, 1940), and *Christian Realism and Political Problems* (New York: Scribners, 1953).

15. *Christian Century*, Dec. 18, 1940, p. 1580.

16. Ibid.

17. Ibid., Dec. 4, 1940, pp. 1506–1507.

18. Reinhold Niebuhr, "The Christian Faith and the World Crisis," *Christianity and Crisis*, Feb. 10, 1941, p. 6.

19. Gustavus Myers, *History of Bigotry in the United States* (New York: Capricorn Books, 1960), and Ralph Lord Roy, *Apostles of Discord: A Study of Organized Bigotry and Disruption on the Fringes of Protestantism* (Boston: Beacon Press, 1953), cover larger periods of time but do provide information on American fascists in the 1930s.

20. Myers, *History of Bigotry*, p. 321.

21. Quoted in David J. O'Brien, "American Catholics and Anti-Semitism in the 1930's," *Catholic World*, 204 (February 1967), 272. See also Leonard Dinnerstein, ed., *Anti-Semitism in the United States* (New York: Holt, Rinehart, Winston, 1971).

22. Quoted in John Roy Carlson, *Under Cover* (New York: Dutton, 1943), p. 167.

23. Statement made by Buchman in an interview in the *New York World-Telegram*, Aug. 26, 1936. Tom Driberg, *The Mystery of Moral Re-Armament* (New York: Knopf, 1965) discusses this incident in detail.

24. Arthur M. Schlesinger, Jr., *The Politics of Upheaval*, Vol. III of *The Age of Roosevelt* (Boston: Houghton Mifflin, 1960), p. 84; Raymond Gram Swing, *Forerunners of American Fascism* (New York: Julian Messner, 1935), p. 148.

25. Carlson, *Under Cover*, p. 318.

26. Walter Johnson, *The Battle Against Isolation* (Chicago: University of Chicago Press, 1944), pp. 164–165.

27. Opinion of Chief Justice Roger Taney in *Dred Scott* v. *Sandford*, 19 Howard 393 (1857).

28. Elmer Sandmeyer, *The Anti-Chinese Movement in California* (Urbana: University of Illinois Press, 1939); Gunther Barth, *Bitter Strength:*

A History of the Chinese in the United States, 1830–1870 (Cambridge, Mass.: Harvard University Press, 1964); Foster R. Dulles, *China and America: The Story of Their Relations since 1784* (Princeton, N.J.: Princeton University Press, 1946).

29. Hilary Conroy, *The Japanese Frontier in Hawaii, 1868–1898* (Berkeley: University of California Press, 1953).

30. This point is underscored by Masakazu Iwata, "The Japanese Immigrants in California Agriculture," *Agricultural History*, 36 (1962), 25–37.

31. Raymond A. Esthus, *Theodore Roosevelt and Japan* (Seattle: University of Washington Press, 1966); Roger Daniels, *The Politics of Prejudice, The Anti-Japanese Movement in California and the Struggle for Japanese Exclusion* (Berkeley: University of California Press, 1962).

32. Homer Lea, *The Valor of Ignorance* (New York: Harper, 1942); Carry McWilliams, *Prejudice; Japanese-Americans: Symbol of Racial Intolerance* (Boston: Little, Brown, 1945).

33. Herbert Feis, *The Road to Pearl Harbor: The Coming of the War Between the United States and Japan* (Princeton, N.J.: Princeton University Press, 1950); Yale C. Maxon, *Control of Japanese Foreign Policy: A Study of Civil-Military Rivalry, 1930–1945* (Berkeley: University of California Press, 1957); David J. Lu, *From the Marco Polo Bridge to Pearl Harbor: Japan's Entry into World War II* (Washington, D.C.: Public Affairs Press, 1961).

34. Dwight D. Eisenhower, *Crusade in Europe* (Garden City, N.Y.: Doubleday, 1948).

35. *New York Times*, Dec. 9, 1941, Jan. 7, 1941.

36. Gordon C. Zahn, *Another Part of the War* (Amherst: University of Massachusetts Press, 1979); Lawrence Wittner, *Rebels Against War: The American Peace Movement, 1941–1960* (New York: Columbia University Press, 1969); Albert N. Keim, "Service or Resistance? The Mennonite Response to Conscription in World War II," *Mennonite Quarterly Review*, 52 (1978), 141–155.

37. The following account draws upon the careful discussion of the moral implications of the wartime bombing by Robert C. Batchelder, *The Irreversible Decision, 1939–1950* (Boston: Houghton Mifflin, 1962).

38. Quoted in ibid., p. 178.

39. Ibid., p. 179.

40. *Congressional Record*, 89 (Sept. 17, 1943), 7586.

41. Hans Rumpf, *The Bombing of Germany* (New York: Holt, Rinehart, Winston, 1963); David Irving, *The Destruction of Dresden* (New York: Holt, Rinehart, Winston, 1964).

42. Ironically, the "most single important cause" of Germany's economic collapse was not the destruction of its urban centers but the systematic attack on its transportation network beginning in September 1944. *United States Strategic Bombing Survey. European War*, Report no. 3, "The Effects of Strategic Bombing on the German War Economy," Oct. 31, 1945, p. 13.

43. Batchelder, *Irreversible Decision*, p. 184.

44. Stephane Groueff, *Manhattan Project: The Untold Story of the Making of the Atomic Bomb* (Boston: Little, Brown, 1967).

45. David Irving, *The German Atomic Bomb: The History of Nuclear Research in Nazi Germany* (New York: Simon and Shuster, 1967).

46. One scientist involved in the project recalled: "Everyone took for granted that the new bombs would be used in Europe if they were ready in time" (Arthur H. Compton, *Atomic Quest* [New York: Oxford University Press, 1956], p. 231). The revisionist historian Martin J. Sherwin, "The Atomic Bomb and the Origins of the Cold War: U.S. Atomic Energy Policy and Diplomacy, 1941–45," *American Historical Review*, 78 (1973), 946, also acknowledges the determination of American officials to use the bomb against Germany as well as Japan. One physicist who had favored using the bomb in Germany, Leo Szilard, questioned the morality of doing so in Japan. He said that it would kill large numbers of civilians in a nation already defeated. Batchelder, *Irreversible Decision*, p. 59.

47. Len Giovannitti and Fred Freed, *The Decision to Drop the Bomb* (New York: Coward-McCann, 1965).

48. Winston S. Churchill, *Triumph and Tragedy*, vol. VI of *The Second World War* (Boston: Houghton Mifflin, 1953), p. 639.

49. Robert J. C. Butow, *Japan's Decision to Surrender* (Stanford, Calif.: Stanford University Press, 1954); Herbert Feis, *The Atomic Bomb and the End of World War II* (Princeton, N.J.: Princeton University Press, 1966).

50. Herbert Garfinkel, *When Negroes March: The March on Washington and the Organizational Politics for FEPC* (Glencoe, Ill.: Free Press, 1959); Louis Ruchames, *Race, Jobs, and Politics: The Story of FEPC* (New York: Columbia University Press, 1953).

51. Richard M. Dalfiume, *Desegregation of the Armed Forces: Fighting on Two Fronts, 1939–1953* (Columbia: University of Missouri Press, 1960); A. Russell Buchanan, *Black Americans in World War II* (Santa Barbara, Calif.: Clio Press, 1977).

52. "The Trial of the Viereckites," *New Republic*, Jan. 4, 1943, p. 21. Among those indicted were Gerald Winrod and the controversial German-American George Sylvester Viereck.

53. The Japanese relocation policy is best described in Roger Daniels, *Concentration Camps USA: Japanese Americans and World War II* (New York: Holt, Rinehart, Winston, 1971); Allan Bosworth, *America's Concentration Camps* (New York: Norton, 1967); and Audrie Girdner and Anne Loftis, *The Great Betrayal* (New York: Macmillan, 1969).

54. Quoted in Daniels, *Concentration Camps*, pp. 55–56.

55. Ibid., p. 68.

56. Ibid., p. 70.

57. Ibid., pp. 72–73, makes this point forcefully.

58. Thomas D. Murphy, *Ambassadors in Arms* (Honolulu: University of Hawaii Press, 1954).

59. About these and other legal actions against Orientals see Milton R. Konvitz, *The Alien and the Asiatic in American Law* (Ithaca, N.Y.: Cornell University Press, 1946).

60. Raul Hilberg, *The Destruction of the European Jews* (Chicago: Quadrangle Books, 1961), is the most thorough treatment of this complex topic. A helpful introduction is Lucy S. Dawidowicz, *The War Against*

the Jews, 1933–1945 (New York: Holt, Rinehart, Winston, 1975).
61. The record of American indifference to the Jewish plight is examined in a popular and highly emotional work by Arthur D. Morse, *While Six Million Died: A Chronicle of American Apathy* (New York: Random House, 1967), and two scholarly studies, Henry L. Feingold, *The Politics of Rescue: The Roosevelt Administration and the Holocaust, 1938–1945* (New Brunswick, N.J.: Rutgers University Press, 1970) and Saul S. Friedman, *No Haven for the Oppressed* (Detroit: Wayne State University Press, 1973), arrive at similar conclusions.

62. Friedman, *No Haven*, p. 43.

63. Ibid., pp. 118–120. Even Roosevelt saw the refugees as a potential fifth column; Feingold, *Politics of Rescue*, p. 46.

64. Friedman, *No Haven*, p. 138. Walter Laqueur, *The Terrible Secret* (Boston: Little, Brown, 1980) shows that Allied leaders knew the extent of the "final solution."

65. Friedman, *No Haven*, p. 174.

66. Ibid., p. 222.

67. Feingold, *Politics of Rescue*, p. xi.

68. Freda Kirchwey, "While the Jews Die," *Nation*, Mar. 13, 1943, p. 366.

69. The tragic story of the forced repatriation of Russians is recounted in Nicholas Bethell, *The Last Secret: Forcible Repatriation to Russia, 1944–47* (London: Futura Publications, 1974) and Mark Elliott, "The United States and the Forced Repatriation of Soviet Citizens, 1944–47," *Political Science Quarterly*, 88 (1973), 253–275.

70. Elliott, "Forced Repatriation," pp. 265–268, 274.

71. Aleksandr I. Solzhenitsyn, *The Gulag Archipelago 1918–1956: An Experiment in Literary Investigation* (New York: Harper and Row, 1973), p. 248.

72. Ibid., p. 259.

73. Robert Leckie, *Conflict: The History of the Korean War, 1950–53* (New York: Putnam, 1962). President Truman declared: "We will not buy an armistice by turning over human beings for slaughter or slavery" (p. 329).

74. Jacques Ellul, *Violence: Reflections From a Christian Perspective* (New York: Seabury Press, 1969), p. 28.

75. Ibid., p. 29.

76. Roger Shinn, *Beyond This Darkness* (New York: Association Press, 1946), pp. 51–53.

77. Long, *War and Conscience in America*, pp. 40–47.

8. THE KOREAN AND VIETNAM WARS

1. Herman J. Otten, *Baal or God* (New Haven, Mo.: Leader Publishing Co., 1965), p. 296.

2. Harold J. Ockenga, "The Communist Issue Today," *Christianity Today*, May 22, 1961, p. 12.

3. George Kennan, "The Sources of Soviet Conduct," *Foreign Affairs*, 25 (1947), 575. In this article Kennan wrote under the pseudonym "X," but his authorship was soon established.

4. Ibid., p. 576.

5. "Special Message to the Congress on Greece and Turkey: The Truman Doctrine, March 2, 1947," in *Public Papers of the Presidents of the United States: Harry S. Truman, 1947* (Washington, D.C.: United States Government Printing Office, 1963), pp. 178–179. Other helpful books that deal with the Cold War include Walter LaFeber, *America, Russia, and the Cold War, 1945–1966* (New York: Wiley, 1967); Daniel Yergin, *Shattered Peace: The Origins of the Cold War and the National Security State* (Boston: Houghton Mifflin, 1977); John C. Donovan, *The Cold Warriors: A Policy-Making Elite* (Lexington, Mass.: Heath, 1974).

6. For the Korean War see the treatment in David Rees, *Korea: The Limited War* (London: Macmillan, 1964).

7. The best way to begin a serious study of the war in Vietnam is to examine the history and culture of that land. For this purpose the following works are especially helpful: Bernard Fall, *The Two Viet-Nams*, rev. ed. (New York: Praeger, 1964); *Vietnam Witness, 1953–1966* (New York: Praeger, 1966); *Reflections on a War* (Garden City, N.Y.: Doubleday, 1967); Ellen J. Hammer, *Vietnam Yesterday and Today* (New York: Holt, Rinehart, and Winston, 1966); Joseph Buttinger, *Vietnam: A Political History* (New York: Praeger, 1968); Van Chi Hoang, *From Colonialism to Communism: A Case History of North Vietnam* (New York: Praeger, 1964); Robert Scigliano, *South Vietnam: Nation under Stress* (Boston: Houghton Mifflin, 1964); Thich Nhat Hanh, *Vietnam: Lotus in a Sea of Fire* (New York: Hill & Wang, 1967).

8. For Ho see Jean Lacouture, *Ho Chi Minh* (New York: Random House, 1968).

9. Alexander Kendrick, *The Wound Within: America in the Vietnam Years, 1945–1974* (Boston: Little, Brown and Co., 1974), p. 53. Additional sources on the Vietnam War may be found in Janis A. Kreslins, ed., *Foreign Affairs Bibliography: A Selected and Annotated List of Books on International Relations, 1962–1972* (New York: R. R. Bowker, 1976) and Milton Leitenberg and Richard Dean Burns, *The Vietnam Conflict* (Santa Barbara, Calif.: ABC/Clio, 1973).

10. Lacouture, p. 171.

11. Kendrick, p. 133. Dooley's books include *Deliver Us From Evil* (New York: Farrar Strauss, 1956); *Edge of Tomorrow* (New York: Farrar Strauss, 1958); and *The Night They Burned the Mountain* (New York: Farrar Strauss, 1960).

12. For an extended treatment of the guerilla action in the south and its relation to the north see Douglas Pike, *Viet Cong* (Cambridge, Mass.: The M.I.T. Press, 1966).

13. John F. Kennedy as quoted in George C. Herring, *America's Longest War: The United States and Vietnam, 1950–1975* (New York: John Wiley and Sons, 1979), p. 43.

14. *Department of State Bulletin*, August 24, 1964, vol. 51, 268, as quoted by John Galloway, *The Gulf of Tonkin Resolution* (Cranbury, N.J.: Associated University Presses, Inc., 1970), p. 167.

15. Michael Charlton and Anthony Moncrieff, *Many Reasons Why: The American Involvement in Vietnam* (New York: Hill and Wang, 1978), p. 158. See also Frances Fitzgerald, *Fire in the Lake: The Vietnamese and the Americans in Vietnam* (Boston: Little, Brown and Co., 1972).

16. Kendrick, pp. 354–355.

17. Herring, p. 188. See Don Oberdorfer, *Tet!* (Garden City, N.Y.: Doubleday, 1971).

18. Robert W. Stevens, *Vain Hopes, Grim Realities: The Economic Consequences of the Vietnam War* (New York: New Viewpoints, 1976), p. 199.

19. Kendrick, p. 200.

20. Neil Sheehan, "Not a Dove, But No Longer a Hawk," *New York Times Magazine*, October 9, 1966, p. 140.

21. Stevens, p. 53.

22. Reston as quoted in ibid., p. 57.

23. John C. Donovan, *The Politics of Poverty* (New York: Pegasus, 1967), p. 92.

24. Arthur M. Okun, *The Political Economy of Prosperity* (New York: W. W. Norton, 1970).

25. Martin Luther King, Jr., *The Trumpet of Conscience* (New York: Harper & Row, 1967), pp. 22–23.

26. Stevens, p. 36.

27. Kendrick, p. 10. On the subject of the nature of American policy during the Vietnam era, see also the staff of the *New York Times*, *The Pentagon Papers* (New York: Bantam, 1971); Arthur M. Schlesinger, Jr., *The Imperial Presidency* (Boston; Houghton Mifflin, 1973); Carroll W. Pursell, *The Military-Industrial Complex* (New York: Harper & Row, 1972).

28. J. R. Saunders, *The Challenge of World Communism in Asia* (Grand Rapids, Mich.; Wm. B. Eerdmans Publishing Co., 1964), p. 7.

29. *Rocky Mountain News* (Denver), Aug. 25, 1965, quoted in Richard V. Pierard, "Billy Graham and Vietnam: From Cold Warrior to Peacemaker, *Christian Scholar's Review*, 10 (1981), 42.

30. Billy Graham, *Our God Is Marching On* (1966 pamphlet by the Graham Organization).

31. Quoted by Pierard from a transcript of "Billy Graham on Vietnam," *Bible Study Hour*, Ben Haden, moderator, pp. 44–45.

32. *Philadelphia Inquirer*, April 25, 1967.

33. Quoted in Marshall Frady, *Billy Graham: Parable of American Righteousness* (Boston: Little, Brown and Co., 1979), pp. 421–422.

34. Billy Graham to Lyndon B. Johnson, Jan. 3, 1969, quoted in Pierard, p. 47.

35. "Quote of the Week," *New Republic*, Jan. 6, 1973, p. 11.

36. Mark O. Hatfield, *Not Quite So Simple* (New York: Harper & Row, 1968), pp. 153–154. This book presents much of Senator Hatfield's position on Vietnam. For more about him and his political thought see Robert J. Eells, "Mark O. Hatfield and the Search for an Evangelical Politics" (unpublished Ph.D. diss., University of New Mexico, 1976; Robert Eells and Bartell Nyberg, *Lonely Walk, The Life of Senator Mark*

Hatfield (Chappaqua, N.Y.: Christian Herald Books, 1979); Mark Hatfield, *Between a Rock and a Hard Place* (Waco, Texas: Word Books, 1976).

37. *Philadelphia Bulletin*, April 17, 1968.

38. Quoted in Eells and Nyberg, p. 62.

39. Hatfield, *Not Quite So Simple*, p. 184.

40. Ibid., p. 207.

41. Mark Hatfield interviewed by T. E. Koshy, "Can a Christian Be a Politician?" *HIS*, Oct. 1967, p. 4.

42. It is difficult to determine exactly the extent of Christian opposition to or support for the war. Billy Graham and Mark Hatfield show the range of opinion, but in what numbers did evangelicals hold these views? We do know that at first Christians in the historic peace churches such as the Mennonites, Friends, and the Brethren were nearly the only ones who spoke out against the conflict. They were joined by a few liberal churchmen and by some socialists. By 1964–65 the strength of this opposition increased as it became apparent that social programs would have to be sacrificed due to the conflict in Southeast Asia. Dr. King and others who were committed to domestic programs formed the mainstream of the opposition. They were joined by individuals such as John C. Bennett and the Berrigans and by evangelicals such as those who published *The Post American* and *The Other Side*. Probably these opponents were never in the majority, and the church establishments were very discrete in their attitude toward the war. For an interesting consideration of the debate on Vietnam see Don Frederick Colenback, "Christian Moral Argument and United States Policy in Vietnam" (unpublished Ph.D. diss., Yale University, 1975).

AFTERWORD

1. Russel B. Nye, *This Almost Chosen People* (East Lansing: Michigan State University Press, 1966), p. 206.

2. Quoted in ibid., pp. 205–206.

3. Martin Evans, *America: The View from Europe* (San Francisco; The San Francisco Book Co., 1976).

4. Sacvan Bercovitch, *The American Jeremiad* (Madison: University of Wisconsin Press, 1979). For an enlightening review essay on this seminal book, see Harry Stout, "Almost Zion," *Fides et Historia*, 12 (1979).

5. Ernest Lee Tuveson, *Redeemer Nation: The Idea of America's Millenial Role* (Chicago: University of Chicago Press, 1968).

6. Ibid., p. 132.

7. Frederick Merk, *Manifest Destiny and Mission in American History: A Reinterpretation* (New York: Alfred A. Knopf, 1963), p. 261.

8. Among Ramsey's books, the most important for present purposes are: *War and the Christian Conscience* (Durham, N.C.: Duke University Press, 1961), and *The Just War: Force and Political Responsibility* (New York: Charles Scribner's Sons, 1968).

9. *The Just War*, pp. 42–69.

10. *Time*, April 12, 1954, p. 33, as quoted in *The Just War*, p. 53.

11. *The Politics of Jesus* (Grand Rapids, Mich.: William B. Eerdmans, 1972).

12. This is discussed with care in ibid., pp. 235ff.

13. Ibid., p. 235.

14. *Politics and the Biblical Drama* (Grand Rapids: William B. Eerdmans, 1976). Especially good, as well as graciously irenic, is Mouw's treatment of "The Anabaptist-Reformed Dialogue," pp. 98–116.

15. See also Mouw's earlier book, *Political Evangelism* (Grand Rapids, Mich.: William B. Eerdmans, 1974).

16. Mouw, *Biblical Drama*, p. 108.

17. Ibid., p. 109.

18. Ibid., p. 110.

19. *In Pursuit of a Christian View of War* (Bramcote, Nottinghamshire, England: Grove Books, 1977). This booklet is a contribution to the series Grove Booklets on Ethics, produced by British and American authors.

20. Ibid., p. 12.

21. Ibid.